Finding Our Way

A Writing Teacher's Sourcebook

Finding Our Way

A Writing Teacher's Sourcebook

Wendy Bishop
Late of Florida State University

Deborah Coxwell Teague
Florida State University

HOUGHTON MIFFLIN COMPANY   BOSTON   NEW YORK

Publisher: Patricia A. Coryell
Executive Editor: Suzanne Phelps Weir
Senior Development Editor: Martha Bustin
Associate Project Editor: Shelley Dickerson
Manufacturing Manager: Florence Cadran
Marketing Manager: Cindy Graff Cohen

Cover image: Writing Home, 1984 by Ditz (Contemporary Artist). Private Collection/Bridgeman Art Library.

Printed in the U.S.A.

Library of Congress Control Number: 2002116637

ISBN: 0-618-41938-1

123456789 – QUF – 08 07 06 05 04

Contents

Part III: Beyond the Classroom

Responses

Responses to the Collection as a Whole

Appendix

About the Authors

Wendy Bishop was born in Fukuoka, Kyushu, Japan, on January 13, 1953, and after a short battle with leukemia, died in Tallahassee, Florida, on November 21, 2003. In her fifty years, she accomplished more than most could even imagine doing in a much longer lifetime—as a woman; as a writer; as a mother to her two children, Morgan and Tait, and to her five step-children, Jos, Jesse, Jeremy, Eowyn, and Dean; as a sister; a friend; a professor at Florida State University; a colleague; a mentor; a collaborator; researcher; and loving wife to Dean, her husband. She greatly enjoyed her life apart from work, especially at Alligator Point, Florida, on the Gulf of Mexico, where her ashes were spread.

Deborah Coxwell Teague is director of the first-year writing program at Florida State University. She trains and supervises over 130 graduate teaching assistants who teach FSU's more than 200 sections of FYW each semester and enjoys working with students of all ages. Deborah loves spending time with her four children–ages 8, 9, 27, and 29–and her 9-year-old grandchild. She is so very thankful to have had Wendy Bishop as a close friend, a colleague, and a mentor.

Introduction

WENDY BISHOP AND DEBORAH COXWELL TEAGUE

ANY text that explores the "touchier" issues of freshman comp would be enormously useful (given, of course, that the subject at hand is treated candidly and with an eye toward practical application).

—Teacher 1

My biggest concerns as a teacher these days usually have to do with students and power. Female students flirt quite a bit to try to improve their grades, and many male students feel that they can argue about their grades and writing issues, I think because of our TA status. They know how little real power we have. A few minutes ago, a student wanted to argue with me about clichés. He was trying to make the case for including clichés in his essay because "they teach lessons," despite the fact that I spent an entire class talking about them, and the class did a group exercise that emphasized figurative language that is fresh.

—Teacher 2

I would like a book that discussed these [suggested] topics (especially if I were a new TA) because I think that these topics are common points of worry for TAs. . . . I wouldn't look to the book to necessarily help me to overcome my anxiety about some of these issues, but rather to provide reassurance that my fears and worries aren't unusual.

—Teacher 3

All writing teachers struggle with power relationships. Some are close in age to their students or are being supervised by senior teaching assistants and program directors or are feeling in competition with peers who value different areas of English studies. Writing teachers have questions about these and other personal relationships: How friendly should they be with students, co-teachers, and supervisors? Should they spend out of-class time with or even date any of these individuals? While determining and developing their own philosophies, teachers have to consider issues like how they relate to students with fundamentalist religious backgrounds or whether or not they as teachers should support co-teachers at all costs or report individuals with problems to supervisors.

Inevitably, writing teachers worry about student resistance, and they constantly renegotiate their sense of self-worth, asking each other about teaching evaluations or disruptive students. How, they wonder, do teachers survive a grade appeal or file a complaint or deal with student disclosures? Undergirding these decisions is another set of complicated career choices, including the decision about whether the teaching life is worth pursuing.

On the basis of our combined experience as teachers of writing, teachereducators, and directors of composition programs and writing centers, we realize teachers often educate each other about issues and topics such as these. They talk, holding discussions that they feel aren't suitable for or able to be covered during their in-service training or pedagogy courses, discussions that will prove crucial to their success and development—as teachers, as potential university professors, as literacy specialists taking up other sorts of work.

Teacher educators have stock responses to some of these topics and questions and avoid others. We know—we've done it. Because of this, we decided to try to bring seldom-discussed topics to the surface in a collection written by relatively new writing teachers for even newer writing teachers.

To confirm the need for a collection like this, we surveyed a group of thirty new teachers during August 2002, after they had completed a training course in the summer of 2001 and their first academic year of teaching in 2001–02. We grouped their concerns into categories and rechecked the currency and utility of our divisions (eventually to group and reduce them) by asking continuing teachers of writing to rank and discuss how or if they had struggled with similar issues. Not surprisingly, we learned that many continue to struggle, far beyond the first year of teaching, as noted in the quotes that open this introduction. Although we have each taught writing for more than twenty years, we know we struggle as well because teaching conditions change.

The subjects that writing teachers in our survey wanted to discuss fell into the following six categories, each of which is followed with a representative sampling of teacher comments.

1. Program Ideology/Conflicts in Teacher Education

    • I feel that we are strongly encouraged to adopt a certain kind of teaching philosophy. The issues I don't feel comfortable discussing are usually issues where my opinion opposes (or at least I feel like it does) the commonly accepted teaching philosophy.
    • [There was] the discomfort I felt whenever political issues seeped into pedagogical discussions; I even feel uncomfortable now as I try to muster the determination to say that I am not superliberal. . . . it appeared that those who conform to the leftist [teacher] majority were allowed to be judgmental and harsh toward their opposition.

2. Student-Teacher Relationships

    • I find it hard to determine whether or not a student is taking advantage of me.

- The main topic that I talk about with other TAs is whether or not the students like us (we say things like "my students hate me").
- One thing that surprised me was how fiercely protective I felt toward my students.
- What I didn't know when I began teaching that I know now is how to deal with my anger toward my students during certain circumstances.
- I wouldn't say it publicly, but I was TERRIFIED of my students. Terrified that they "wouldn't like me" and that they would think that I was just some passing teacher. . . . I have a problem with confrontation as well. . . . I didn't expect any student to have the audacity to complain about my grading.
- I did not know the nerve of some students. I never in a million years imagined how some students will cut corners.
- We didn't touch on what to do when we really dislike a student.
- I think we needed more advice on the appropriate level of contact with our students outside class. . . . I find myself wanting to develop an intellectual relationship with them.
- As a new teacher in an age of such violence, I often feel that I distance myself from my students.
- Although they are legally adults, the lack of emotional and intellectual maturity in most college students is almost baffling. Their moods and emotions are as unpredictable to them as they are to teachers.

3. Gender and Race Politics

- After I got into the classroom, I was much less sure about coming out to these kids. For one thing, I really don't want them to think of me as primarily a sexual being.
- There are, of course, conversations about male and female relationships, and they seem to differ from person to person. Men, it seemed, more than women, had trouble, but struggled valiantly with ethical boundaries.
- Certainly, the issue of romance/sexual attraction is on the minds of TAs. . . .Teaching is a form of performance, and most teachers enjoy being the center of attention. Though we can all get to sleep at night feeling noble about doing something "meaningful" and "important," nothing feeds the ego like a room full of attractive, adoring teenagers of the opposite sex.
- I have a personal investment in making them aware of issues in diversity, especially with regard to race and sexual orientation . . . how much of my job is it to teach writing, and how much of it is to do consciousness-raising and diversity training?
- The knowledge that I am a lesbian seems to shift my role as an instructor to that of an anomaly, a sexual object, or a poster child. These are not options I wish for my students to adopt in our relationships.

4. Saving Face/Confidence as a Teacher

- I really needed to understand at first that if I tried something and it didn't work it didn't mean that I was destined to be a bad teacher.

- We talked endlessly about being too young, unprepared, and inexperienced in front of a classroom of kids expecting us to be teachers.

5. Peer-to-Peer Relationships

- I learned that all teachers are different and that just because someone has a different philosophy doesn't mean they are a worse or better teacher.
- The lessons that are likely to last the longest and make the most valuable impressions are the value of honor and personal integrity and accountability both to oneself and to one's colleagues and supervisor.

6. Relationship to Graduate School/Own Education

- How important is teaching?
- What really gets to me, though, is the attitude of some TAs concerning their teaching obligation. I want to teach—I know that. Some TAs don't. That's fine, but they are still obligated to give the their students the absolute best of what they have to give.
- Generally, I did not know how to manage my time. I have to always remind myself that I am a student first and that I have to budget my time and energy.

As we read and reviewed the many candid responses that had been shared with us, we felt confirmed in the need for this collection. We love our profession because it is demanding and rewarding; we love it as well because it is collaborative—teachers easily share with other teachers. Our surveys confirmed that there was much that could be learned from and grown from, and we used the above categories to focus our request for contributions when inviting teachers to join this collection.

In *The Composition Instructor's Survival Guide*, Brock Dethier reports that "nearly forty thousand people teach college composition and writing in the United States" (xiii). Although our book began as a sourcebook for new or retraining teachers of writing, we know that a large number of that general college writing-instructor population will also find much of interest here. As noted earlier, teaching challenges shift and change throughout a teaching life as instructors move to different institutions and undertake new classes, as they become more adept at old skills and move on to new challenges, particularly the challenges of new technologies and conditions for composing.

You can see by this brief history how *Finding Our Way* developed into an edited collection of essays by college writing teachers, for college writing teachers. While new teachers of writing generally receive a solid grounding in contemporary theory, research, and practice in composition studies through pre-service or workshops or term-long teacher-education courses, they—and we—felt that many issues of concern to them aren't dealt with in the general curriculum. As we arranged for the contributors to address peers about topics of their choice, we suggested they imagine they were sharing in a more organized and reflective manner the same subjects they discuss in the privacy of their offices. For instance, after talk, a teacher might learn (and share the insight) that

> It is essential for the teacher to be interested in the class in order for the students to be interested. If I walk into a class worried about a paper I have to write, paying the rent, or anything other than what I need to teach, then my students recognize that instantly. If I'm not there mentally, then neither are the students. When I teach I am not a student myself; I have to be the teacher.—Teacher 4

These essayists are joined by respondents, a wide sampling of reflective practitioners who range from second-year teachers to writing-teacher educators to long-time writing-program administrators. Fifteen agreed to respond to the three individual parts of the collection (Approaching the Classroom, Inside Out, and Beyond the Classroom) and two others to respond to the whole. All were encouraged to write as if they were prefacing this material for their own course discussion. Therefore, in their responses these compositionists share many of their own teaching experiences, offer helpful advice, but also complicate and enrich the discussions you are about to join.

In the appendix, we have shared a listing of the composition texts kept handy on our bookshelves; the ones we pull down time and again for illumination, advice, and confirmation about the choices we are called upon to make as writing teachers. No doubt we've left many fine texts off this admittedly idiosyncratic list, but we trust that you will continue to create your own collection, your reference shelf standards, by adding the voices of colleagues and specialists who address your particular teaching concerns. We trust that these resources will start you on that search.

Meanwhile, we sincerely hope you enjoy reading this collection—that it, too, finds a necessary space on your teaching reference shelf. We'd like to think that you'll pick up this volume for what you thought would be just a few minutes of light reading and instead find yourself unable to put it down. We believe it likely that you'll identify with at least some of the experiences and concerns our teacher-writers share and that you'll realize that the doubts, fears, questions, and concerns you have as a teacher are shared by many of us. Remember, having doubts, fears, questions, and concerns does not make us flawed teachers; quite the reverse—our shared experiences serve to help us grow and learn, and *our* learning sets the stage for our students' learning.

Acknowledgments

Thanks to Suzanne Phelps Weir, who walked into our offices one day and encouraged us to work together on a topic we all care deeply about. She has been supportive at every step of this project, offering encouragement, expert advice, and friendship.

Thanks to the many writing teachers who shared their ideas and opinions in initial surveys and to those who shared more extensively in this collection.

These contributors all practice what they teach; they write and revise with energy, commitment, and good humor.

They are joined, as well, by a generous group of respondents. They have negotiated complicated professional roles, often simultaneously, and include teachers; teacher educators; writing-program and college administrators; and teachers who love literature, creative writing, composition, and rhetoric. Each readily agreed to support and improve this collection. Thank you, once more, for making time in your schedules to share with us and for putting up with our e-mails and editing.

Without sounding grandiose, we want, as well, to thank all the first-year writing students who educate us. Sometimes we don't get it exactly right, but always we want to do so.

Finally, our families—Dean, Tait, and Morgan; Everett, Caylah, Kyler, Casey, Christy, and Aidan—who make life in Tallahassee rich and full.

PART I
APPROACHING THE CLASSROOM

1

Your Culture, Their Politics: What a Teacher Should Know When Entering a New Writing Program

KENYA M. THOMPKINS

On the first day of class, the teacher began by introducing herself and going over the syllabus. She asked if there were any questions regarding what she had covered. Then, she asked us to do what most students dread, introduce ourselves. Always the nervous one, I decided to go first, especially since this was my first course with this professor. After all of us had said something about ourselves, the professor informed us that she had no problem with our addressing her by her first name, especially since we were all adults and this was a graduate-level course. Her consent seemed to allow the students to relax, except for me. All that semester, the other students addressed her by her first name; I continued to address her as Dr. __. During the last week of class, she jokingly said, "Kenya, you can call me by my first name." My response to her set in motion what today has evolved into a wonderful relationship, for I said, "Dr. __, you have to understand I address you as such because I respect you and because I was taught to do so. You see, it's a part of my upbringing, it's a part of my culture." She smiled and said, "I understand." As I reflect, I, now, understand too.

By now, most of you have reached a point in your educational experiences where professors welcome their graduate students to establish a more personal relationship with them. But I use my story to illustrate how cultural norms, values, beliefs, and expectations influence all of us at some point during our enrollment as students or tenure as employees in the educational setting. As an African American male reared in South Georgia, I was constantly reminded to address my elders or superiors, especially my teachers, as Mr., Mrs., Ms., Dr., etc., for to do otherwise would possibly lead to some form of punishment. This cultural practice was further reinforced during my undergraduate and graduate matriculations as a student at a Historically Black University (an HBCU). I never questioned it, nor ever had a reason to do so. In fact, I took (take) great pride in showing this level of respect to my professors, supervisors, colleagues, and students.

I've learned there are many more cultural practices that define an institution's identity, determine its missions, shape its students, and guide the instruction rendered between its walls. On your first day as a freshman in college, you saw some kids who looked and sounded just like you. However, these similarities paled in comparison with the many students who were different, all representing their cultural backgrounds. Yet, you were all drawn to that institution. And whether you'd admit it or not, you probably all had more in common by the time you left that school because the school shaped your experiences. Now as a teacher entering a new writing program, you must realize that this new institution has its own cultural practices and that department you will be teaching in is a subculture within that college or university. And if you wish to be an effective teacher you definitely need to recognize and accept that axiom and learn about the culture(s) you are entering. Before I go any further, I offer my experience as a teacher entering a new writing program as a point of discussion.

As I indicated earlier, I am an African American male. I was reared in the South, attended schools in the South, and now teach at a university in the South. I have taught English composition (in the classroom and in a writing center environment) for over five years. Much of my teaching practices reflect what I was exposed to during my undergraduate years. In my first-semester English course, I learned how to apply the different modes (narrative, cause and effect, comparison-contrast, definition, argumentative, and position paper) to a five-paragraph theme. During my second-semester English course, we read and discussed literature. Our writing assignments required that we provide some type of critical analysis of some literary work and research the topic for further support. Once I became a teacher I did as I had been taught, and there were no problems because the educational setting where I taught espoused the same teaching practices and philosophy that I had learned as an undergraduate.

What I didn't know during my undergraduate years was that much of the instruction I had received in composition was based on a current traditional model. In this model, the skeletal structure of the essay is emphasized. Students learn how to write well-organized, developed essays that possess clear thesis statements usually in the form of a three-pronged statement or road map in the introduction. I'll spare you the five-paragraph class discussion, but I'm sure many of you have either received this type of instruction or heard of it at some point during your matriculation. And some have even taught it. But what happens when you enter a new English department that has a different teaching approach and encourages teachers to adopt a different (and possibly contradictory) teaching philosophy? What do you do? I was faced with these and other questions when I accepted a teaching assistant position during my doctoral studies program.

Having taught English composition prior to entering the program, I felt quite confident in my abilities as a teacher. However, I learned quickly that some of what I had been accustomed to teaching was different from what was expected of me at this new school. To make the transition smoother, I opted to attend a six-week intensive summer training workshop for first-year teaching assistants (TAs).

After completing the workshop and eventually entering the classroom, I was glad that I had attended the training program. I learned early during the program that we were not to teach the five-paragraph theme in our composition courses because the program believed most incoming freshmen already knew how to write those kinds of papers. Also, we were told that first-year writing courses were not grammar classes and that we should not teach grammar in class; however, teachers were encouraged to review grammar from time to time, especially on an individual basis. Again, it was assumed that these students should already know the basic rules of grammar. And though we were taught other things, what was emphasized the most was that teaching writing as a process was to be our aim. Of course, my initial response was that I always teach writing as a process. But by the end of the summer program, I understood clearly the differences between the process I taught within the product-oriented instruction I was accustomed to (a linear process of plan, prewrite, write, revise, publish) and the process-oriented pedagogy this new program emphasized (which was much more recursive).

The other thing I learned was probably the most useful to my growth as a teacher and as a person. I learned that it was okay that my previous school emphasized a current traditional model and encouraged its teachers to provide some grammar instruction. And it was okay that this new program emphasized writing as a recursive act. I was able to accept the different teaching philosophies because it was apparent that both programs had designed their writing curricula to meet the needs of their students, a point that became more clear after I fully understood the missions of each institution. Once I came to this realization, I was ready to co-exist in both environments and help students do the same. Based on my experiences, here's a set of suggestions to consider as you leave one institution and enter another:

1. Recognize that you are both a teacher and a professional.
2. Recognize that you bring your cultural experiences to the classroom setting.
3. Recognize that each institution has its own cultural values and beliefs.
4. Recognize that the environment you are entering is highly political.

1. Recognize That You Are Both a Teacher and a Professional

Sometimes it's hard to accept our new roles in life, especially when we've been accustomed to receiving instruction. As a new teacher, especially a new TA, you have to remember that you are entering a profession. Granted, as a teacher you will forever be a student because of the nature of the discipline. But now you are the primary facilitator of learning. If this is your first time teaching, you're going to be nervous; that's okay. I still become nervous each semester because with each class there's a level of uncertainty. My advice to you is that you be honest with yourself first. You know your strengths and your weaknesses. Of course, rely on your strengths, but constantly work to improve where you are weakest. And remember, you always have something to offer your students. Many of your students in freshman composition will be freshmen; some might be sophomores. As a TA, take some comfort in knowing that you have satisfied the requirements to receive a bachelor's degree and that you are now in a graduate program. As a new teacher, you should find solace in knowing that you have completed both undergraduate and graduate studies; by virtue of your degrees and education, you have something to offer your students.

Also, often new teachers are nervous because they feel they don't know everything. I'll let you in on a little secret; the wisest of veteran teachers will gladly admit that they don't know everything. In fact, some will admit that they learn something new every semester. A few will tell you to keep your personal resource text(s) available in the event that you do need to review a rule of grammar, syntax, and so on. And don't be afraid to ask your students questions about various topics. They bring with them their own literacies and understandings of the English language. The writing classroom is a wonderful place for the exchange of ideas and no longer are teachers expected to assume the traditional authoritative role where they demonstrate their level of expertise by lecturing for an entire hour. Most writing programs encourage teachers to design their classrooms around collaboration between student-teacher and student-student. Remember, you're there to provide positive experiences that will improve your students' writing.

After you have settled into your new role, you might want to join a professional organization such as the National Council of Teachers of English (NCTE)[1] and its many constituent organizations. There are local, state, and national professional organizations that you might consider joining because they are excellent resources/support groups for educators/students at all levels. Also, become familiar with the various learning sites on your campus. Although writing centers are typically housed in most English departments, don't assume all learning/resource centers are located in that department. There are other sites of learning that provide support to English faculty and students.

2. Recognize That You Bring Your Cultural Experiences to the Classroom Setting

You bring with you certain educational values and beliefs to this new setting. You've been developing those values and beliefs since you were first educated informally at home and formally in an educational setting. For instance, students who attended small, private schools (K-12) and then attend small, private universities might have drastically different expectations than students who attended public schools in urban settings (K-12) and then attend state-funded institutions. Students taught at parochial schools will have different expectations than students who attend all-male military academies.

At a certain level, these different educational settings do reflect class and socioeconomic hierarchies, and with these classifications come certain stereotypes and assumptions. I don't mean to imply that you hold such beliefs, but there are some who strongly believe that access to higher education should only be available

---

[1] See http://www.ncte.org.

to certain people and socioeconomic groups. Problems that often arise as a result of these attitudes are further complicated by issues concerning alternative admission policies. At some point you will have to consider how you feel about open enrollment and affirmative action, especially if you intend to teach at a state-funded institution. Such reflection will force you to consider how you feel about your colleagues and the students you teach. As a TA and a new teacher, you have to realize that you bring with you certain expectations and attitudes, which might be different from the expectations and attitudes of your colleagues and/or your students. These underlying expectations form your and their ideologies. Recognizing these differences doesn't say that one ideology is better than the other. But such recognition does allow us to enter a discourse community and exchange healthy and insightful dialogue. Remember, as teachers, we also add to the cultural tapestry that exists on college campuses.

3. Recognize That Each Institution Has Its Own Cultural Values and Beliefs

Do you know the differences between a Tier 1 (doctoral-granting) research-oriented university, and a Tier 2 and 3 (master's; baccalaureate and associate degree) teaching-oriented institution? (I combine the latter because arguably few differences exist between Tier 2 and Tier 3 institutions in the relatively minimal amount of pressure to produce original, publishable research.) If you don't, I strongly urge you to learn the differences and consider the following. Tier 1, doctoral-granting, research institutions are vastly different from the other tier institutions.[2] For one, the research institutions typically enroll more students than do other tier schools. More important Tier 1 schools usually receive a substantial amount of grant money that goes toward senior fellows, research activities, and teaching assistants. Although Tier 2 and 3 institutions offer MA, BA, and AA degrees, they usually don't generate the same amount of research/grant money. Teaching assistants at doctoral-granting research institutions provide much of the instruction taught in first-year writing. Because it's less expensive to pay a TA's salary than it is to pay a tenured faculty member's salary, more TAs can and will be hired, thus decreasing, in many cases, the number of composition courses regular faculty members teach. Also, having this type of labor affords many institutions the luxury of capping the enrollment in each composition class.

The scenario is noticeably different at Tier 2/3 institutions. At these schools, many regular faculty members teach composition courses; in some cases, two of

---

[2] In 2000, the Carnegie Classification system of Institutions of Higher Education (found at http://www.carnegiefoundation.org/Classification/) was reordered to include the following categories: Doctoral/Research Universities (Research I and II), which is divided into Doctoral/Research Extensive (averaging, in 1998, about 20,000 students) and Intensive (averaging, in 1998, about 10,000 students). The next category is Master's Colleges and Universities (Comprehensive I and II), followed by Baccalaureate Colleges (Liberal Arts I and II), then Two-year, Associate of Arts/Associate's Colleges and a variety of specialized institutions. While the categories are meant to be descriptive, they are, in fact, also used to determine funding and ranking by federal and private agencies. The institutions themselves use the rankings to attract faculty and students.

their courses per semester are composition. I've even heard of faculty teaching four composition courses per semester, despite having a literature/creative writing background.

Also, Tier 1 schools share certain values, values that are different from those at other institutions. Nationally, Tier 1 schools have more stringent admission requirements. Therefore, many of their students will probably have graduated in the top twenty percent of their high school graduating class. It's expected that these students already possess basic writing and language skills. Therefore, there should be more emphasis placed on developing these students' writing styles and less focus on rudimentary skills. Remember, as I mentioned in the background information I shared, the new writing program I entered did not endorse teaching the five-paragraph theme, the modes of writing, or grammar in classes. As a Tier 1 research institution, it believed that its students already possessed those skills.

Tier 3, baccalaureate-granting, institutions usually have a more flexible enrollment policy. The quality of education rendered is usually superb. However, these institutions typically pride themselves on admitting some students who might not have received the highest scores on entrance exams but who have demonstrated in other ways that they are extremely competent and are capable of competing in the college setting. High school students who graduate in the top twenty percent do enroll in these schools, but the majority of the student population will consist of other students (i.e., returning students, first-generation students, students from local and state areas, etc.).

Of course, these are generalizations and the tiers, being descriptive, do not have entirely fixed boundaries, but my point is that as a new teacher, you must recognize that institutional values and missions will dictate the kind of student you teach and thus dictate the kind of instruction you provide. As I mentioned earlier, my undergraduate and initial teaching experiences were greatly influenced by the kind of institution I attended. As part of its mission, the university provides quality education to those who are often first-generation college students. Sure, the school continues to attract some of the best high school students according to their secondary placement and entrance exams; in fact, it has been recognized for attracting just as many African American merit scholars as some Ivy League schools. However, the university welcomes students who haven't always received some of the same educational experiences. So, introducing a current traditionalist approach to some of these students provides them with certain writing experiences that they either did not receive or do not remember. Is this sub-par instruction? No! Is it different? Yes! As a new teacher, it's imperative that you recognize what type of institution you are entering and what kind of students you will be teaching.

4. Recognize That the Environment You Are Entering Is Highly Political

It is important that new teachers realize that the cultural identity of an institution of higher education breeds politics. Whether you like it or not, part of your role will be to negotiate the dynamics at the college or university, particularly within an English department. By now, I'm sure you are well aware of the funding discrepancies that exist on some campuses. The business, engineering, computer, sciences, and health departments often receive more assistance from the university or from external sources in terms of financial support, institutional respect, and attention. (At least it seems that way.) Seemingly, disciplines in the arts and social sciences are treated less favorably. And though it might sound self-serving, the English department seems to receive the least amount of respect even among the latter groups. To make matters worse, many administrators, faculty, staff, and students view the English department, especially the composition component, *only* as a service unit of the university. If students perform poorly on a state test, English faculty are blamed. If it's determined that students don't write well during or after their matriculation, the English faculty are usually chastised.

So, don't be surprised if you enter a situation where university administrators influence the type of instruction rendered in those classes. Or because of budget woes, don't be surprised if the department has to close sections, thus increasing the enrollment in your sections. I'm glad I didn't encounter either of those situations, but if you are unfortunate enough to encounter anything remotely similar, the first thing you should do is *not* take it out on your students. For whatever reason you became a teacher, the fact is you are one. And your first obligation as a teacher is to uphold the standards of the profession and provide experiences that will allow your students to improve their writing. Sometimes it's easy to forget that, and sometimes it's even easier to lash out at students because the real culprit is out of arm's reach or is considered invincible. But remember, you are there to do a job, so do it to the best of your ability.

As a "junior political agent" at the university, I'd suggest that you go through the appropriate procedures. First speak with your director of composition or first-year writing and express your displeasure with the class size. More than likely, you will encounter a sympathetic listener who knows all too well what you're experiencing. But talking to the director will prove to be a good way of releasing any internal frustrations you might be developing. Also, ask to serve on composition committees. Doing so may allow you to gain a better understanding of the writing program, the department in general, and, possibly, the university at large. It's worth mentioning that class size is just an example of some of the issues you will encounter. Pay per class, benefits, office space, general working conditions, and retention policies are others. Try to avoid being a complainer who doesn't offer any solutions, suggestions, ideas, or insights that might solve problems, or at least address them. This latter suggestion brings me to another point.

As a new member in a department, you will not be fully aware of the politics that exist in that department. Groups form for different reasons. Depending on the situation, faculty will align themselves with members who were a semester ago their foes. This formation of subgroups is natural. But if possible, during your first year you may want to remain neutral with regard to "political affiliation." Go to work, teach your classes, do your research, and go home. Yes, I'm taking it to the extreme; you will form relationships with people. You will develop opinions about working conditions, colleagues, students, etc. But you don't want to appear (so soon) as an ally of this group or an enemy of another one. During that first year, you will be learning your way around that campus and within that department. Also, as a TA, you will have to take classes from professors, so you don't want them to perceive you as a foe. These suggestions will be equally useful when you enter a department on a tenured line.

Early in your first year you will also want to gauge the formality level of this department. If you recall, in the opening narrative, I shared that it was difficult for me to address my professor by her first name. Don't be surprised if you enter a department that is extremely formal. I have seen departments where everyone addresses each other by titles (Dr. ___/Professor ___). And I've seen departments where they address one another by first name. Find out what's the norm in that department and go from there. Usually you'll discover early on what's expected. Just remember that as a new faculty member, you must be willing to negotiate the politics and norms at the university and within the department.

Entering a new writing program can be challenging and exciting at the same time; it was for me. I had my expectations as a teacher and my preconceived notions of what this new writing program and its faculty and students represented. But I'm glad to report that many of my preconceived notions were false and that my teaching skills have improved. Also, I've come to realize that the different teaching philosophies I've encountered actually complement one another. I was able to understand this because I was honest with myself and made an effort to recognize the cultural dynamics of this new institution. Doing so has allowed me to become part of the department and share in its mission to provide excellent, effective experiences that will improve the communicative skills of students via writing. There are many other things I could share with you as you enter a new writing program, but doing so would rob you of the best experience of all—self-discovery. But I will leave you with some suggestions that might help you situate yourself in this new environment:

- When you get a chance, go outside, sit among the students (i.e., on the student commons), and observe their interactions. If possible, speak with students about the institution in general and about writing at the institution. Write down what kinds of students you observe and what some of their habits are. Then consider how you feel about what you observe. Do the same thing with the faculty.
- Get to know the office staff. I urge you to become familiar with the office manager, program assistant, and student workers. They usually run the office, and they know what's going on in the office and on campus. Sure, some of the information they share is borderline gossip, but these individuals can be a great support, particularly as you learn your way around campus. So, when you're feeling frustrated because of your dismal paycheck, or overwhelmed because of the number of papers you have to grade, remember there is someone who makes even less than you, but who has to deal with your complaints and many students' ill-mannered behavior. I just hope you show them the respect they deserve, for the office personnel may prove to be the greatest confidant you might have as a new teacher.
- Consider the type of elementary and secondary school you attended. What role did that experience play in your decision to attend college?

- Categorize your socioeconomic upbringing: low, middle, upper classes? What effect did (does) it have on your educational choices?
- Consider the tier of your undergraduate college and your graduate school. When choosing those institutions, did the tier matter? Now that you have considered your institutions' rankings, is there a particular tier institution you would rather teach at?
- Consider the type of writing instruction you received during undergraduate studies? Is your writing pedagogy similar to the instruction you received?
- What is your teaching philosophy? If you don't have any type of response to this question, it's time you start working on one. In fact, some job applications require that job candidates include such a statement with their application portfolio. More importantly, you should know, or at least be willing to question, why you've become a teacher and how that decision influences your pedagogy and interaction with your colleagues and students.

Investigating these questions and suggestions in discussion with peers or a teaching journal during your first year will help you adjust to your new setting. Good luck on this new journey!

2

"We're Not in Kansas Anymore": Negotiating a Teaching Philosophy

KATE BROWN

In high school, I earned A's in all my English classes. I could whip out a five-paragraph essay complete with a solid thesis statement, supporting details, and a summarizing conclusion in no time at all. I thought that I had mastered writing. In college, however, my A's changed to B's, and the comments on my papers went from "nice work" and "good clear purpose" to "no original ideas here" and "your argument is too simple." I would sit in front of my computer believing that if I could just think harder to generate some original ideas, then my writing would improve. Though I never became an A student in college with my "just think harder" philosophy, my college experiences shaped my ideas about writing.

When I started my summer teacher-education course to prepare for my graduate assistantship, I learned that the first-year writing program had a very different view about writing than I did. I heard terms like process-centered pedagogy, collaboration, drafting, portfolios, and personal discovery used in discussions about writing for the first time. When the professor talked about drafting I thought *any student can write a good paper if she can write endless drafts,* and when she talked about personal discovery writing I thought *anyone can write about their personal experiences; it doesn't involve real thinking.* But in the third week of my summer teacher education course, something happened that made me question my beliefs about writing.

I sat down with my mentor TA, Sarah,[1] to discuss her students' first set of papers. Sarah had asked me to read each of the papers the previous night and grade them so that when we met we could compare and discuss the rationale behind our

---

[1] Teacher and student names and specific details about events have been changed to preserve the anonymity of those involved.

decisions. After reading countless papers about cheating boyfriends and deaths of grandparents, there was one paper that I remember vividly. Becca, a minority student, who frequently struggled with her writing, had written an essay describing in painful detail an experience when her stepfather sexually assaulted her, and to make him stop attacking her, she stabbed him several times with a pocket knife. I was unsure of how to react to this paper. I wondered *does a grade trivialize Becca's experience? Should Sarah or I talk with Becca, or possibly recommend counseling?* Initially, I was uncomfortable dealing with these issues in the writing classroom, and questioned whether or not a program pedagogy that encourages students to write about similar, intensely personal experiences would work for me.

Keeping an Open Mind

From my undergraduate experience I had developed a hierarchy in my mind where researched critical writing was the most valuable and most scholarly kind of writing, whereas personal writing and creative writing did not rank on my scale because I believed that these genres did not involve thinking. But for some reason Becca's essay stuck in my mind, and I wondered: *what is it about this essay that is so powerful?* I considered what would happen if Becca changed the genre of her paper to include research and analysis of her experience, but, despite my hierarchy of writing, I felt that her essay was presented best in a narrative form. Her personal, informal voice, and the way the essay made me feel as if Becca were sharing her story with *me*, friend to friend, in confidence, convinced me of this. Becca's essay made me start to question the validity of my ideas about writing, because I had observed that sometimes personal narrative is a more appropriate way to convey a message than research writing.

I knew from the start that my writing program emphasized the value of many types of writing, but I was skeptical about the theories I was being offered. I realized that I did not have to agree with or accept all of the program's ideas and pedagogical philosophies, but I needed to be able to articulate why. Without reading Becca's essay, I am not sure whether I would have questioned my ideas about writing that summer, or investigated the reasoning behind my beliefs. Once I began to question them, my approach to teaching and writing slowly began to evolve.

When I first questioned my beliefs, as a new teacher, I was not ready to dive headlong into personal-discovery writing. I decided to try some of the methods that my teacher-education instructor talked so much about. I overcame my initial suspicion of process-centered pedagogy and tested drafting on my own papers. For example, in one of my first attempts at drafting, I wrote a case study about writing-center tutoring. I decided to experiment with a theme in the introduction of the first draft:

> My undergraduate experience as an English major can be summed up by the scene in *The Wizard of Oz* as Dorothy and her friends approach the "Great Wizard of Oz" for the first time. I almost expected green

smoke and flames to spring up behind the professors as they entered the room, and I was certainly feeling "small and meek" during most of the classes. As a tutor for the athletic department during my senior year of college, I saw that a different atmosphere could be created when student and teacher learn through conversation. I was pleasantly surprised that I did not have to assume the persona of the "great and powerful" to be an effective tutor. Tutoring was difficult at first because I had to try to adapt to the needs of each student, and be in tune to his or her strengths, weaknesses, and problems. The conference style atmosphere of tutoring makes it easier to adapt than in the classroom, but many of the same strategies can be applied.

Though *The Wizard of Oz* is my favorite movie, I realized after this attempt that incorporating this theme into my case study was not the best way to convey my message. I went back to the computer and drafted another introduction with a different tone:

Why should a student come to the Reading/Writing Center? I asked myself that question every time I walked by the mysterious room with the fluorescent light streaming through the white, gauzy curtains at my undergraduate institution. Not only do many students wonder, as I did, about the purpose of the Reading/Writing Center, but there are also widespread misconceptions about its function. Stephen North points out in his essay entitled "The Idea of a Writing Center" that two common misconceptions about writing centers are that they are for people who have "special problems" or that writing centers can be used as "fix-it shops" (North 24–5). Is there a hint of truth in these so-called "misconceptions"?

After this trial test of drafting, I realized that it offered the opportunity for me to change ideas, writing techniques, and rhetorical approaches without losing the benefits of each strategy. Now this realization seems like common sense, but my former idea, that there is one way to write a paper and that thinking is the key to good writing, prevented me from experimenting and really having fun.

Though I did enjoy experimenting with *The Wizard of Oz* theme, I chose the research-oriented approach to the case study. Even now, I look at that example and think, "See—research writing *is* better." But if I recall Becca's essay, I correct my oversimplification and think, "Research writing is better *in this rhetorical situation*." Recognizing the strengths and limitations of my ideas about writing is a difficult process that sometimes feels like a 12-step program.

When it was time for me to create a course syllabus for my first writing class, I took a step toward process-centered pedagogy. I was still uncomfortable with and suspicious of personal writing, but I wondered if there were a way to ease toward it. Fortunately, my program offers strands, which provide a structure for the first-year writing classes. I chose a strand entitled "Awakening Natural Curiosity," which includes several interesting paper assignments that center on ethnography. What interested me about this strand were its objectives:

> This approach to first-year writing encourages instructors to guide students as they develop their curiosity about the world around them. . . . This strand awakens students to the value of observing others, reading texts related to various communities, and considering how others would perceive their lives and surroundings. The paper assignments center on observation of activities from an outsider's perspective (Garrett, Hall, and Hunley).

I knew that this strand would reduce likelihood of having to address sensitive personal issues in the classroom, while maintaining the focus on the students' experiences and observations. It provided a way for me to experiment with a personal writing pedagogy, and to continue to gather information to develop and revise my ideas about writing.

Talking Constructively about Teaching Concerns

The first-year writing strands were an important resource that helped me to find a pedagogy that I was comfortable with as a new teacher, but talking with experienced and supportive teachers about their methods and ideas contributes significantly to the continued development of my pedagogy. I enrolled in a Theories of Composition class during my first semester, in which many knowledgeable teachers were eager to talk to me about the reasoning behind their teaching choices. Though I often did not share their pedagogical philosophies, I continued to learn to articulate and clarify my own through these discussions.

This group of encouraging teachers suggested readings that helped me to orient myself as a teacher in a new environment. Donald Murray's "Teach Writing as a Process Not Product," James A. Berlin's "Contemporary Composition: The Major Pedagogical Theories," Peter Elbow's "Being a Writer vs. Being an Academic: A Conflict in Goals," and Richard Straub's *The Practice of Response* were just a few readings that helped me to understand my role as a teacher and to develop my teaching philosophy.

Stepping Out of the Comfort Zone

Once I had I started to question my teaching philosophy, investigate new ideas about writing, and read about different pedagogical methods, I knew that I had to continue taking steps out of my comfort zone. Even today, after two years of teaching, I am still slowly changing my ideas about writing and taking steps in different directions from my original teaching philosophy. Talking to my peers, I find I am not alone. Many of my colleagues have struggled to understand how to match their teaching expectations to the realities of the classrooms they enter. For example, Ryan Holt had taught literature to high school and middle school students but had never taught writing. To aid his adjustment to teaching writing, he incorporates a novel, usually Kerouac's *The Dharma Bums,* and explains, "I teach a book because I am more comfortable with teaching literature than teaching writing. New teachers need to find the reward that they can cling to. Mine is the novel." Ryan uses the novel to ease his transition into teaching writing, but instead of a novel as the focus of his course, he limits its presence to one essay assignment: "The final paper will be a personal reaction/reflection on the book. You will write about the effects it had on you as a reader and the experiences you had reading the book" (Course Information Fall 2001).

Similarly, Keri Sanburn was influenced by her past teaching and undergraduate experience. Keri earned a position as a writing teacher at her undergraduate school after graduation and taught an intensive basic writing course with a focus on grammar. At this school she adapted to the pedagogy and explains: "My old school was really into grammar, so I was really excited about it. I had to be to make it interesting!" When Keri came to graduate school and faced the challenge of adapting to a process-oriented approach, she adapted her pedagogy again; however, she maintained a brief grammar component to make her feel comfortable in the new environment: "During my first semester in the new program, I started out with two grammar days, but now I do 10–15 minute grammar lessons and sometimes hold special office hours for students who need grammar help." Keri is gradually stepping out of her comfort zone by reducing the amount of time she spends on grammar in class.

Ryan, Keri, and I all had to adapt to a new pedagogy when we became part of the writing program, and now I realize that *all* teachers, whether they are experienced or not, have to adjust. Actually, by thinking through issues like these, I've come to see that teaching is a constant series of adjustments, and after almost two years of teaching in my program, I continue to look for ways that I can become a better teacher. Initially, adapting to a new pedagogy and academic environment might be scary, and though you cannot rely on ruby slippers to deliver you back into your old environment, here are three steps that might help you on your way:

1. Keep a double-entry journal where on one side you write what you believe to be your new writing program's goals, and on the other side write the goals that you bring to the writing program. This journal will help you to recognize the similarities and differences between your teaching philosophy and the philosophy of the program.
2. Once you have recognized the differences between your philosophy and the program's philosophy, you should explore the reasons behind both. To start your inquiry, in your double-entry journal, write lists of questions about both sets of ideas. For example, in one column I would ask: *Why do I believe that creative writing does not involve as much thought as researched critical writing*? and in the other column I would ask: *Why does this writing program value personal writing*? Questions like these provide entry points through which you can start to understand your own beliefs as well as your program's beliefs.
3. Find answers to your questions through reflection and research. It may take a long time to unpack the reasons behind your beliefs, but reflection through freewriting, through talking with friends and colleagues, or in other ways,

will help you reassess and recalibrate your beliefs. To learn more about your new writing program, pay close attention to written materials, like mission statements and teacher handbooks that might provide insight into the program's goals. Again, talk with your colleagues, both new and experienced, to compare thoughts about the adjustment process and to discover how others view and understand the program's goals.

Most important, let the adjustments come naturally. If you are feeling uncertain about your teaching philosophy in relation to the program's philosophy, don't merely accept the program's beliefs because you feel like you *must* in order to fit in. It will take brains, heart, and courage, but through confronting and understanding your and your program's ideas you will continue to learn, adapt, and grow.

Works Cited

Garrett, Caimeen, Kelly Hall, and Tom Hunley. "Awakening Natural Curiosity Approach." First Year Writing Teacher's Guide. <http://writing.fsu.edu/fyw/tguide/p2/part2e.htm>

North, Stephen M. "The Idea of a Writing Center." *The St. Martin's Sourcebook for Writing Tutors*. Ed. Christina Murphy and Steve Sherwood. New York: St. Martin's Press, 1995. 22–36.

3

What to Do When You're Not Really New

SANDRA L. GILES AND TOM C. HUNLEY

"But first, are you experienced? Have you ever been experienced? I have."
—Jimi Hendrix

We (Sandra and Tom) are both PhD-level creative writing majors and composition/rhetoric minors, active as scholars in the area of writing pedagogy. We came as graduate teaching assistants to a first-year writing program at a large liberal arts university almost three years ago, both of us having several years of experience teaching at the college level. As new, but experienced, TAs, we went through an afternoon orientation session in which the program's First-Year Writing Mission Statement was discussed, as was the basic philosophy behind process pedagogy. Then during our first year, we, along with all the other TAs in their first year of the program, attended a weekly pedagogy workshop, for which we received academic credit.

We adapted to the department's philosophy and enriched it through sharing our previous experiences during the pedagogy workshop. We also sought ways to take leadership roles, helping the brand-new TAs adjust to teaching by acting as both official and unofficial mentors. We frequently discussed the challenges these tasks presented: the challenges of fitting into a coherently designed program even though we had not been trained by that program, of how to make use of what we already knew how to do, of holding onto what was of value in our previous experience and bringing it with us into the new environment. When asked to write about these subjects for *Finding Our Way,* then, we readily agreed. The following essay transcribes e-mail conversations between the two of us in late fall of 2002.

SANDRA: I don't know about you, Tom, but my adjustment to our current composition program and philosophy of teaching was much easier than adjustments I'd had to make previously. Let me explain.

I was trained to teach composition in the summer of 1991, at the small state college where I'd just received my master's. There were only three of us in training, so we had a lot of personal attention and supervision. Our leader was a young, new assistant professor whose degree was in literature, but she'd been through TA training, and it was apparently pretty comprehensive training, having studied under people like Joseph Williams. We saw parts of his famous book on style while they were in early draft form. She grounded us in the idea of writing as a process, which was a wonderfully exciting paradigm shift for me. I'd never thought of writing that way before. When I'd been a student, we'd written timed essays and studied grammar and paragraph development in class. And that's all. It blew my mind to rethink all of that, to view writing and writing instruction as a process of clarifying thought and language, to bring a few readings into the 1101 classroom not to become the focus of the class, but to stimulate ideas and to get the conversations flowing. Our mentor also taught us to do the task of what Ed White calls the critically reflective teacher: to reflect constantly about whether what we were doing in the classroom was effective for student learning, and to listen to what the students themselves had to say about that.

So that was the foundation of my training. I was an adjunct for one year and then taught at that school for the next five years as a full-time temporary, which meant that I had all the advantages and responsibilities of a regular faculty member except those dealing with tenure. I participated in committees and department discussions about the composition program. I participated in the composition and rhetoric study group. I also read in the field on my own, and of course picked my colleagues' brains. The school's composition program was in a transitional phase in that there were many newer faculty who were grounded in process pedagogy, but there were also many established faculty who hadn't been trained that way and truly didn't see the point in it. There had been some tension, so the department did not have a unifying philosophy other than that students needed to be doing a lot of writing and getting a lot of feedback. Other than that, we were encouraged by the administration to do what we deeply believed was best for the students. So I did. And I learned a lot by trial and error—for example, that organizing a freshman writing class according to the old rhetorical modes was far too easy for them, and too superficial. And boring.

Then in the fall of 1997, I managed to land a tenure-track position at a junior college, which both is and is not like a community college. The mix of students is really interesting: open admissions students, students who could have gotten scholarships to any place they wanted but chose to stay close to home for the freshman year and then transfer, and everyone else in between, including a large percentage of nontraditional students. This school's comp program was also in a transitional phase: newer faculty grounded in process pedagogy, some established faculty who had shifted to it, but others who resisted. The administration here, though, had decided to handle the situation differently. And by the administration, I mean every level from the department all the way up to the academic dean. They decided to force everyone to adopt process pedagogy, by which they meant their version of it, which was never clearly defined. At the same time, because we were such a small school, we were under much stronger pressure from the governor and the state board of regents to deal with the whole assessment and accountability issue. The statewide attitude in education became, at that time, that we teachers didn't really know what we were doing, that we had not been doing a good job, and that we would need to be forced to do a good job. So all of that began to hit the fan the year before I came on board. Imagine.

My first day on the job at the junior college, I was handed the department's mission statement for the composition program. The department's philosophy made total sense to me. It emphasized writing as a recursive process of developing ideas and drafting and rewriting. It called for students to be exposed to writing by both their peers and professional writers. It stated that students should get frequent feedback from both their peers and their instructor, and that the feedback should be encouraging. That philosophy matched both my training and the teaching style that I had developed for myself. I felt very much at home, at first. But I soon became as confused and frustrated as the rest of the department because the administration apparently wanted something very, very specific. They would gather us together in long meetings to chide us for not having a one hundred percent pass rate (in an open admissions junior college, no less). They would berate us for not running our classes the "right" way. We'd ask what the right way was, and they'd tell us we should go read up on pedagogical theory. As if we weren't doing that already. One meeting would stress the need to provide a real, actual audience and purpose for the students. The next would emphasize the need for total and free self-expression for the students and their development of their individual voices. The following meeting would present academic writing as the be-all, end-all purpose of a comp class. Each meeting's emphasis would be presented as the one "right" approach to teaching. We were confused, and our administrative evaluations depended on our figuring out what the heck the administration wanted.

For a while, I tried to figure out what they wanted. Then I gave up and did what my own experience and conscience told me worked best. My students said, in their evaluations and in their reflective writings, that they were learning more about writing in my class than they ever had before. But the pressure from the administration was intense. I was almost frustrated enough to look for other types of jobs, but then I spent five weeks one summer in a National Writing Project Summer Institute, which renewed my enthusiasm for teaching. And then in my third year at the junior college, I went through a pretty grueling pre-tenure evaluation, in which instructional effectiveness was the main factor evaluated. My evaluation was positive. Still, the overall atmosphere in the department was extremely tense, confused, frustrating. I felt I wasn't adjusting at all to that program.

And then the following year, I found myself in graduate school, pursuing my PhD and serving as a TA. That's when you and I met, Tom. Since by that time I'd had almost ten years of teaching experience at the college level, I wasn't required to go through the teaching assistant "boot camp." We TAs who had previous experience met one afternoon before fall semester began, during which time the First-Year Writing Program's Mission Statement was explained to us. Once again, here was a mission statement that fit with my own teaching philosophy.

I was still a little edgy, though, because of the tense three years I'd just been through. Even here at this huge school with somewhere around a hundred composition TAs, it seemed that something more specific than just the underlying philosophy of process was expected. Here, though, I wasn't under the same kind of scrutiny, or the same terribly confusing set of contradictory expectations. Still, it seems like one of the hardest things about adjusting to a new program is figuring out what the heck "they" want.

TOM: It sounds like administrative pressure at that junior college made for a tough atmosphere, but at least the department made efforts to ensure that its teachers were engaged in critical self-reflection. (I'm thinking of the pressure of the merit raises but even more about requiring instructors to read the latest journals.) When I think back to my community college adjuncting experiences, the title of this book, *Finding Our Way,* seems apt. I was given a set of textbooks (and in one merciful case, a sample syllabus) and wished good luck.

In 1994, I began work on my MFA in creative writing, which I believed would be my ticket to a satisfying teaching career. I was not awarded a teaching assistantship, and it wasn't long before I was collecting food stamps, an important part of the graduate school experience, I suppose. I desperately wanted to teach, and it killed me to hear some of the teaching assistants talking about their TA duties as if they were odious chores. I decided that if I minored in composition/rhetoric, the department would be bound to offer me an assistantship during my second year in the program. During my first term, I enrolled in a course called "The Composing Curriculum." We read books by James Moffett, Peter Elbow, and others. We read one book about portfolio grading and another about ebonics and standard English. We kicked around terms that were new to me such as "process era" and "post-process era," and we tried out writing exercises that my classmates could use with their students. Since I wasn't teaching, I packed away a lot of the theory, but I didn't have any way to connect it to practice. In my second term, I took Research Design and Evaluation in Composition Instruction. I ended up giving a presentation on peer mentoring, but again, it was all abstract to me. At that same time, I began working in the school's writing center, which they called a "writer's center," because they were devoted to producing better writers rather than better pieces of writing (process rather than product). Before getting to work one-on-one with student writers, we had to receive some training which included reading a packet of essays about using Bakhtin in the classroom and issues such as that. We were called "responders" rather than "tutors." This was a chance to begin connecting theory to practice.

My comp/rhet minor didn't get me an assistantship, but it did get me the next best thing: a pair of instructional internships at the local community college. There I worked with a wonderful master teacher. During my first quarter with him, we team-taught World Literature and Basic Writing. For a few weeks, I observed while he taught. Then we took turns, and after class he would give me pointers. Then, once he was satisfied that I knew what I was doing, he more or less turned the classes over to me. During our second quarter together, we taught an on-line composition class. It was something the school was just trying out, and my master teacher was doing it for the first time, just as I was. It wasn't going very well; about half of the students ultimately dropped out. Because of this, I think, I wasn't given as large of a role, and I didn't get a chance to try out many of the theories I had learned about in my composition and rhetoric classes.

Then I was out of teaching for one and a half years, though not outside academia. I was working as a public relations writer at a community college on the East Coast. After I'd gotten pretty adept at the PR job, I decided that while I was there, I'd like to adjunct as well. The English department didn't answer my inquiries, so I started teaching continuing-education classes (creative writing, basic grammar, and developmental writing). I was given a book and bidden good luck. I didn't even have contact with any other teachers. From my master's-level comp/rhet classes, I remembered the importance of stressing revision, but that was about it. The textbooks were current-traditional, walking students through paragraphs and essays based on the modes of discourse.

I found it enormously satisfying to be working with these determined students, most of whom were trying to get up to speed so that they could start taking college-transfer courses. So, when my wife and I moved to the West Coast in August 1998, I applied for adjunct positions at every college in the vicinity. During the week before classes started, I received offers from two colleges and accepted them both. One school furnished me with textbooks, a grade book, and a sample syllabus. The other school, which hired me on a Friday to start teaching the following Tuesday, just gave me the textbooks. So I quickly cobbled together syllabi and weekly planners for three sections of composition, using readers, the modes, grammar drills, peer critique, and multiple revisions of essays. Between those two colleges, I taught full-time for the next two years. I made various modifications in my courses based on suggestions from faculty members who observed my teaching and others who just shared their ideas with me. I also paid a lot of attention to the evaluations I got from students, and I was pleased to see those getting better each quarter.

One change I made was to stop drilling on grammar, opting instead to integrate grammar lessons with their revision process through what I call "debugging" assignments. When my students debug, they look at a handbook such as Chris Anson's *The Longman Writer's Companion* or Ann Raime's *Keys for Writers* and use it for help with revising specific features of their drafts-in-process. For example, if a student's draft contains an abundance of distracting comma splices, I might point out specific pages in the handbook that will help the student figure out how to rewrite one of the comma splices three ways: as a complex sentence, as a compound sentence joined by a comma and a coordinating conjunction, and as a simple sentence with one of the original clauses enclosed by either parentheses or dashes.

Another gradual change I made was to make paper topics more open-ended, less canned. This was in part for my own survival. Could I stand to read very many more essays comparing and contrasting apples and oranges? How many more argumentative/ persuasive essays could I read about the death penalty or abortion? So I did start to be more creative with paper topics, but I still wasn't deeply involved with constructive conversations with other teachers about what works and what doesn't. I wanted some training that consisted of solid (up-to-date, though not "trendy") ideas and clear ways to put them into practice.

I'd like to hear more about that National Writing Project Summer Institute that you participated in. Was it very helpful in integrating theory and practice?

SANDRA: Oh yes, it was a wonderful experience. I attended the South Georgia Writing Project Institute in the summer of 1999. We met for five weeks, five days a week. There were about twenty of us, I think: all teachers interested in incorporating writing into their teaching were invited to apply. Most of us were English or language arts teachers, but there were also math and P.E. teachers, for example. From all levels—kindergarten to high school, college TAs-in-training to me. We read and discussed and argued composition theory, traded ideas for classroom applications, led each other through classroom activities, and so on. I spent an awful lot of time making things out of construction paper (when an elementary teacher was leading class) and at first I turned my nose up at that kind of thing, but then I realized I needed to put more creativity back into my own classroom, to make class a richer experience for the students. I revisited my lesson plans and added more hands-on activities, brought in different types of media, and found ways to encourage creativity. I found the whole experience inspiring. It reawakened my enthusiasm for teaching, gave me a lot of ideas. Plus, it was really interesting to see how first-grade teachers, for example, teach writing and get their kids interested in learning. It was also particularly interesting to work with high school teachers, to see how they do things and why they do them that way, to understand the administrative and other types of pressures they're under. It helped me to think about my own students' writing in the context of their whole education, the arc of it. Very eye-opening. I have to admit, though, the major thing I learned from the Institute was so basic, I don't know how I hadn't known it before: to write with my students.

Tom, it sounds like in your earlier experience, you made a very determined individual effort to connect theory and practice, and to hold them both against actual student performance and attitudes. That, I think, is the key to effective teaching. And I think that there are a lot of adjuncts out there who take their work very seriously, but often don't get noticed for it because they're not around the department for meetings and such.

I'm curious about the on-line course you were involved with. Why do you think so many students dropped out? The reason I ask is that I've heard of that happening quite a bit with on-line freshman classes, and not just writing classes.

TOM: I can briefly address my experience with the on-line class. It does relate to our topic, I think, in that it was a trial-and-error learning experience for me, and one thing that experienced teaching assistants can bring to a composition program is the benefit of their own teaching history, including (and perhaps especially including) their past mistakes.

In my case, I think my co-teacher and I would have had a higher retention rate with an honors class, perhaps, or in a second-semester composition class whose students had already been acclimated to college. Or it might have worked as a continuing education class for self-motivated learners. The class was supposed to attract nontraditional students such as single parents living in remote locations, but I think it attracted a lot of students who just didn't want to get out of bed and head to class. Also, I think they just needed more personal contact, more encouragement. I'm a big fan of computer classrooms and of integrating course management systems such as Blackboard in writing classrooms, but students need to feel like part of a vital, living community of writers. This means having them write together, writing with them, holding conferences (both one-to-one and with groups), having students share their invention exercises with the class or reading selected invention exercises out loud ourselves, singling them out as examples worthy of public praise. I guess I'm saying that, for whatever reason, my co-teacher and I weren't able to get the energy level up the way we can in a live classroom. We could try to prod, cheerlead, and motivate via e-mails and announcements, but somehow we weren't able to share our enthusiasm for the writing process as effectively in the virtual classroom as we would have in a shared physical space. It's been several years, though, and I would be willing to try teaching an on-line class again. After every less-than-successful classroom experience, there's always the urge to tinker and try again.

So one of the questions for you and me to address in this conversation, I think, is how experienced teaching assistants can make themselves available as a resource in terms of lessons learned through trial and error, such as the one I just described, and lessons learned through formal training and brainstorming, such as what you described with National Writing Project Summer Institute. How can experienced teaching assistants most effectively bring their past experiences into the forefront to the benefit of the program they find themselves teaching in? A separate issue, also important, is how an experienced teaching assistant can adapt his/her teaching practice to conform to a department's carefully theorized ways of running classes in a fairly consistent way, without discounting his/her training and experience picked up in other places. In other words, if the experienced teaching assistant is used to a different pedagogical model than the one practiced within the department, how can he/she teach within the program's accepted parameters without completely discarding what he/she has learned elsewhere?

SANDRA: I think you've homed in on the two most important issues for experienced TAs: integrating into the department, but also valuing and making use of their prior experience. So I guess the first step is that somehow, experienced TAs should make sure that the department's TA trainers and mentors know just what their prior training and experience consist of, while showing a sincere desire to be oriented into the new department.

Some departments could facilitate this by offering an orientation session longer than just one day or one afternoon, like the one we went through. If the new TAs understand that they will be contributing to the training, sharing their prior experience and training and being valued for it, rather than just sitting through a standard orientation, then they should be willing to devote the time and effort. And a longer orientation session, for experienced TAs, would ensure that the new people understand the department's missions and goals. For example, here at the school where you and I are now, the first-year writing program is very dedicated to process pedagogy. If some of the new folks have been trained in some other approach, then it will be quite a paradigm shift to align themselves with our philosophy. If I had come here not knowing what process pedagogy was, or not really understanding what it was and how it affects daily classroom methods, then I would have needed an extended opportunity to rethink thoroughly what I'd been doing. Being handed the formal mission statement and the TA guidebook would not have been enough to help me make that paradigm change, no matter how willing I was to try. I think that a longer orientation at the end of the summer, say a weekend-long session, would be valuable because it would allow people to replan their classes, if needed, before those classes actually started.

In departments that don't offer extended orientation sessions, experienced TAs might have to go out of their way to make sure that those in charge are aware of the nature and extent of their prior training and experience. This might mean handing out copies of their *curriculum vitae* with cover letters, or it might mean scheduling informal meetings with TA trainers and mentors. They will also have to learn as much as they can independently about the department's teaching philosophy to make sure their classroom practice is in line with it.

TOM: You suggested that a longer orientation session for experienced teaching assistants would help the department make use of those assistants' prior experience. That could be valuable, but the other obvious avenue is the year-long pedagogy workshop. I think that all TAs in a pedagogy workshop, both the experienced TAs and the first-time teachers, could benefit from two types of presentations: (1) second-year PhD students with experience teaching at other institutions could offer special insight into the culture of the department's writing program, the shared philosophy of its senior instructors, as it compares with the culture of other programs with which they have been affiliated; (2) experienced TAs who are new to the department could prepare and deliver presentations to the brand-new teaching assistants. I think this would be a great way to value what experienced TAs have learned from their prior teaching experiences, and it would give the new teaching assistants a broader understanding of the full range of theories and practices that exist in the field. For example, if one of the experienced teaching assistants has a background in writing across the curriculum (WAC), in distance learning, or in community service pedagogy, he/she could share that experience with the beginning pedagogy workshop. Other TAs with previous experience might choose to discuss what they've learned through trial and error about handling discipline problems, confronting plagiarism, encouraging participation, and various other classroom management issues.

SANDRA: You mentioned several areas in which experienced instructors could offer their expertise—community-service learning, distance learning, etc. I know that you and a few others who came into the program the same time could have offered a lot. You, for example, have much to offer because of your experience teaching creative writing.

I'm sitting here thinking of topics on which I could have contributed: I have taught upper-division business writing, basic or remedial writing, and literature. You and I both have a lot of experience working with nontraditional students. I've been a writing center coordinator and have served on committees whose charge was to define the writing program's mission in line with the college's overall mission. I served on a committee whose job was to facilitate the remedial writing department's move from a separate developmental studies division to the English department, and to then redefine remedial writing's philosophy. There's the National Writing Project Institute.

TOM: Since you had experience as a writing-center coordinator, a worthy project for you to pursue might have been to prepare and give a presentation to the tutors and/or administrators in the university's Reading/Writing Center. They, in turn, could have taken whatever tidbits they liked, presumably those that gelled with the department's shared philosophy, and discarded the rest. The point is that the department would have been valuing your input.

As far as creative writing, I had taught it seven times before I came to FSU, and I could have given a presentation on that to the pedagogy workshop. I did informally recommend textbooks to several TAs. But, as you know, I advocate separate pedagogy workshops for everyone who wants to teach creative writing, and I'm delighted to hear that our university is considering offering such a class.

SANDRA: Well, I'm not sure I agree that creative writing pedagogy should be entirely separate; for one reason, a lot of teachers use CRW-type assignments and activities in class. But I know what you mean; you want a space where CRW pedagogy can be the focus, and I do think such a space has been sorely lacking in the field.

There's another thing you and I could offer our less experienced colleagues. I think you and I both have taught at schools that are more like the schools where most of them will eventually teach, don't you think?

TOM: I agree that a lot of our classmates, particularly those MA students who don't have immediate plans for pursuing doctorates, would benefit from knowing more about junior colleges and community colleges. They might also benefit from hearing from experienced TAs who have previously worked as adjuncts at universities. A couple of our classmates came to this department with backgrounds as university adjuncts. What if we had put together a panel addressing the various rewards and pitfalls associated with each of these different teaching situations? It might have been very enlightening for some of the less experienced TAs, especially those who intend to go directly onto the job market after completing their master's degrees.

SANDRA: Oh, I definitely agree that folks who are about to go onto the job market should be aware of differences in student populations. The students here at our university are not like the majority of students the TAs will eventually teach. At the schools where I've taught before, there were students who were fabulous writers, highly experienced writers, but they would sit in class beside students who'd never before been asked to write anything longer than a paragraph, because they had not been in the college prep track during high school. The writing potential was there, but the students had virtually no experience and desperately needed help, needed to learn a lot of the technical aspects of writing, if they were going to survive this or any of their other college classes.

I would never argue that composition classes are solely service courses—they can and should be so much more than that—but there are certain skills that we need to make sure students have before they leave us to go to their future college classes, and to their futures in general. And while that may not be such a big issue at universities like ours, a Research I university, it will be an issue in other places. Graduating TAs should be aware of this, or they'll be thrown by the questions they'll be asked when interviewing at smaller and less prestigious schools. And they'll really be thrown for a loop when they start teaching in those places.

And that kind of advice is something we experienced TAs can offer to our classmates, since our program's administrators understandably would rather focus their efforts on training instructors for our program in particular. As you suggested before, maybe we could design a panel for the end of the year in a pedagogy workshop, or the following year as a one-time workshop, a sort of "here's what to expect when you leave" kind of thing.

Or maybe these issues should be addressed earlier. Even here at our university, all students must complete the first-year writing sequence, and must do so in their first year. There's a reason behind that requirement; the courses are prerequisites to other classes, all over campus, for a reason. When I served as a mentor here last year, I sensed that the experienced TAs were aware of this issue but that the new TAs were not necessarily aware of it. They tended to see the composition class as being divorced entirely from the context of the students' overall education. That attitude, I firmly believe, encourages students to view what they learn in comp class as being divorced from their own overall education, and then there's no transfer of learning.

In closing, I'd like to suggest that folks who bring experience to a TA composition program do a couple of things. First of all, they should find out the basic philosophy of the program. Any program will design its philosophy around the types of students it gets, as well as the type of university it is (technical, or pre-professional, or liberal arts, or what have you). If they're lucky, there will be some sort of orientation program which will be comprehensive enough at least to introduce that philosophy. If not, they should sit down and talk with the program's administrators and a couple of TAs who have been there awhile. If the new-but-experienced TAs then have to change their classroom practices to be in line with the new program, they should see it as an opportunity to expand their repertoire, a chance to broaden their understanding of different types of pedagogies and various types of students with widely varying needs. This kind of broadened understanding can only help them when they begin interviewing for jobs, and when they actually begin the jobs.

TOM: Well stated, Sandra. I'd like to add that new-but-experienced TAs have a responsibility to their fellow incoming TAs who have never taught before. A new-but-experienced TA can speak to an entirely new TA from the unique perspective of someone who is making the same kinds of adjustments but has been down similar roads before and encountered many of the roadblocks and potholes that the novice TA is liable to encounter. Whether this informal mentoring takes the form of classroom visits, topical presentations delivered in front of the pedagogy workshop, or kind words of advice offered in the hallways, it can make the transition to a new school smoother for everyone involved, and it can make for better, more confident, more satisfied teachers throughout the department's TA pool.

4

When You Look and Sound "Un-American": Advice for Foreign-Born Teachers of Writing

PAVEL ZEMLIANSKY, FADI AL-ISSA, HSI-LING HUANG, AND MASOOD RAJA

Introduction

In this discussion, we share narratives and reflections about being foreign-born writing teachers in the United States. Each of us came to the United States to attend graduate school and very soon found ourselves teaching writing to American students. All four of us use English as a second, and, sometimes, third language, and despite years of learning and using English, when we began teaching writing in America, we faced a set of unique problems which our US counterparts have never had to face. In addition to overcoming the usual challenges facing new teachers, we sometimes had to convince our students and administrators that our English skills were sufficient for the classroom and that we were qualified to teach writing.

To put our teaching histories into perspective and to examine how they fit into the broader picture of foreign-born teachers' work, we connected our narratives in this essay with an analysis of existing published research about the work of international teaching assistants (ITAs) in this country. At the end of the essay, we share our recommendations to foreign-born writing teachers and to the program and department administrators who train and direct them.

* * *

Before Teaching Writing in America

Before coming to America to attend graduate school, we were proficient users of English with significant teaching experience. We had studied English for many years and had

taught students of various ages and ability levels. After coming to the United States, however, only Fadi and Masood were given teaching responsibilities immediately. Pavel and Hsi-Ling had to take research assistant positions for their first year of graduate school and were only allowed to teach one year later.

Pavel

I had long studied and used English in my native Ukraine before deciding to pursue graduate studies in the United States. I began studying English in elementary school as a six-year-old, with an experienced and dedicated English teacher. Having forgotten all my other school classes, I still vividly remember my earliest English lesson. On the first day of school, the teacher brought paper cut-outs of traffic lights and taught us the colors in English.

I took English for ten years in secondary school before becoming an English and translation major in a fiercely competitive department of foreign languages at Kharkov State University in Ukraine. At the end of each semester, all students in my department were ranked according to our exam scores, and the rankings were made public within the department. In addition to high grades, top achievers won free semesters of study in England, France, or Germany and other perks. Being near the top of that rating list during my third year in college won me a semester at the University of Bath in England.

After graduating, I got a job with the Cultural Section of the British Embassy in Ukraine, where I used English daily to communicate with my British bosses and to teach English-language teaching methods to teachers of all levels. Simultaneously, I was teaching English and translation courses to university students and tutoring privately. By the time I decided to come to the United States, I was a proficient user of English with substantial teaching experience.

During my first year in graduate school in the United States, I was a research assistant to three faculty members. The work was in general enjoyable, and I gained useful experience about the workings of an American university. I even ended up being a de facto co-editor of a scholarly book. I adjusted socially and became more confident about my English. I was "working my way up" to becoming a writing teacher.

All twelve graduate students in our small department shared a large office, where each of us had a desk. While not really resentful about not teaching, I could not ignore the fact that, while my fellow first-year graduate students held conferences with their students or taught writing or literature, I was making photocopies of articles or preparing the next mass-mailing for the department's Visiting Writers Program fund-raising campaign.

Hsi-Ling

Before I came to America in 1996, I had been teaching English, from kindergarten to adult levels, for years. When I applied to graduate schools in America, I discovered that the requirements for creative writing, which I was interested in, were higher than for most other areas. Most majors require a score of 550 on the Test of English as a Foreign Language (TOEFL), which is administered by the Educational Testing Service and is required of all foreign applicants to US colleges. To enter a creative writing program, however, I was required to have a score of at least 600 along with a thirty- to fifty-page writing sample. I was accepted by Bowling Green State University in Ohio and awarded a teaching assistantship by the Creative Writing Program. However, as the only international student among the new and old students in the program, I was not given a class to teach. Instead, the English Department—which determined who was qualified to teach but was not responsible for my assistantship—assigned me to tutor in the writing lab for my first year, and expected me to teach the second year.

Fadi

I learned English as a child, at the same time as Arabic, which is my native language. My father, who is a professor of English literature, taught me English in my early years. Then I traveled with my family to England, where I stayed for four years. While in England, I was able to use English daily and adapt to the new environment without any problem. My grades were high, and I was one of the top students in my class. When I traveled back to my native Syria, I had no problems in English classes. In fact, I helped my classmates with some of their problems with English. In addition to that, in seventh grade I began tutoring. I was not paid for my work, but it was a way for me to maintain my English-language skills. I helped my cousins, my friends, and the kids in the neighborhood with their homework.

Private English-language institutes began offering me teaching positions as soon as I became a freshman in the English department. I declined the offers because I wanted to focus on my studies. During my senior year in college, I transferred to Damascus University in the capital city. There I was able to take a teacher-training course at the American Language Center. I took this course to be informed of the latest teaching methods and theories and to sharpen my teaching skills further. Immediately after graduating college, I went back to my hometown of Lattakia and took a full-time teaching position at the most prestigious and well known language institute there. That is when I began to make a living out of teaching English to ESL students ranging from the ages of five to fifty. I enjoyed an excellent reputation because of my proficiency and fluency in English, and this success enabled me, in February 2001, to establish and run my own language institute that teaches only English. At the Institute, I taught courses in English for communicative and educational purposes. I even taught literature-appreciation and essay-writing courses.

Masood

I moved to the United States in 1996 after ten years of military service in the Pakistan army as an infantry officer. I spent the first five years of my stay in America obtaining a bachelor's and a master's degree at Belmont University. While working toward my master's degree, I did not teach a class of my own, primarily because the English department at Belmont did not employ TAs. I did, however, help several professors with their classes by participating in their class discussion panels, giving occasional lectures, and sitting in as a graduate participant in their undergraduate courses. This experience was completely different from being a TA, for various reasons. The students didn't have to take me as an authority figure, and to them I was only a guest speaker who was there to enhance their learning experience. Thus, the student response in this phase of my teaching in America was quite positive.

International Teaching Assistants in US Higher Education

Hiring foreign-born teaching assistants is a common practice in US higher education. This practice is especially widespread in science and mathematics departments of large public universities. Yet, as the review of research below shows, there is an uneasy feeling among many educational administrators, students, and their parents about the quality of their foreign-born teachers, especially about their language skills.

According to the 1992 study "Crossing Pedagogical Oceans: International Teaching Assistants in US Undergraduate Education," by Rosslyn Smith et al., "Changing scientific and technical education demographics have led in the late 20th century to the appointment of significant numbers of international students as graduate teaching assistants at US institutions" (2). The authors attribute this growth in the numbers of ITAs to the fact that "many American students turn to careers that do not require graduate study" (2).

Traditionally, science and mathematics departments have employed larger numbers of ITAs than have departments of English, writing, and foreign languages. At least two factors can account for such a disparity. First, many undergraduate science and math courses are organized around the "lecture and discussion" format. Within this format, a full-time, experienced professor delivers lectures to large classes, which are then broken up into smaller groups for seminar-style discussions led by teaching assistants. In such courses, teaching assistants are given only a supporting role. They help the professor in teaching the course by leading class discussions and, sometimes, by grading exams, but they rarely have control over the course design and pedagogy.

Second, the subject matter of science, math, and other lecture-based courses is often seen as separate from the language used to teach it. Language is seen merely as a communication device used to impart the content of the course to the students. In popular perception, language is not the substance of instruction here and is, therefore, subordinate to the course content. In writing and literature classes, on the other hand, language is at the center of instruction. In order to teach American students to write in English, an international teaching assistant must be a good writer in English.

As the numbers of foreign teaching assistants in American universities grew larger, policymakers in different states responded to what Smith et al. (1992), Rao Nagesh (1995), and other researchers have called "the foreign TA language problem." Smith states that, since 1992, following student and parent complaints about ITAs' lack of language proficiency, eighteen states "have passed laws or implemented system-wide mandates to assess the language skills of ITAs" (3). For instance, one of us was requested to submit additional evidence of language proficiency to the state while already teaching writing in the United States.

The hiring of many ITAs may have started as a "necessary evil" some years ago when universities could not attract enough American applicants. Since then, however, it has yielded the benefit of bringing into this country many qualified and highly motivated foreign nationals ready to learn and work. Still, as Smith et al.'s study suggests,

> For many US students, parents, and academic and political leaders, the demographic change is viewed as part of the crisis in undergraduate education, the overhauling of graduate education, and the research function of the university and its faculty. Critics call for the use of regular full-time faculty in undergraduate courses rather than graduate teaching assistants. (2)

That research and publishing distract faculty from teaching is, of course, a charge familiar to many academics, especially those working in research-oriented universities.

Smith et al.'s assessment of the public reaction to the increasing number of ITAs in American universities adds an extra dimension to the problem. Not only do American universities have to use more graduate students to teach classes because full-time faculty are too busy researching and publishing, but now they also have to turn to foreign-born graduate students to fill teaching vacancies. And while the proficiency of ITAs in their areas of study is often beyond question, their lack of English language and communication skills often prevents them from teaching effectively.

*   *   *

First Day in Class

We believe that our "first-day-in the-classroom" experiences are different from those of our American counterparts. We have foreign names and accents. Over the years, we have developed methods of introducing ourselves to our students in ways that would help them see us as teachers first and as foreigners second. The need to develop these special introductions may sound trivial for some of our readers. Yet, writing teachers know that the success of every given course depends, in a large degree, on the class chemistry and the interpersonal relationship between the teacher and the students.

Pavel

I don't recall the details of the first class that I taught in America five years ago. As all beginning teachers, I was probably nervous and anxious to do well. Even with several years of experience in teaching English as a foreign language and teacher training, I must have wondered how American students would react to my foreign name and accent. Before, when I taught English in Ukraine, I could enter the classroom with a feeling of linguistic superiority. I could speak, write, and teach English much better than any of my students. Now that I was facing my American students, I could not be sure. After several years of teaching writing in America, I can not count on my students' mostly benevolent reaction when I enter the classroom in the beginning of each semester.

"Hello and welcome to the course."

A mild surprise in their eyes. They have picked up the accent.

"My name is Pavel Zemliansky. You can call me Pavel."

By now they know they have a foreign teacher. Some smile while others frown. A few are probably thinking "Oh, no!"

"I have a foreign name and I hope you can learn it. I will do my best to learn your names quickly," I say smiling and trying to sound friendly but firm.

To break the ice, I always ask students to interview each other, to learn each other's names and other basic information. After that, I invite them to ask me questions about myself. The first of these questions is usually "Where are you from?"

A lot of what I do here is no different from other teachers' first days in the classroom; yet, I am always conscious of the additional task that I have. I must allay any potential concerns about my English skills and prevent any of my students from thinking that they got the short end of the stick by being in a class taught by a foreigner. During more than five years of teaching writing in America, I have never encountered students who were openly hostile to me as a teacher because I was a foreigner. The criticisms I receive in their end-of-semester evaluations of me usually stem from some other aspects of my teaching.

Hsi-Ling

My first teaching job in the United States was tutoring in the writing lab. My experience there was generally positive even though I encountered the "Oh No! Syndrome" on a daily basis. My students began to show appreciation for my teaching only toward the end of the semester. Some seemed to feel embarrassed that a foreigner could identify their problems in writing. It was very rewarding that the following semester many of my returning tutees insisted on being my regular students.

Not all was good, though. At the end of my first year in the lab, the English department's graduate advisor had a talk with me. He made up stories about my writing-lab supervisor complaining about my poor performance and said that he couldn't let me teach anymore. On top of that, he was going to discontinue my assistantship. Fortunately, my teachers in the creative writing program were very supportive and reassured me that the English department had no authority to cancel my assistantship, which was awarded by the creative writing program. I was allowed to continue working in the writing lab for another semester and made a research assistant the following semester. Although the department's graduate advisor who had confronted me earlier was later on let go from the job because of allegations of racism and sexism, I felt that I was denied teaching opportunities unjustly. Ironically, while my ability to teach was being questioned, I won a summer fellowship in a competition which was judged anonymously by a creative writing professor from another school. Still, none of my fellow graduate students congratulated me.

When I moved to Tallahassee to start my doctoral studies at Florida State University, I was happy that the English department provided a six-week TA training session. The program was intense, and we nicknamed it "boot camp." Given my previous negative experience with tutoring, I would have felt much less confident as a teacher had I not participated in the summer training.

On my first day in class, I was a little nervous, but since I had been a tutor for so long, I felt that I was able to handle any situation. When I entered the classroom, I immediately noticed some of the students' expression had changed to "Oh, no!" Before I even exposed my accent, I wrote down "Hsi-Ling Huang" on the board and asked, "Anybody know how to pronounce my name?" Silence. "Extra credit?" A couple of brave souls raised their hands, but, of course, didn't say my name right. But my humorous introduction relaxed them and put a smile on their faces. I told them I was originally from Taiwan and, most recently, from Ohio. I thought that sharing my experience could help them appreciate me as a teacher. It was a mistake.

My students seemed to mistake my friendliness for weakness. They began to make fun of my pronunciation or intentionally asked me to repeat what I said. I tried to talk in a firm tone, but it didn't work very well, since I am only five feet one and skinny, and have a soft voice. Some students disagreed with my criteria when I graded their papers because they didn't trust a nonnative speaker's ability to judge their writing in their mother tongue. Many students either talked back or rolled their eyes when I lectured. Coming from a culture where the distance between teachers and students is bigger and where students rarely disagree with their teachers out loud, I was shocked to discover how disrespectful American students could be toward their teachers. I was also disappointed by how many of my students cared only about their grades and not about improving as writers.

Masood

It was at Florida State that I first planned and taught two courses without the direct supervision of a professor. My earlier classroom teaching experience was from Pakistan, where I had taught small arms and minor tactics to young officers at the School of Infantry and Tactics. With my Pakistani experience and my experience at Belmont University, I felt quite ready to teach a class on my own. Still, when I walked into my classroom, I was a bit apprehensive. Even though I was quite sure of my ability to teach, I wasn't quite sure how the students would respond to a teacher from Pakistan in post–September 11 America.

Well, I walked into my classroom, introduced myself, and then asked the students to introduce themselves to each other. I could tell that some of the students weren't sure about my ability to teach them, which, of course, was expected on their part, for not only was I foreign, I also had a very thick foreign accent. At the end of the class, I told them: "I am here to teach you how to write from your hearts, and if you trust me during this semester, we will all become better writers together."

My personal approach to teaching writing is very simple: as a teacher I must care about my students' writing. Also, when I ask my students to write expressive essays about their personal lives, I feel the need to share some of my own personal experiences. I was aware that I had to prove my competence and my beliefs to them in many overt and subtle ways. During the semester, I used one class session just to answer my students' questions; most of these were about my person, my country, and my experiences. This attempt at making our relationship more personal and open paid off. In a class survey, administered to the students at the end of the semester, more than seventy percent of them declared this activity as the event that made them trust me more as their teacher.

As an ITA I do not necessarily carry a chip on my shoulder, but I do understand that we have to prove our worth to earn respect, just like every one else. Foreign-born teachers simply have to work a little harder. During the semester, I shared one of my essays about September 11 with the students. I had written this essay at my previous university; it captured my feelings and emotions on that day. *The Belmont Literary Journal* chose the essay as the best prose piece. There were two reasons to share the essay with my students—first, to show them that I felt the same sense of loss as they felt about the tragedy of September 11, and second, to show them a piece of writing that also functioned as a mark of personal achievement in writing. This experience worked well, and over fifty percent of the students surveyed felt like trusting me more as a teacher and a human being after this reading.

Another thing that I have always admired in my own teachers is kindness. Thus, in my own teaching role, I tried to be as kind as possible. Now, kindness does not necessarily mean weakness. I was always polite, but firm. I tried to convey to my students that I would listen to them if they had any problems and that I would try to work with them if any class rules were hurting a student unduly. Thus, my class policy was fair but fluid and took into account the various responsibilities, problems, and personal dilemmas of students. This really worked well, for I did not know that one of the biggest fears these students had was that, being a foreigner, I would be either too strict, too rigid, or too pedantic (eighty percent of my students reported feeling this way). Thus, a little bit of genuine kindness—which is my moral code, anyway—went a long way in winning the students' trust.

Fadi

When I started teaching my first course, I had been in the United States for only two months. So I was a little bit nervous because I was not accustomed to the American educational system, nor did I know about the things students were taught in high school. So one way that I got over my nervousness was by arriving to class ten minutes early. It started at 10:10 a.m. I was there at 10 a.m. I went in and sat in the corner as if I were one of the students. I began having discussions with them and asking them things like "Do you have a map of the campus? What is the time? What is your major?" They might sound like simple questions, which they are, but this was an icebreaking activity for me. I stayed seated and talked until it was 10:15. Yes, I was intentionally late starting the class. However, I was in class without that hierarchy of teacher-student. Everything was in harmony without such a distinction. After I stood up and introduced myself as the teacher, most students were not as nervous as they had been when we talked about the class before it started. Neither was I. Why? Because we had talked without being divided by the teacher-student hierarchy. That was how I kept the class functioning "all for one and one for all." Everyone had a responsibility, and I made it clear that they were more responsible because they were twenty-four different minds, twenty-four unique experiences, and twenty-four majors while I was only one of them. I did not have a problem because I was an international teaching assistant. Although I had the accent, I was able to make up for it with my fluency in English and sense of humor.

*   *   *

How American Students Perceive Their Foreign-Born Teachers

The following section summarizes and explains research data on how American college students perceive their foreign-born teachers. The data are scarce, but what is available shows that often students do not go beyond their foreign teachers' less-than-perfect English skills in evaluating their teaching. Also, students often tend to expect a low level of English proficiency from their foreign-born teachers.

Little research on the topic exists, but what is available shows that the relationships between American students and their foreign-born instructors are not always great. In his 1995 article "The 'Oh No!' Syndrome: A Language Expectation Model of Undergraduates' Negative Reactions toward Foreign Teaching Assistants," Nagesh Rao cites a study of over three hundred undergraduate students, many of whom came into classes taught by foreign teaching assistants with low expectations of their teachers' language abilities. According to the study, foreign TAs with "heavy accents" were perceived as "difficult to follow," and many students felt "angry and anxious" in a class taught by a foreign teaching assistant. The study also showed that many students were likely to drop the course taught by an ITA when low expectations about their teacher's language proficiency were confirmed during the semester. Similarly, in her 1995 article "When It Comes to My Major, It Matters If You Are Foreign or Not," Georgia Smyrniou found that students who are required to take a course taught by an ITA complain more about their TAs' language skills than those who take the course as an elective. Students generally care more about courses in their majors, whether required ones or electives, and Smyrniou's study seems to confirm this. They believe that the language barrier between their foreign teacher and themselves prevents them from learning.

Both studies seem to indicate that in evaluating their foreign-born teachers American students rarely went beyond evaluating those teachers' language skills. The foreign-born teachers' lack of English skills overshadowed other factors of their teaching.

*   *   *

Training for Foreign-Born Teachers

Some of this discontent with ITAs' English-language proficiency is well founded. When one of us taught in North Carolina, the state legislature mandated that all publicly funded universities in the state provide extra proof that their ITAs' language skills were good enough to teach. The lawmakers were responding to a flood of parent complaints about language proficiency of ITAs at several of the state's universities. As awareness of the "foreign TA language problem" has grown in universities across the country, so has the number of training programs for ITAs. Most of these programs train foreign-born teaching assistants together, regardless of their discipline. The following section reviews existing trends and programs in ITA training.

As Hsi-Ling mentioned earlier, before we began to teach writing in our program, we underwent a six-week-long summer training course. It was a "crash course" in composition theory and in methods of teaching writing, both of which were particularly useful for new teaching assistants with backgrounds not in rhetoric and composition. The training does not separate American and foreign teaching assistants and does not include any special language or cultural awareness training for ITAs.

We were fortunate to have such thorough and discipline-specific training to prepare us for teaching writing. Most ITAs across the country, however, are likely to receive only general training focusing on issues of cross-cultural communication and language skills. Alternatively, when special training courses for ITAs are not conducted, universities offer teacher manuals and other printed materials designed to prepare foreign-born ITAs for teaching in America.

A typical ITA training program is run by the University of Delaware. According to the program's Web site, the program screens ITAs from different departments "in terms of oral language proficiency and helps prepare them for their instructional duties at the University, a great deal of which involves understanding the culture of the undergraduate and graduate environment" (U of Delaware ITA Training Program Internet site). The program runs for four and a half weeks in the summer and includes such courses for ITAs as Oral Intelligibility and Culture and Pedagogy. ITAs are therefore instructed in both the English language and the culture of the American university. The same training is provided to all ITAs, regardless of their department and discipline.

The Graduate Assembly of the University of California–Berkeley prepared its own publication for the university's ITAs in 1985. It is called *Teaching at Berkeley: A Guide for Foreign Teaching Assistants* and is written by ITAs themselves. The handbook includes advice on overcoming the language barrier and on adjusting to the culture of the American university.

What Foreign-Born Writing Teachers and Their Program Administrators Need to Know

If recent years are any indication, the numbers of foreign-born teachers of writing in the United States will continue to grow. New graduate students in English and writing and rhetoric departments will accept teaching assistantships.

Graduates of those programs will take full-time teaching positions. The review of research in the previous section shows that available training for ITAs is usually generic and not adjusted to the specific needs and interests of these teachers of writing. What recommendations, then, can be given to writing-program administrators and teacher trainers who hire and work with foreign-born teachers of writing? What do foreign-born teachers or those considering coming to the States need to know and understand before they accept teaching positions in US higher education? How can composition as a discipline begin to work toward a coherent theory and practice of preparing foreign-born writing teachers for their work in the United States?

First, some thoughts for those who are considering teaching in the United States but are not sure about their English-language skills or teaching abilities. If you have been accepted for graduate study at an English, composition and rhetoric, or linguistics department, your English is probably good enough to teach. It does not matter if you have an accent or a foreign name or don't look "American." Most students are openminded and willing to learn, and it does not matter to them whether their teacher is American or not. Although you will get an occasional "Oh, no, my teacher is foreign!" look, especially on the first day of a new semester, those feelings soon disappear as you show your students that you are a good teacher, that your English is excellent, and that you care about their learning.

Writing is a universal art, and you are qualified to teach, not because your first language may or may not be English, but because you are trained to teach it and love to write yourself. Remember all those endless lessons and exercises in English grammar you took when you were in school? Now may be a time to put them to good use. When you teach your US students grammar and style, you may actually be able to do so much better than your American colleagues. You learned English grammar by dissecting and understanding its difficult rules. This is why you can probably teach those rules better than some of your colleagues who know them only intuitively because English is their native language.

Perhaps one of the largest adjustments you will need to make as a teacher in the United States is getting used to the ways in which students interact with their teachers and the kinds of relationships that exist between teachers and students here. Many foreign-born teachers come from cultures where teachers are highly respected, even revered, figures who keep their distance from students. In many foreign cultures, teachers dress up for class and expect students to treat them as figures of authority. Questioning a teacher's teaching method or grading criteria out loud is completely off limits.

Not so in the United States. Some students find it difficult to learn to pronounce your last name correctly, and, to save themselves embarrassment, they will prefer to address you by your first name. Even those students who can say your name correctly may still prefer to call you by your first name. This is not a sign of disrespect, and you will need to decide how informal a relationship you want to build with your classes. You can certainly set your own rules in your classes. Other essays in this collection continue to address issues of relationships between teachers and students.

To hire dedicated and well-qualified foreign teachers of writing, writing-program administrators and department chairs need to realize that many of their prospective international teaching assistants have probably had significant teaching experience before coming to the United States. Many make the decision to continue graduate studies in the United States some years after graduating from college and after holding full-time teaching and other jobs where they were required to use English daily. During their employment, they may have undergone rather extensive teacher training and probably already have their own teaching philosophies and ideas.

Whenever possible, writing-program and department administrators should arrange face-to-face meetings with foreign applicants for teaching positions. Such meetings will not only allow both sides to have a conversation about teaching but also help the administrators make sure that the candidates' English-language skills are adequate. Unfortunately, such meetings usually can be arranged only if the applicant is already in the United States.

A few more words about ITAs' English proficiency. As we said before, a vast majority, if not all, applicants for teaching positions in writing programs in the United States arrive with superior command of English and the ability to teach a class. At the same time, administrators should not rely on test scores alone to determine the applicant's level of English. The Test of English as a Foreign Language (TOEFL), which all foreign applicants are required to take before being admitted to an American university, measures only listening, reading, and grammar skills. Those skills are traditionally seen as useful to a student who plans to attend lectures, take notes, and study from textbooks. The test gives little or no information as to how well the applicant can speak or write in English. To overcome this deficiency, many graduate programs require applicants to submit writing samples. Face-to-face meetings with applicants, which we mentioned earlier, can also help make sure of the future teacher's English proficiency.

Finally, writing programs and English departments should regard their foreign-born teachers not only as experts in their discipline but also as cultural resources capable of showing to students ways of writing and learning they may not have encountered in the past. As graduate students, international teaching assistants are in the process of learning academic writing in America themselves. Issues other than language come into play: cultural awareness, contrastive rhetoric, and so on. Their writing senses are heightened as they explore new discourses, conventions, and styles. In a way, they are like the students they teach, but they are also acquainted with the latest composition theory and teaching methods. Given this combination, foreign-born writing teachers may be able to teach difficult concepts and techniques of writing to their students quite effectively because they are, themselves, going through a learning process radically different from the learning process of their American colleagues who teach composition.

A Concluding Vignette

Pavel

After completing my doctorate in 2002, I now teach writing and rhetoric at James Madison University in Virginia. Toward the end of my first semester there, one student in my first-year writing class said to me, "I can't believe you were able to come from a foreign country and learn how to teach us, Americans." Hearing the note of appreciation in her voice felt good.

Hsi-Ling

A couple of months ago, I had a conversation with a humanities professor from China. Something she said really inspires me—"I love teaching so much that I will do it for free, and I am especially proud of my Chinese accent!" Whenever someone bugs me about my pronunciation, I answer, "I'm a foreigner; leave me alone."

Fadi

During each class I teach, I have students write two evaluations: one after the first paper is turned in, the other at the end of the semester. I instruct the students not to write their name, so they can evaluate freely and talk about whatever they want concerning the class. The first evaluation helps me focus more on which techniques and activities the students thought were helpful and productive in making them better writers. The second one helps me in preparing for the class that I will be teaching in the following semester. In both evaluations, one comment that always reoccurs is how I have changed my students' view on writing. They feel that they are not writing to meet a deadline anymore but, rather, writing for the sake of writing because of my flexibility and emphasis on the act of writing itself. In addition to that, the most rewarding comment in the anonymous evaluations is "I have become a better writer due to our work together."

Masood

I know my whole experience seems quite unreal. Maybe I was lucky to have fifty good students during my first semester of teaching. I am also not trying to prove that I am an exceptionally good teacher—I am just an average guy who loves teaching. What I am trying to say is that as ITAs we will always have to come up with something extra to motivate our students. We will also have to prove, in many subtle ways, our level of competence to our students. But most of all, I think, we will have to genuinely care about our students. I have been told time and again that I should always keep in mind that I am here for my own coursework, and that being a teacher is secondary to being a PhD student. I do not agree with this belief. If I do well in my own courses at the cost of my students, then I have failed anyway, for the only reason I am studying at the PhD level is to become a teacher, and I should, therefore, not wait until I finish my PhD to become a kinder, caring, and giving professor. I should, rather, be willing to be all that right now as an ITA.

Works Cited

Cohen, Robby, and Ron Robin, eds. *Teaching at Berkeley: A Guide for Foreign Teaching Assistants.* Graduate Assembly of the U of California–Berkeley, 1985.

Rao, Nagesh. "The Oh No! Syndrome: A Language Expectation Model of Undergraduates' Negative Reactions toward Foreign Teaching Assistants. ERIC Document ED 384921, 1995.

Smith, Rosslyn M., et al. "Crossing Pedagogical Oceans: International Teaching Assistants in U.S. Undergraduate Education." George Washington U, 1992.

Smyrniou, Georgia. "When It Comes to My Major, It Matters If You Are Foreign or Not." *Reading Improvement* 32.4 (1995): 227–235.

University of Delaware. *International Teaching Assistant Training Program.* December 2002. < http://www.udel.edu/eli/programs_ita.html>.

RESPONSE

Taking Off

CHRIS M. ANSON

Imagine what it would be like to have studied a complex field, such as aeronautical engineering, and then be asked to fly a 757 bound for Houston with 150 passengers on board. You'd certainly be familiar with the plane itself, with ailerons, wing structures, elevators, rudders, trim tabs, and flaps. You'd know about the operation and design of inlets, compressors, burners, turbines, and nozzles. You'd be familiar with aeroelastic constraints, control effectiveness, unsteady aerodynamics, and flutter. You'd know about the kinematics and dynamics of homogeneous turbulence, Reynolds stress and heat-flux equations, second order closures, and two-dimensional and three-dimensional hydraulic and environmental flows. All this and much more. You might even be able to design your own plane and make it airworthy.

But could you fly that 757 to Houston? Without any experience in a cockpit, could you begin to taxi to a designated runway for takeoff? Without ever having communicated to a tower and ground crew, interacted with a lead flight attendant, coordinated with a first officer, or addressed a plane full of businesspeople and tourists and folks visiting their relatives, would you even know how to talk? You might have experienced flying in a commercial jet many times as a passenger, but as the pilot, you wouldn't have a clue.

The history of higher education is filled with examples and anecdotes that parallel such a situation. Newly minted scholars with PhDs in history, engineering, anthropology, management, turf science, psychology, and literature—all growing experts in their fields—are put into classrooms because they have knowledge of a subject, not because they know how to teach. Even if the consequences of uncertainty or inability or inexperience aren't quite as life-threatening to the students who take seats in their classrooms, the principle is the same. Many new teachers are given assignments to do an extraordinarily complex activity—in some ways, more complex than flying a plane—without so much as a book of FAA rules and a flight plan. Ironically, the most highly prized new scholars, those who ride through graduate school at prestigious institutions on full fellowships and are eagerly pursued on the job market—are often the ones least prepared to coordinate and teach their first college courses. It is difficult to find any other advanced profession in which a significant portion of one's job requires absolutely no experience or training.

The essays in Part I of *Finding Our Way* help us to understand the complexities and nuances of college instruction in composition. They push against the dominant ideology of teaching and learning that has led to this situation, the one displayed in the media and echoed in the common social discourse about instruction. In this system (depicted somewhat crudely in Fig. 1 below), a teacher comes into a classroom—a closed space for learning—bearing knowledge acquired through advanced study: facts, information, details, references, conclusions. The teacher's job seems unambiguous: within that defined space, convey or impart or transmit some of that knowledge to the learners, passing it on like a street vendor selling newspapers. The new teacher who lacks pedagogical preparation and whose own experience has matched this model of instruction may also construct himself or herself as a knowledge holder and knowledge transmitter. In composition, this may mean lecturing about grammar and style, giving students preformulated interpretations of assigned readings, or leading Socratic-style discussions designed to coax the students toward a specific conclusion. Yet plentiful evidence suggests that such methods fail to engage students, improve their critical acumen or intellectual abilities, and provide them with skills and strategies for more advanced kinds of learning and literacy.

In Essay 1, Kenya Thompkins helps us to think about classrooms and educational institutions along the lines of what Mary Louise Pratt calls "contact zones,"

Figure 1
Dominant Model of Teaching and Learning

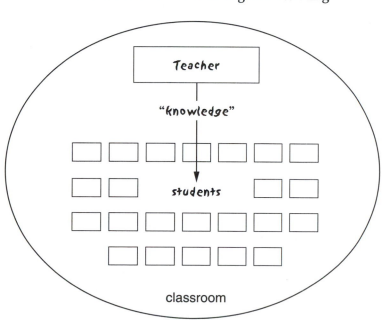

the "social spaces where cultures meet, clash, and grapple with each other, often in contexts of highly asymmetrical relations of power" (Pratt 79). In classrooms designed to foster students' intellectual development and acquisition of new abilities, the interaction of teacher and students involves, as Kenya puts it, the influence of "cultural norms, values, beliefs, and expectations." In part, these influences come from the personal, familial, political, and cultural/regional backgrounds of students and teachers. In part, they are also shaped by the dominant ideology and values of the institution itself, which surround and seep into individual classrooms.

Consider, for example, the institutional influences at three schools I have visited: Liberty University in rural southern Virginia, founded by fundamentalist minister Jerry Falwell; Hostos Community College in the Bronx, part of whose (secular) curriculum is taught in Spanish; and Sinte Gleska University, a historically tribal college located on the Rosebud Indian Reservation in rural South Dakota. Each institution is inspired by very different philosophies and systems of beliefs: Liberty by fundamentalist religious principles that reject evolutionary theory in favor of creationism; Hostos by the inspirational and liberatory teachings of Puerto Rican educator Eugenio Maria de Hostos and by the mission of "providing educational opportunities leading to socioeconomic mobility for first and second generation Hispanics, blacks, and other residents of New York City who have encountered serious barriers to higher education"; and Sinte Gleska by the principles and philosophies of its namesake, Sicangu leader Sinte Gleska ("Spotted Tail"), and its commitment "to its earliest purposes: to preserve and teach Lakota culture, history and language" and "to promote innovative and effective strategies to address the myriad of social and economic concerns confronting the Sicangu Lakota Oyate." Being a sensitive and successful teacher at these institutions requires an acute awareness of the complex relationships among institutional values and leadership, curricular goals, local context, and the students as learners. As Kenya points out, entering into a classroom at any institution means negotiating one's own values and heritage, those of the students (who themselves represent a range of views and beliefs), and those of the institutional culture and history.

In Essay 3 of this section, Sandra Giles and Tom Hunley offer personal accounts that place many of Kenya's ideas into specific contexts. Sandra and Tom both had prior experience and preparation when they entered a large state university's writing program. As they moved across different teaching positions and institutions, the beliefs and ideologies of their educational cultures shaped the way they taught college composition, but also provided them with a kind of experiential template against which they could judge new situations and methodologies. Imagine, for example, that you have prior experience at a highly progressive and well informed institution and are now considering accepting a position in a more conservative or traditional program, one ill-informed by new research, theory, and practice. In such a scenario, you need to artfully navigate the department's or institution's political landscape, making decisions about the nature and timing of certain proposals for reform. You can have a significant impact on such an institution, but doing so requires a lot of political sense, diplomacy, and understanding of people's motivations, needs, and interests.

In Essay 4, four foreign-born teachers explore the complexities of their relationships with predominantly American-born students, focusing in particular on the relationships between culture, speech, and writing. From the perspective of many American students entering college, someone with a foreign accent who learned English as a second or parallel language is suspect: how can such a person be an "expert" in written communication? Falling prey to the dominant model of teaching and learning, such students believe that teachers come into classrooms to impart knowledge. Lacking "native knowledge," having acquired English "second-hand," how can foreign teachers possibly impart as much as someone born and raised in the United States? In dealing with these sometimes deeply held beliefs, Pavel Zemliansky, Fadi Al-Issa, Hsi-Ling Huang, and Masood Raja share classroom experiences and strategies for helping students to acquire a new understanding of the classroom and the roles of teachers and learners.

For new instructors, the complexities and nuances of teaching opened up by these essays may seem bewildering when they may be anxious about "simpler" things, such as filling an entire class session and doing so with some semblance of authority and confidence. In Essay 2, Kate Brown offers some ways to make sense of the many feelings, experiences, puzzles, and contradictions that any teaching situation yields. Without a context for exploring experience, teaching becomes a lonely and frustrating activity—or one with little reflection and improvement. Kate's essay suggests both personal and communal ways to explore some of the issues raised in Essays 1, 3, and 4. Writing is crucial, not only because as teachers of writing we ought ourselves to be prolific writers, but also because writing is such a powerful medium for reflection and exploration. (Consider not only Kate's suggested modes of writing but also the interesting mix of genres represented in the essays here: narrative dialogues, pastiches of research and personal reflection, anecdotally supported tips.) Teaching philosophies, which are continuously evolving texts, can be a good start, and can become one document in a larger collection that makes up a teaching portfolio. "Talking with experienced and supportive teachers about their methods and ideas" is another. Finding opportunities like these to engage in safe, supportive explorations of teaching helps us, in Kate's words, to see teaching as "a constant series of adjustments."

As you consider the experiences and thoughtful suggestions of these eight teachers, consider also the way that they transform the dominant model of teaching and learning depicted earlier in Figure 1. As Kenya reminds us, the classroom is not an entity unto itself but is situated within an institution and a culture whose values and ideologies cannot be ignored. As Sandra and Tom remind us, new teachers are no more like tabula rasa than are students; they all bring into classrooms a wealth of experience and knowledge, affording, when a context is new, many opportunities for growth and change. As Pavel, Fadi, Hsi-Ling, and Masood remind us, no teachers or students can ignore their culture and background—these are not veneers of self; they *are* self. Teaching means understanding, sharing, and melding such uniqueness into a community of learners. Finally, if our model is to be complete, it needs a temporal dimension that shows it moving through space and time as teachers and students grow, mature, learn, and change. As Kate reminds us, teaching is a lifelong journey. Systematic reflection—alone and with others—allows us to explore and record those changes, and gives us a way to cycle the "scholarship of teaching" back into our continuously improved practices.

Figure 2
Classroom as Complex Cultural Space

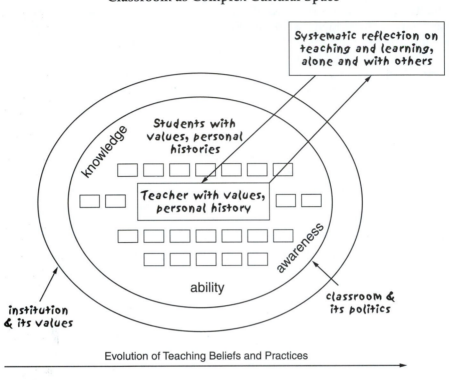

Systematic reflection on teaching and learning, alone and with others

knowledge

Students with values, personal histories

Teacher with values, personal history

awareness

ability

institution & its values

classroom & its politics

Evolution of Teaching Beliefs and Practices

Work Cited

Pratt, Mary Louise. "Arts of the Contact Zone." *Profession*, 1991. MLA. 33–40.

RESPONSE

A View from Writing-Program Administration

AMY GOODBURN

Dear Fadi, Hsi-Ling, Kate, Kenya, Masood, Pavel, Sandra, and Tom,

First, thank you for your stories. Reading them reinforced for me the power of teacher narrative as knowledge-making, illustrating how reflecting on our experiences can lead to shared critical inquiry (Ritchie and Wilson 2000). Indeed, many of your stories remind me of the time, less than ten years ago, when I was a graduate student experiencing the confusions, joys, and tribulations of teaching for the first time in a college writing classroom. Now, as Coordinator of Composition at the University of Nebraska–Lincoln, I find myself reading your essays from a different vantage point. This semester my colleagues and I are embarking on a revision of our first-year writing curriculum. So I've been immersed in thinking hard about the identities of first-year students who take our courses, the diverse experiences and backgrounds of the graduate teaching assistants and lecturers who predominantly teach these courses, the various pedagogical and theoretical approaches to the teaching of writing that could be emphasized, and the diverse— and often contradictory—beliefs about purposes for first-year writing courses. So while I am no longer a new teacher, I am continuing to "find my way" into these discussions as an administrator, and your essays have helped me to think, again, about the complicated and rich contexts that support teacher inquiry and professional development within postsecondary English departments. In this response, then, I touch on a few themes that rose to the surface for me across the boundaries of your individual essays.

First, I was interested in how your essays conceptualize the social location of the teacher. Your essays illuminate how the identity of a teacher is, in many ways, a social script read by peers and students in ways that teachers often cannot control. Kenya illustrates how a moment as simple as deciding how one will be addressed speaks to larger cultural and social scripts of what it means to be a teacher, scripts which are inevitably tied to social locations of race, gender, class, geography, and so on. Similarly, Hsi-Ling's account of students making fun of her pronunciation speaks to the politics involved in trying to claim a space from which to gain authority in the classroom. Your accounts are important reminders that not all teachers come into the classroom with equal authority and power. Here at the University of Nebraska, where over ninety-three percent of students come from Nebraska (and the majority of teachers do not), I regularly see how teachers struggle with issues of authority, especially when they do not look like, talk like, or act like their students.

And your stories remind me of when I began teaching at the ripe old age of 21. I wore braces on my teeth and looked, on my best days, all of 16. I was mistaken not only for an undergraduate, but for a first-year student! I remember how hard I tried to acquire a sense of authority those first few years and how much of a mask it felt. This struggle led to my interest in literature on feminist pedagogies and, as I see now in retrospect, to my dissertation topic on authority issues in composition classrooms. So while your essays focus mainly on issues involved in becoming a new teacher of writing or in entering a new writing program, they also point to possibilities for research and inquiry in the field of composition.

A second theme that crosses your essays is the importance of negotiating differences within one's teaching context. Several of you discuss moving to a new teaching program with a different philosophy about what constitutes effective writing instruction and the importance of productively negotiating, reflecting upon, and understanding these differences. You speak about the importance of skepticism, of situating yourself in relation to a program's values, of being open to discovery, and of learning to articulate what works for you as a teacher and writer. Indeed, a central question that many of your essays ask is "How can experienced teachers adapt their teaching practices to conform to a department's carefully theorized way of running classes without discounting their prior teaching and learning experiences?"

That question invites me, as a writing-program administrator, to consider the "flip side." That is, how can I value the diverse teaching experiences and literate life histories of teachers in my writing program while also developing a coherent curriculum and common pedagogical course experiences for first-year students? I was especially interested in the various ways that the "administration" was represented across your essays. In some essays, I sensed anxiety, frustration, and suspicion about "what the administration want." Of course, administrative structures for writing courses vary across institutional contexts, but I am interested in how teachers "read" department culture, particularly my position as a writing-program administrator, and ways that I can not only respond to teachers' concerns but also work against these binaries of "teacher" vs. "administrator" to develop shared ownership and collective responsibility for our writing program. Your essays have given me some new ideas for how I might better sponsor bridges between experienced teachers, new teachers, and program administrators. Toward this end, I was especially interested in the last thread I saw across your essays: the importance of sustained and multiple opportunities for collaboration and shared inquiry with other teachers.

Your essays depict a stunning variety of professional development contexts that have supported your thinking about teaching-mentoring partnerships, National Writing Project Institutes, teaching circles, summer workshops, composition theory seminars, year-long pedagogy workshops, team-teaching, writing-center tutoring, conversations with peers, e-mail exchanges, and so on. While some of you describe what used to be the typical experience of being given a set of books and a syllabus and told to teach, for the most part you seem to have been invited into many rich contexts for supporting your teacher development. I was especially struck by Sandra's discussion of how she learned about the teaching of writing from K-12 teachers in a summer writing project. As she suggests, these experiences can promote powerful paradigm shifts, helping us to recognize connections across contexts and to develop richer understandings of how literacy is sponsored throughout our schooling. Your essays invite me to consider more fully how the curriculum revision I am currently working on needs to be conceptualized in concert with revised teacher-development structures as well.

Welcome to the profession and thanks for contributing to my thinking and learning about teaching!

Sincerely,
Amy Goodburn

Work Cited

Ritchie, Joy S., and David E. Wilson. *Teacher Narrative as Critical Inquiry: Rewriting the Script.* New York: Teachers College Press, 2000.

RESPONSE

Blind Spots

THOMAS BLIGH

The essays in Part I touch on some of the issues most relevant to a college instructor: authority, empathy, confidence. Effective teachers, consciously or not, constantly shift roles in order to respond to classroom situations. Whether you're an experienced teacher working at a new school with a different atmosphere and student body than what you're used to, an international teacher standing before two dozen students who may doubt your abilities as an effective communicator, or an accomplished recent college graduate with confidence about what worked for you but few ideas about what might help your students, these four essays provide inspiration and useful tips on how to meet these challenges.

Kenya Thompkins' excellent advice touches on lessons most of us had to learn either the hard way or through observation and the steady accumulation of semesters as teachers. Like Kenya, I've taught at more than one university and have had to adapt my teaching methods to fit both the students and the departments. Many methods of teaching college composition exist and what's taught today may be universally rejected a few years from now as theories change and teachers meet various degrees of success and failure with their methods. It's wise then, to try several pedagogical models. As a graduate student, you're most likely an adaptable person. Each semester you must adapt to a new group of students and a new situation. You won't teach just one way for the rest of your career. As a graduate student and a teaching assistant, realize that now is the time to get used to that fact.

I strongly agree with Kenya on this point: "Your first obligation as a teacher is to uphold the standards of the profession and provide experiences that will allow your students to improve their writing." You'll teach hundreds of college writing courses during your career. But each one will be different, and each will be populated with individuals who will look to you for the instruction they'll need to succeed in college and in life.

Kenya's essay is useful for teachers at any level, as it provides a clear overview of the different types of colleges and universities and how their individual missions attract students of various backgrounds and interests. Universities that emphasize research often have different goals for their writing courses than community colleges or smaller, private colleges. Teachers need to recognize how their geographic or academic surroundings influence both their students and the courses designed to benefit their students. To date, no blanket approach exists which will prove successful to all students—a useful fact to keep in mind during discouraging moments.

For an engaging account of the modifications a writing teacher must often make, consider Kate Brown's essay, in which she explores the beliefs about writing she formed as an undergraduate and how she attempted to reconcile them with the pedagogical training she received as a teaching assistant. Early in her essay, Kate brings up a good point: resistance should be investigated. Kate began her teaching career unsure of the value in creative writing and in personal writing and gradually came to see the benefits of approaches other than research and analysis. Instead of stubbornly clinging to these notions, Kate questioned her beliefs and eventually reached a compromise. It's useful to note that Kate reached her new appreciation of the different forms of writing through the act of writing itself. Kate's discovery did not result from a Zen-like moment of clarity or an especially insightful mentor—it sprang from her own attempts to relate her experiences in writing by using different approaches. Kate figured out what she needed to know by stepping out of the teacher role and assuming the role of writer; she left her comfort zone. That's an activity we can all practice.

New teachers spend more time than they'd probably prefer in what might be called the "discomfort zone," an area of uncertainty, nervousness, and fluctuating confidence. A good mentor can really help. Sandra L. Giles and Tom C. Hunley speak on the role of mentoring, which has always been a facet of academic life. Mentoring occurs on several levels: professor to professor, professor to student, and experienced teacher to new teacher. I've found the most useful ideas for classroom activities often come from casual conversations in the graduate lounge. Small-group work! Why didn't I think of that? Portfolios due before the last week of the course? Brilliant! First-time teachers often have blind spots; mentors, having learned from experience, observation, and research, can kindly point out those spots.

Speaking of blind spots, when I was a new teacher, my mentor taught me something which to this day I can't believe I didn't figure out myself. It was so simple, yet incredibly helpful. Like many writing teachers, I asked my students to arrange their desks in a circle, believing that this set-up allowed for greater face-to-face contact and a decentered place for the teacher. After observing my class one day, my mentor told me that he noticed the circle had the opposite effect: my students, consciously or not, made a large circle that was more like a square. Students scooted their desks back against the walls, giving themselves plenty of distance from each other and from me. The circle that was supposed to supply an informal openness had become a means of distancing. Often the students on either side of me would back up their desks so that I couldn't really see them unless I turned around halfway in my seat. I would have needed to mount side mirrors to my desk in order to see these students, and even then I would have likely missed out on the full picture. A few students had found my blind spots and they retreated into them. Students who positioned themselves in these areas were less likely to receive eye contact from me, which also meant I was less likely to call on them to participate in class discussions. My mentor pointed out that a circle, if large and spread out, fails in its aims. Old-fashioned rows would be better than a circle that allows students to opt out of participation.

The good news: if you ask your students to make the circle smaller, they will. As a new teacher I doubted my authority and persuasive power. But I shouldn't have. When I asked them to bring the circle in closer, they did it. Ask nicely and firmly, and your students will usually agree to reasonable requests. Today, as a teacher who's taught college writing for more than five years, I know what to expect when I ask my students to sit in a circle, and I'm ready for their wallflower behavior. I'll say, "Let's circle the wagons," and then wait for them to create a circle. Then I'll survey the circle and ask them to bring it in closer if need be. Sometimes my students don't want a smaller circle. But I don't start class until the circle is a close one, without blind spots. This is a small thing I probably would have figured out eventually, but it really helped to have a helpful, more experienced teacher observe my class and give me constructive suggestions based on his own experience in the classroom.

Classroom architecture is but one of the areas to keep in mind as a teacher; the students who fill these desks provide a variety of interesting opportunities to refine one's pedagogy. Sandra and Tom discuss a unique dilemma faced by graduate students who received training at one university and now teach at a different one. This happened to me—I taught for three years at the school where I received my master's degree and then taught at a small, private college. When I went on to pursue a doctorate at a different university, I found I had years of teaching experience but little experience in teaching writing the way my new university believed writing should be taught. My folders of exercises and activities that had proved successful at other schools were not appropriate for a composition course that emphasized process. Sandra and Tom identify the challenge for the graduate student with prior teaching experience: "integrating into the department, but also valuing and making use of their prior experience." In my new teaching environment I found I had to modify or discard old methods, learn new approaches, and then measure the success of these combined techniques.

The value of prior experience is particularly evident in the achievements of international teaching assistants. "When You Look and Sound "Un-American": Advice for Foreign-Born Teachers of Writing" showed me some things I didn't know about international students who teach writing while depicting the universal struggle of first-time writing teachers: the struggle to establish authority in the classroom. What makes a person competent to teach college writing? An advanced degree? An exemplary undergraduate record? Extensive training? Those questions probably enter the minds of many new teachers, foreign-born or not. I had those doubts as I taught my first writing class after a three-week training course. I was 23; I'd been a college graduate for just one year, and here I was trying to teach twenty-four first-year college students. Would they challenge my authority? I decided I needed a ready-made reply in case one of my students questioned my competence. Here's what I came up with: "I'm 120 undergraduate credits ahead of you." I don't know how rude or arrogant or even effective that retort would have been because I never uttered it. None of my students ever challenged my competence or training. As a new teacher I tried hard, made mistakes, enjoyed successes, endured frustrations and disappointments, and learned a lot. As a more experienced teacher, I still do.

My efforts to shore up my confidence as a new teacher seem somewhat less significant after having read this essay. After all, I was born in this country. My favorite part of this essay comes when the authors point out that what makes international teaching assistants qualified to teach writing is their love of language and their past success at learning a second language. ITAs may have recently learned verb forms, homonyms, subject-verb agreement, and other intricacies of English grammar that American-born undergraduates may have long forgotten. ITAs are unique role models for their composition students who may see them as successful writers who have overcome cultural and linguistic obstacles in order to communicate effectively with others.

The sub-theme of these four essays may well be that trial and error is an acceptable approach to a first teaching experience. The successful techniques of your favorite teachers or your trusted peers may not work as well for you. Your personality will play a part in determining what kind of teacher you'll be. Ultimately, you'll be the one to decide what works best for you. Recently I taught in a classroom too small for a feasible circle of desks. Even worse, a pillar in the room's center blocked visibility. My students sat in rows. To compensate for this situation, I walked around the room frequently as I spoke to my students and as I listened to them. I wanted to be able to see and hear everyone and I wanted to keep my students' attention. I found I had to keep moving. So will you.

Critical Self-Reflection in Teaching

CARRIE LEVERENZ

For many of us, the joy of teaching comes from the opportunity each class, each semester, to learn something new from our students. The four essays that open *Finding Our Way* evoke a similar pleasure—the pleasure, as a teacher, of learning from other teachers. As someone who has been involved for the past ten years in preparing graduate students to teach writing, I am happy to say that I am still learning about teaching. With each new pre-semester workshop, each staff meeting, each visit to a new teacher's classroom, each response to a teaching portfolio, I am the beneficiary of these new teachers' insights about teaching, insights that are the product of what I see as the most important tool in a teacher's toolbox: the capacity for critical self-reflection.

Although the essays by Kenya Thompkins, Kate Brown, Sandra Giles and Tom Hunley, and Pavel Zemliansky, Fadi Al-Issa, Hsi-Ling Huang, and Masood Raja offer different perspectives on the challenges of being graduate-student teachers, they share several key insights: that it is important to understand who you are in relation to where you are, that identities are multiple rather than unified and singular, that difference is to be valued, that collaboration is a key to learning, and that having a sense of authority is an important step to agency—to being able to act in this world. What strikes me is how similar these insights are to what many of us hope students will learn from our writing classes.

Understand Who You Are in Relation to Where You Are

In "Your Culture, Their Politics: What a Teacher Should Know When Entering a New Writing Program," Kenya Thompkins reflects on the dissonance he initially felt as a black man schooled in the South to be polite and to write tidy five-paragragh essays when confronted with a writing-program director who asked to be called by her first name and who allowed composition classes to be sites of personal discovery rather than grammar lessons. As Thompkins remarks, new teachers need to understand "how cultural norms, values, beliefs, and expectations influence all of us at some point." He also advises "as a teacher entering a new writing program, you must realize that this new institution has its own cultural practices." The dissonance Thompson experienced between old and new cultural norms is not unlike that many first-year college students experience in our composition classes when asked to write in ways that violate what they've been taught to expect. Thompkins's advice—remember where you came from and understand where you're at—is relevant to anyone struggling to feel comfortable in a new place, to successfully meet a new challenge.

Identities Are Multiple Rather Than Singular and Unitary

Another insight that all these essays share is the difficulty of adjusting to new expectations—those of students and of mentor/supervisors. For many new teachers, that challenge can feel like pressure to change who they are, a pressure that can make some feel excluded or alienated from the university they were so eager to join. In "What to Do When You're Not Really New," Sandra Giles and Tom Hunley discuss what it's like to begin a PhD program and a new job as a teaching assistant when one already has a full-blown teaching identity. Giles in particular describes her previous experience teaching at a community college where she spent a lot of energy trying to "figure out that they wanted" teachers to be and to do. Even in a program in which teachers were not the victims of narrow, contradictory expectations, Giles admits, "[O]ne of the hardest things about adjusting to a new program is figuring out what the heck 'they' want." Sounds a lot like what our students might say. Entering the profession of higher education, making a commitment to study literature or rhetoric or creative writing, learning to teach composition are all part of a new identity just as beginning students are asked to take on a new identity when they come to the university and enroll in our composition classes.

The answer, as these authors reveal, is not to change who we are or what we teach every time we enter a new institution. Instead, we need to recognize that multiple identities are inevitable, even valuable, and that we can believe more than one thing, even potentially contradictory things, as Kate Brown tells us in "We're Not in Kansas Anymore: Negotiating a Teaching Philosophy," in which she describes how she came to value a student's personal narrative in spite of Brown's belief that academic writing is the best form of writing. Brown's coming to value multiple kinds of student writing led her to experiment with different genres in her own writing—a particularly apt example of how we learn from our students. She also lauds her colleagues for figuring out ways to bring some of their best former teaching practices into their new writing programs, a move that illustrates that it's not just teacher identities that are multiple and contradictory, but program identities too. No matter how well defined the mission statement of a program, the wide variety of teachers in the program ensures that differing perspectives will prevail.

Value Difference

In spite of, or perhaps because of, this inevitable multiplicity of identities, being new and a little unsures of ourselves can make us wary of the very differences between people that promise to enrich our experience as teachers and learners. The challenge—and benefits—of cultural difference is perhaps nowhere more salient than in the American college writing classroom taught by a graduate student whose first language isn't English. The authors of "When You Look and Sound 'Un-American': Advice for Foreign-Born Teachers of Writing" make a compelling case for the value to American students of being taught by foreign-born TAs. As a WPA, I've listened to student complaints about international TAs not being able to speak English or not having the right to teach them composition, even as I've read those same teachers' beautifully written prose in my graduate classes, heard them talk eloquently about their goals as teachers, admired the sacrifices many of them make to live and study in another country, and marveled at their ability to speak two or three or four languages, as many do. Ironically, perhaps, as Zemliansky, Al-Issa, Huang, and Raja attest, these international teachers who seem so different from their American undergraduates are in an excellent position to understand their students' anxieties about whether they will succeed in this strange place—as Al-Issa makes clear in his story about sitting in the back row and pretending to be a student on the first day of class. From that point on, students knew that he was willing to identify with them. Would that his students also learned to identify with him.

Collaborate

Certainly one of the best ways to learn to value both similarities and differences in others is through collaboration: working together for the greater good of the group. What do we learn from collaboration? That our own ideas are not so crazy, but that sometimes our ideas need to change. Having to make a case for our ideas in the face of opposing others teaches us to give good reasons and to think hard about others' reasons, certainly one of the most important outcomes of a liberal education. All the essays in this section highlight the benefits of collaborating with other teachers, both more experienced teachers (who may or may not share your values and beliefs about teaching writing) and other new teachers. Giles and Hunley formed a bond as experienced teachers coming into a new writing pro-gram, a bond that led to their extended conversation that constitutes their contri-bution to this volume. Kate Brown's epiphany regarding the benefits of narrative writing came through sharing student writing with her mentor-teacher. Zemliansky, Al-Issa, Huang, and Raja already share a bond of "difference" as international teaching assistants, but as their narratives attest, their experiences vary considerably. Acting together, though, in the writing of this essay enabled them to make a more persuasive case than any one of them might have made writ-ing alone. Indeed, much as we want students to learn to collaborate in order to enhance their own individual work, we also want them to see what they can accom-plish when working as a group. Similarly, Thompkins advises new teachers to join professional organizations and to become a "junior political agent" by working with administrators, the composition committee, and other teachers to make the program better.

Assume Agency

One final message comes through strongly in all these essays—the importance of writing as a means to act in this world. It was the great insight of the National Writing Project that to improve their teaching of writing, teachers needed to learn to act like writers. These essays, written by graduate-student teachers for other graduate-student teachers, illustrate the point. The authors are using writing to reflect on and make new knowledge about their work that can enrich the lives of others: an important message to send to teachers of writing as well as students.

PART II
INSIDE OUT

5

Voices in Progress: Creating Confidence in the Writing Classroom

CARLYN C. MADDOX

When I entered college in 1985, I considered myself a decent writer but not necessarily a confident one. My high school classes taught me how to formulate airtight thesis statements and produce organized analytical papers, so I felt prepared—up to a point. I had little experience with personal essay writing or research papers, so I was squeamish about measuring up to a college professor's standards. When I took the required English 102 composition class my freshman year, I thought my teacher would expect what all my previous teachers had expected—perfectly constructed essays in perfect five-paragraph forms. Fortunately, for that class and my professional career, my teaching assistant had other ideas for me and my writing.

My teaching assistant, whom I will call Mr. B, was a self-proclaimed "Literature Freak" who rhapsodized in every class about the writings of Wolfe, Salinger, and Kerouac. In every class, he read passages from their books, noted their "soaring and unique voices," and encouraged us as young writers to imitate our favorites and write toward finding *our* voice. He said that voice was the most important part of a young writer's craft, and that our voice was what he was most interested in hearing.

Of course, this was all new to me; I had never been called a *writer*, and finding my voice sounded way too sophisticated for my writing at that time. But Mr. B was determined we all had voices hiding somewhere in the muck of our prose, and, during a conference, he decided to show me mine. He had assigned us several "free" writings, and I had written a passage in my journal about my grandmother's hands.

"I see you've tried something new," he said, pointing to the entry.

"Yes," I said. I didn't know why I was nervous; I think it was because I never had any teacher conference with me and talk about my writing.

"This is *exactly* what I want you to do," he said. "I can see your grand-mother's hands as you perceive them. The bony, white knuckles and the big dia-mond rings. This is what I mean by voice—the images come from you."

He asked me to read the paragraphs out loud and pointed to specific places where I could expand or condense. With relief that he liked my writing, I listened as he talked to me about stretching this voice and trying new ways to write.

"I think you have a very imaginative voice," he told me. "You should keep writing about your family like this."

I walked out of his office and thought about his words while a tiny and excited flame jumped through my body. My writing had been seen, a teacher had complimented it, and I felt for the first time my young voice had been heard.

This experience stayed with me many years later as I became a creative writer and a teacher of writing, for Mr. B taught me to feel confident as a writer and also how to teach confidence. He always said our names in class, looked us in the eye, and continually pointed out the student work he felt illustrated his points or showed good writing. Instead of simply saying "good detail" or "explain more here" on my papers, he underlined what he thought was intriguing and asked me to expand particular details in order to punch up the writing. And, most important, he seemed excited to watch us grow as writers. This excitement was contagious, and it hasn't left me yet. As I stand in classrooms today, I remember his energy and drive—his "Lit Freak" spiels—and I remind myself that we as teaching assistants should instill in our students a confidence they may not have yet about their writing. We need to remember that their voices are unique and dis-tinct—and that we may never know how we will inspire them to love language.

Of course, knowing about our students' histories can help us build their confidence, and we must understand their backgrounds and their perceptions of writing. Unfortunately, many of their views are narrow because they were taught writing by nonwriters who viewed student writing as an engine to maintain or fix. Students have approached me countless times and said, "I just can't write . . ." and "I will never be a writer," and I always wonder: where do they learn such defeatist attitudes? They learn these attitudes, of course, from the test-driven curriculum of our present educational system. Writing, for many of them, has been an exercise in mistake making and mistake correcting. And many see writing as an assignment and not as a tool for imagination, clarification, or academic exploration.

In my classes, motivating students toward confidence about their writing is my ultimate goal. If a student walks out of my class and feels strong about his or her ability, then I have done my job well as a writing instructor. I want students to feel invested in what they write in my class; I don't want to see their abandoned portfolios strewn in the hallway the next semester. The questions are, how can we as teaching assistants instill this confidence? How can we motivate students to care about their writing?

One of the first things I learned as a teacher was that knowing the curricu-lum and creating exciting writing assignments wasn't enough to build a confident classroom. The other important element in motivating students is establishing a genuine rapport with them. A good classroom is a good conversation—there is a continual verbal back-and-forth that is centered on learning. Fostering this con-versation is easy; all a teacher has to do is ask questions. Students have stories and will love to tell them to you—if you ask. The key is to focus on your students' stories so that you remember them. When the time comes for students to write and invent ideas for their assignments, draw upon previous conversations with them and ask them about specific interests or situations in their lives. This sounds simple, but many teachers do not realize the power of personally connecting to their students in this professional way. The students also sense you are connected to their lives, and they believe you have been listening and that their stories are worth listening to.

Giving good feedback on student writing is another hallmark of building student confidence. Rick Straub's essay "Responding—Really Responding—to Other Students' Writing" and his essay "Managing the Paper Load, or Making Good Use of Time" are excellent resources for providing feedback on papers. I have found that his idea of having students respond to my responses is an excellent one because it opens the dialogue further between us. I usually ask them to keep a list of my responses in their journals and make notes about them. Sometimes I have them freewrite about my responses in order to clarify again what they might need to look at more closely. This practice empowers students to feel that they have a voice about their papers, and, again, it promotes our working together for their improvement.

First-year student writers respond to the question, "How can teachers build confidence in their students?"

DERRON HANSON: "One can tell a teacher's confidence by the tempered show of authority and the 'sureness' of how she addresses questions. They smile! They are friendly yet firm. They encourage different styles; break away from traditional essays and explore some options that certain students will respond to."

KATHERINE REESE: "Positive criticism is very successful. Students need to be told what they are doing wrong in a way that will not deter them from wanting to fix it. If a teacher writes all over my paper, I don't automatically think I did everything wrong; instead, I realize that my teacher really cares about my paper and put a lot of time into helping me with it."

NATASHA ARNOLD: "A teacher can instill self-confidence in her students by giving advice on how to better their work. …A truly effective teacher cannot be a timid or shy person. They need to be confident and outgoing."

CRYSTAL WHITTAKER: "Teachers are able to instill motivation through feedback. When a student is writing a paper, they more times than not have no clue if they're on the right track. The only way a student is able to feel confident is if the teacher is able to criticize."

MATHEW HOWE: "Teachers should let students write on stuff that is important to them and at the same time teach them proper grammar/techniques so the student feels he or she has a good overall paper."

Other confidence-building factors that come to mind when I teach are learning and knowing my students' names early on, making clear my expectations for the class, and trying to understand their writing histories and goals for their writing future. I try to always call them young *writers* (à la Mr. B), and, as much as possible, I ask them to bring in texts they feel represent good writing so we can discuss styles and forms. In process notes at the end of their papers, I ask them to assess their workshop experience and what they have learned in each paper. I also ask for feedback on what needs to be changed in the classroom environment—or what they need to help them strengthen their writing.

I would love to say that all my students are happily motivated and feel they are on their way to becoming *writers*, but of course this isn't always the case. I remember one student from last spring who wore this I-HATE-WRITING look on his face every day in class. He would shuffle in late, slump in his chair, and rarely hand in assignments on time. One day, I asked him to meet me in my office to discuss the assignment he had not turned in. He was to read two essays—Ward Churchill's "Crimes against Humanity" and Alex Shumatoff's "The Navajo Way"—and respond to their thematic similarities and differences about Native Americans in a journal entry.

"I need to ask you why you haven't completed this week's journal," I said after he sat down in my office.

"I don't know," he said.

"This is the second one you haven't turned in," I told him. "At this point, your grade is suffering. Is there something wrong here?"

"I just don't *like* to write," he said and sighed. He had said this to me before, during our last conference when I brought up a late assignment. He also informed me that he was going to be a computer programmer and thankfully would *never* need writing in his career.

"Is the problem this assignment?" I asked.

"Not really. I don't like any of the assignments." He shrugged and stared at me, and I was at a loss. What could I say to motivate him? I didn't want him to fail, but his grade was certainly headed south in a big way. Then I remembered one of our conversations at the beginning of the semester. He had talked about coming to Florida State University and playing trumpet with the Marching Chiefs. It was obvious to me that he loved the trumpet and was as excited about playing as he was about being a computer programmer. This gave me an idea for a compromise that just might motivate him.

"What if you substituted three of the journals to write about playing trumpet or being in the Marching Chiefs?"

His eyes brightened a little, so I went further.

"You could explain to me, a non–trumpet player, what playing the trumpet is all about. I'd like to hear about your favorite musicians, and I'd like to hear about the band practices."

"That sounds okay. . . ."

"I mean, the Marching Chiefs put on quite a show. Why not open that world up to me in your journals?"

"Oh," he said. "So I don't have to do that other reading? I can just write about being in the band?" He was excited now.

"Well . . . You can substitute three of the readings for the trumpet writings. But you still have to do the rest of the readings. We'll work on the journal schedule and see which ones you will substitute."

He thought about this a moment, and his I-HATE-WRITING expression had faded.

"I guess that'll work, Mrs. Maddox," he said. "I could probably think of a thing or two to say."

"I hope so," I said, and he left.

After this conference, he began arriving at class on time and participating in discussions. He put more effort into his papers and tried to join our workshop community. The trick was to connect with him about his interests and to become flexible with my journal assignments in order to motivate him. I think once he saw my willingness to work with him about his writing, he was willing to meet me halfway and try harder.

Building confidence in our students can—and will—yield success. Every teacher, however, will approach classes and students differently. The key for us as teaching assistants is to remember that we may be the first teacher ever to take a real interest in a student's writing. We may also be the first teacher ever to tell a student that we think he or she is a good writer—or a great writer. Here are some ideas I've incorporated into my classroom that may help you build confidence within yourself as a teacher and with students as writers:

1. Understand the power of your voice. Have you ever listened to yourself present material? Is your voice too soft or loud? Too fast or slow? Do you know how to pause and ask questions and how to emphasize material? Do you know how to lead class discussions? Voice intonation, volume, and speed can affect the way a student learns. Getting to know how you present material can help your teaching.
2. Prompt yourself before each class with these questions: What are my goals for my classes today? What questions might students have about the syllabus, schedule, or workshop agenda? What questions should I ask my students about their progress? These questions will keep you connected to any changes or problems you need to address as the semester goes along.
3. Assess your class discussions and workshops. Try different scenarios to see how the class responds best. Do your students respond better to working only with partners, or would they workshop better with larger groups? Do the students understand the purpose of workshop and their role in giving feedback? Do students sense your presence in the workshop process, and are you accessible to them during this time? What is working or not? For example, when your class is workshopping research papers, are the students clear about how to use and cite resources correctly? Chances are some will know very well and others won't know the MLA from the NFL. Pace your instruction to fit the needs of the students: if they need mini-lessons over citations or punctuation, make sure they are equipped with this knowledge before a workshop. Assessing your progress will help you fine-tune class progress.
4. Read aloud examples of good student writing from the class. Make sure you read each student's writing at some point in the semester. Be specific about the

sentence structure, descriptions used, tone, or "voice" shown in the writing. Tell the class what is good—and what could be improved. You may want to check with the student beforehand, though most in my classes are excited to be in the spotlight.

5. Feedback, feedback, feedback. This is what students in my classes feel is the most important part of the writing and workshop process. I usually comment extensively on the first and third drafts. I try to note what is strong about the writing and suggest places for improvement. Identify concepts that the whole class could review, and stress these in the workshop agenda.

6. Use conferences as a time to address problems or show students where they can improve in their drafts. I always require my students to bring either a draft, notes, or a list of questions for me to address in the conference. If the students are doing research for their papers, this is an excellent time to interview them about their processes and interest in the topic. Also, if you have students who are normally quiet during class, ask them if they wouldn't mind you calling on them from time to time or asking them their opinions in class discussions.

7. Use humor as much as possible when teaching the writing practice and process. I read excerpts from Anne Lamott's *Bird By Bird* or Natalie Goldberg's *Writing Down the Bones* and talk to students about the necessary prewriting and "composting" that these authors stress. Bring in humorous quotes or advice from writers. Let your students hear about the "writing life" in this way.

Creating confidence as a new teaching assistant won't be a challenge when you become comfortable with your syllabus and your students. Once the students know your expectations and sense your enthusiasm in presenting material about writing, many will try hard to write their best. Remember my story of Mr. B—he took the time to recognize my writing in a genuine and excited way. This led me on a path toward confidence as a teacher and a writer, and I hope to carry his enthusiasm for language and its beauty into all my classes.

Works Cited

Goldberg, Natalie. *Writing Down the Bones*. Boston: Shambhala, 1986.

Lamott, Anne. *Bird By Bird*. New York: Panetheon, 1996.

Straub, Richard. "Managing the Paper Load, or Making Good Use of Time." *The Practice of Response: Strategies for Commenting on Student Writing*. Cresskill, NJ: Hampton, 2000. 253–260.

___. "Responding—Really Responding—to Other Students' Writing." *The Subject Is Writing*. Ed. Wendy Bishop. 3rd ed. Portsmouth, NH: Boynton/Cook Heinemann, 2003. 162–172.

6

Am I a Failure? Coping with Challenges in the Classroom

AMY L. HODGES

Students challenge us all—some students challenge us in the classroom; others correct our language or other students' opinions; some complain about our evaluation methods and our teaching styles. How do we cope with challenging students and remain confident in our teaching abilities? As you read the following stories of conflict, consider your own challenges in the classroom. It is possible to learn to embrace our challenges, to see that they can strengthen, not weaken, our pedagogical beliefs and practices.

Shared Stories of Conflict

True or False: Students Who Fabricate Experiences and Essays

Conflict has not spared my classroom; in fact, I faced my most profound teaching challenge in the fall of 2001. I taught two sections of first-year writing that fall semester, and class was in session on September 12, 2001—the day after the national terrorist attacks. Because of my commitment to a pedagogy focused on writing and healing, I decided to encourage my students to write about the attacks of the previous day.

> One student, Kelly,[1] stayed after class to share her writing with me. She explained how directly the tragedy affected her; her cousin was on the Boston flight that crashed into the second tower of the World Trade Center. She cried; I listened. I felt a strong connection as she shared her loss, and I felt compelled to allow her room to grieve, work through her

---

[1] All students used in this chapter were assigned pseudonyms, and major identifying details about each student were changed to protect the student's privacy.

pain, and I even went to great lengths to make sure she was seen by the Counseling Center.

Kelly seemed thankful for my help, and I remained concerned over the next two and a half weeks when she didn't make it to class. I assumed she was attending the funeral and had gone home to be with her family. When she returned for the peer review of the personal experience essay after more than two weeks away, I was both relieved and excited to see her. Kelly's workshop group seemed drawn in, even mesmerized, by her story, and I knew she had written about her cousin.

Then it was time for me to read Kelly's personal experience essay. I waited until I got home to read her paper. I turned off the television and the phone so I could completely concentrate on the essay that I had encouraged Kelly to write. As I read her narrative of the events on September 11, I began to question the truth in Kelly's piece. The flight number was not one of the numbers I had heard or seen flashed on the television screen for weeks; wait, she was on the 7:00 a.m. flight from Boston to San Francisco? It was Boston to Los Angeles, right? Her cousin's name sounded more like an Amarillo diner than a girl's name. And she was the lead in the Boston Ballet's production of *Cleopatra*? But that didn't make sense—my friend had just attended the ballet, and they were performing *A Midsummer Night's Dream* in September. Kelly was with her cousin the day before the attacks? How was Kelly in my class and in Boston on Monday, September 10? Everything about Kelly's essay seemed eerily disjointed, and nothing added up. Her telling of the event was much too confusing, and I saw clear indications that Kelly had created and dramatized this personal experience.

I felt taken in by her story. I had encouraged Kelly to write and discover the power this event held in her life. How had I read or misread her as a student and a writer? Suddenly, what I embraced as the key principles of personal writing and healing were called into question. My principles had been used against me.

At the time, I questioned if my 9/11 writing exercise and my encouragement for students to write and grieve had led Kelly to write what she believed I wanted to read; had my pedagogy led Kelly to fabricate an essay on the death of her cousin? Had that teaching moment failed?

As a new teacher of writing, I had been skeptical that failing moments in the classroom should be welcomed, and even embraced. Now, when I reflect on the challenge I faced with Kelly, I am almost thankful for what our interaction taught me about myself as a teacher. The incident encouraged me to follow the advice Lad Tobin offers when he reminds teachers to

[M]ove beyond the edited fairy tale, the basal reader of our own teaching experience. Like any good narrative, this new story will be a little unsettling, sometimes even downright scary. But that's all right: as long as we keep telling it to each other rather than keeping it to ourselves, we'll be strong enough to take it. (149)

Through this conflict, Kelly caused me to reflect on my teaching principles. Yes, she took advantage of a tragedy and my teaching philosophy, but she did not cause me to abandon my commitment to personal writing. Perhaps I even have greater faith in students' need to tell their stories of life and loss, and Kelly taught me the importance of listening to students. Above all, she helped me realize the importance of all stories, good and bad, from the classroom.

He Has a Knife: Students Who Subvert the Classroom

A teacher with six years of experience and a poet, Meg Scott faced the challenge of violence in her classroom.

> One of my students, James, was a good writer and as enthusiastic student, so I noticed when he began acting strangely over a period of three or four weeks. He was sleeping through class, completely distracted, and uncooperative with class instructions on several occasions. His appearance had also changed, and I suspected he was using drugs heavily. The students in his peer review workshop group complained about his behavior, but I just failed to find an opportunity to talk with him before I was forced to confront the situation.
>
> I still remember that class—James began mumbling in class, though his words were all incorrect and confused. He then reached into his pocket and took out a knife, and he began to speak lines as if he were in a movie and about to encounter a knife fight. I asked him to step outside with me, and he complied. When we got outside the classroom, I confronted him about his distracting and frightening behavior. He didn't seem to understand me, and I was afraid of what he might do in this altered mental state.
>
> He reentered the classroom, but did not pack up his things as I had asked. I immediately pulled him out of class again and asked another student to pack up his things. We stood outside, and I explained that he should go to the Student Counseling Center and seek help. I asked him what drugs he was using, and he said, "All of them." The student who gathered James's things arrived at the door with his bags, and he grabbed them from her angrily. He cursed at me, and then got on his bicycle. He fell off his bike about ten feet from the classroom, and I instructed one of the students in the class to call for help on a cell phone. I cancelled the rest of class, and I waited with James, who was crying, until health care professionals arrived.
>
> Now that time has elapsed, I realize I should have talked with James sooner—as soon as I detected a problem. By ignoring his disruptive behavior, I was sending him a signal that it was acceptable to show up for class under the influence. I may have even joked with him about having a "rough night," which could have led him to believe that I was amused by his antics.

This teaching challenge involved my entire class, and I felt I should share the conflict with the class, because they, too, had experienced a student go crazy, get kicked out of class, then hurt himself just outside the classroom, resulting in a class cancellation and a medical emergency. As it turns out, James was sent to a mental health facility for drug treatment and counseling, and he sent the class a letter apologizing for his behavior and for scaring any of us with the knife. We talked about the situation as a class, and we even sent James a card. And our class discussion about James prompted an interesting dialogue about the connection between drug abuse and mental illness. Two students chose this as their research topic for their final paper. As a class, we recovered and grew.

In the end, this situation of conflict strengthened my pedagogical values. We, as teachers, never know what is going on behind the faces of the hundreds of students we teach. I feel called to work with people, and I hope to help student-writers find a means of expression. An overwhelming majority of my students are fundamentally good people. There is some cost to consider in opening myself and my pedagogy to them, but the power of shared experience and, occasionally, shared conflict is well worth the risk.

You're Not Like Me: Students Who Challenge Our Beliefs, Our Cultures, Our Pedagogies

Another teacher and poet, David Higgenbotham, has always encouraged his writing students to write about their interests and passions, and one semester his pedagogy and personal philosophies were challenged.

A student in my freshman composition class wanted to explore his family's Iranian heritage. He wanted to write his research paper on his father's involvement in the Iranian revolution. Amir was a very charismatic student, and I hoped his enthusiasm for his topic would show some of my more reluctant students how personal involvement with a topic might make a research paper fun.

Amir conducted interviews with his father and crafted outlines. We discussed the form his paper would take. Everything went well until I read his first draft. There was no documentation. His father was not quoted. His father did not even appear in the paper. He wrote about the revolution, tangentially, by attacking Jimmy Carter. He made extravagant claims about the Carter administration's secret dealings, and, whether that was true or not, he had no evidence or sources.

I spent a few minutes with his draft before I asked him to explain. After I pointed out the paper's obvious structural weaknesses, Amir became confrontational. When I asked him where he had found his information, he replied, "My father." I asked Amir to define how his father was an authority, and encouraged him to quote his father directly. He said, "My dad *was there*." I assumed he meant Iran.

In his second draft, close to fifteen pages, the assertions had become more outlandish. His father was still not in the paper, and the paper was filled with careless syntax and grammar. I asked Amir to make his own revisions to the paper and to meet with me outside class.

I had his third draft in hand before our conference, and I spent an hour marking places where it needed work. When Amir arrived, I began by talking about where his evidence was still weak. "You are American; you don't understand."

"Yes, I am," I said. "But I'm not talking about the revolution. I'm talking about backing up your paper's assertions." He looked down at the paper.

"You're from Georgia." I wasn't sure what he meant, but it wasn't sympathetic. I changed course and pointed to some recurring syntactical errors. I was introducing the apolitical comma when he interrupted, "I bet you are a Democrat."

"Well, yes, I am. I am a teacher. I am poor. Go figure."

"I bet you voted for Carter." I was three. But I *would* have. He had me there.

Our next meeting was not so friendly. After our conference, he skipped the next week's classes. I thought he might have dropped, until he showed up in his pajamas on the day the project was due. He came into the classroom thirty minutes late, barefooted, eating an ice-cream cone. He did not have his paper. He didn't have his books, or anything to write with. The interruption was so sudden and absurd that I completely lost my place. I asked him to leave, and he did not. I told him to leave, and he told me that I didn't have the authority. I walked to the door, opened it, and silently held it open. After a while, Amir huffed up out of his desk and left. I went back inside to a focused, attentive class.

Amir waited for me outside the classroom. After everyone had left, he cried and apologized, asked what he could do to get caught up, and would I take him back. I felt sorry for humiliating him in front of his classmates. He promised to bring his final draft to the next class, and I agreed.

The next class held some of the energy of the last. I was at my desk as my students were coming in when a student, very proper in his Air Force ROTC uniform, clomped into the room and stood at attention. "Sir, I just saw Amir on the quad and I heard some guy say to him, 'Here's your paper,' and then Amir gave him some money." Before I could ask him to clarify, Amir stepped in behind him, his paper in hand. I took him outside and confronted him, but he denied the accusations.

I wish I could rewrite the ending. I had hoped to nail him, but couldn't. The words were his. The paper had been rewritten exactly as I had hoped it would, but not by Amir. And is it my fault? I had provided him with a complete edited draft. While the words were Amir's,

Five Considerations for Dealing with Conflict in the Classroom

1. Clearly state, orally and in writing, your classroom objectives, grading criteria, and classroom community standards at the opening of each semester to help clarify your teaching philosophy.
2. When you are challenged in front of the classroom community, don't resort to sarcasm, humiliation, or other inflammatory comments that will exacerbate the conflict. Stay outwardly calm and encourage the challenging student(s) to remain calm as well.
3. Focus on the conflict, not the individual.
4. Take responsibility—ask yourself what you might do to help resolve the conflict.
5. Seek advice. Make sure you understand the entirety of the situation, consider ways to deal with conflict, and talk with your supervisor, mentor, or fellow teachers about ways to resolve the conflict.

Conflict in the Classroom: Questions

As you think of ways to negotiate and cope with your challenge in the classroom, answer the following questions:

1. Briefly examine the conflict and, as neceasary, write about it. How did it come about? When did you first notice the situation or student? What has been the progression or key conflicting moments?
2. Write down at least three ways you might resolve the conflict. Whom might this involve? What has to happen to reach a healthy resolution?
3. If time has elapsed, how did you cope with/resolve the challenging student/ situation?
4. Did you remain confident in your teaching abilities, or did you question yourself as a teacher during this challenging situation? Explain.
5. Did this challenge strengthen or weaken your teaching standards?
6. What will you do differently or the same the next time a similar situation arises?

the corrections were mine. All the unsupported claims in the paper had been removed, and there were even a few citations. I couldn't dispute Amir's claim, but I had other ways of pushing him, and though he did pass my class, he had to fight for every point.

Coping with Conflict

Now, even though you may be more aware of the way conflict occurs in every teacher's teaching life, solutions and ways to deal with conflict may still seem blurry. How do you embrace conflict when you do everything you can to avoid it? And how do you *really* deal with students who lie, challenge, and act out inappropriately? After talking with many teachers, new and experienced, I found that the most important step in coping with conflict is identifying the problem. After you have consciously identified the situation of conflict, it is important to involve the challenging student in the resolution of the conflict. Make him or her responsible.

I talked with Kelly about her fabricated experience, and she cried and apologized profusely as she shared her "real" story. I asked Kelly to withdraw from the course, and she seemed as heartbroken as I was. Interestingly, she continued to attend class for the remainder of the semester—maybe so that her peers wouldn't know she lied, or maybe to show her sorrow. She did not withdraw from the course that semester, but she did fail.

Meg identified her situation of conflict by involving the class with James's disruptive behavior and drug problem. The class was involved in the discussion and resolution of the conflict, and together they negotiated what learning was available. David confronted Amir about his faulty paper and inappropriate actions within the class, and David, too, finds that his experience with Amir paved the way for a stronger classroom community for future students. David reevaluated his course plagiarism and grading policies, and now his writing students begin each writing sequence in class.

Conflict causes doubt; sometimes we allow conflict to call our confidence as teachers into question. It shouldn't, though. Remember that challenging students make teaching interesting, for often, these are the very students who are the most inventive, creative, and passionate. And they often stretch our teaching philosophies, and even embarrass, surprise, and teach us.

When I first began teaching, I found myself hesitant to share failing or failed teaching moments with anyone—fellow teachers, friends, or my mentor. I now recognize the power that all stories, good and bad, from our classrooms hold. As challenges arise in your classroom, look for safe forums for sharing your experience. Sometimes you will confide in your teaching journal, sometimes you will share in a pedagogy seminar, sometimes you will consult your mentor or advisor. Sometimes you may even have reason to share the experience with your students, and at other times, you may find it more useful to wait until a future term to use the lesson to improve the way you teach. You will find, as a teacher, that these stories will teach you, lifelong.

When dealing with conflict in the classroom, you must always consider ways to deal with the issue and then negotiate and cope with your situation. Use the suggestions that appear on the preceding page to help you do so.

Work Cited

Tobin, Lad. *Writing Relationships: What Really Happens in the Composition Class.* Portsmouth, NH: Boynton/Cook, 1993.

7

If I Had a Penis and a Mustache

JULI HONG

When I called my mother the night before teaching my first freshman composition course, I was looking for maternal comfort—for her to say, "You'll be fine. You'll do a great job." Instead, my mother only increased my anxiety and unease.

"Wear lots of make-up," she said in Korean. "It'll make you look older. And pull your hair up; that'll help. What are you going to wear? Have you decided?"

"No, not really," I said with a sigh. That was a lie. Although the university didn't have a specific dress code for instructors, I still wanted to look older and professional. The problem was that my wardrobe that summer consisted of spaghetti-strapped tanks and cartoon-ridden T's.

As if my mother read my mind, she told me, "Well, don't wear any of your shirts with those silly little people on them."

"Yes, Oma," I said.

"Heels," she continued. "The higher, the better. See what you get for not eating enough rice as a little girl? You'll be shorter than them all."

I began gnawing on a hangnail, but then my mother said, "It's all about respect, Juli-ya. Never forget that."

The words triggered another onslaught of stomach cramps, and I contemplated taking a second dose of Mylanta. My mother was unaware that her concerns had already been preoccupying me for weeks. With small eyes, round cheeks, and a 4-foot, 11-inch build, I could have passed for an incoming freshman student myself. My students would expect someone older, and upon seeing me, they'd be filled with skepticism.

The next morning, the alarm didn't have to announce the beginning of the day. I was already awake and had been twisting and tangling myself in the sheets throughout the night, as if that could thrash the anxiety out of me. I got out of bed, pulled my hair up into a severe knot, and applied make-up to my face. Finally, after hours of deliberation the previous evening, I settled on black slacks and a conservative, scoop-necked blouse. While waiting for the bus to take me to campus,

I rehearsed everything I would say and do. When I walked to the Diffenbaugh Building and entered, I ducked into the bathroom to make sure my make-up hadn't melted in the Florida humidity. Minutes later, I found the classroom, took a deep breath, and opened the door.

Most of the students had already arrived and were seated. I could feel their gaze crawling all over me as I made my way to the front of the classroom. I was Miss Cleo, reading into their stares and half smiles. They were all thinking how young I was and that maybe this would be an easy class for them. I set my things down and glanced at my watch. Time to begin.

"Everyone here for ENC 1101?" I asked with a low but sure voice I didn't recognize, and a polite but perfunctory grin.

The students nodded.

"Great," I said. "Welcome, everyone. My name is Juli Hong, and I'm your instructor." As I handed out the syllabus and course information sheet, I continued to attempt the demeanor that I had already done all this before—that it was as natural as blinking my eyes. While I might have looked poised to the class, my throat was parched and I was sweating. I thanked God that I had chosen to wear a dark-colored shirt.

After going over the rules and expectations of the course, I ended with, "Are there any questions?" I half-expected one of them to pipe up and say, "Yeah. How old are you?" But no one did, and after a short freewriting exercise, class ended twenty minutes early. It was over. My heart no longer felt like it needed a pacemaker. I had made it through my first day.

As the semester went on, it became easier to stand in front of the classroom. Yet, I was always conscious of my age and how young I must have looked to my students. Therefore, I dressed professionally, made sure that I was prepared with minute-by-minute lesson plans, and did not tolerate unruly behavior. If students would talk while I was teaching, I would snap, "Didn't I just tell you to quiet down? So, do it!" Maybe it wasn't the most subtle way of dealing with problem situations, but it certainly got their attention, and although I must have appeared schizophrenic to them, that didn't matter as much as maintaining my authority.

Luckily, I had a well-behaved class that fall, so there weren't too many issues I had to face. I did notice that many times, the students either seemed unprepared or didn't take responsibility for keeping track of their assignments and coursework. This behavior led me to believe that they weren't taking the class seriously because they had a young, female teacher. I kept telling myself, "They're straight out of high school. They're not used to college responsibilities." Still, this did nothing to ease the frustration.

Unfortunately, my hypersensitivity about my age and authority affected the way I handled what would have been a minor situation with one of my students, Sharice. She had the manners of a good student, and in the beginning, she was. Always well behaved, she participated in class discussion and had assignments in on time. However, by midsemester, she was forgetting to hand in work, failing the pop quizzes, and missing class. The students were currently working on their third papers and had scheduled mandatory individual conferences with me the following Monday through Wednesday. Sharice had signed up to meet with me that Monday morning, but failed to attend. It wasn't until Tuesday evening that she e-mailed me.

She wrote, "I'm sorry I missed conference, but I had a medical emergency, and have a written excuse to prove it. Is there any way I could reschedule my appointment?"

I responded by telling her there were only two slots available on Wednesday.

She wrote back, saying, "Can I meet with you Friday during class time?"

When I told her that conferences were only being held Monday through Wednesday, her response took on an argumentative tone. "But I have class during those times. We have English on Mondays, Wednesdays, and Fridays. I don't understand why you wouldn't hold conferences on Friday during class time. That just doesn't make sense."

Her attitude agitated me. She would never have responded to me that way if I had a penis and a mustache. Speculations began to race through my head. *She probably wants to meet with me as late as possible because she doesn't have her draft written!*

In my response, I made no effort to hide my anger. "I'm the teacher, and conferences are when I say they are. As I mentioned already, there are two available slots tomorrow. Take one or don't."

She wrote back within the hour. "But I have class during those times. Please, isn't there any other time?"

Her written tone was now entreating. I reminded myself that she had begun the course as a conscientious student and that perhaps she was trying to reestablish responsible behavior. I relented and we agreed on a time for Thursday afternoon.

As I waited in my office two days later, watching the second hand on my clock make another cycle past the numbers, I grew livid. Sharice had stood me up for the second time. I had made a special trip onto campus just so she could keep me waiting. I felt that she had taken advantage and had no regard for me as a teacher. She encouraged me to make an exception for her, just to throw it back at me, unappreciated. I realized later that Sharice had no such thoughts or ulterior motives, but at that moment, I felt affronted by her actions.

Sharice didn't even e-mail me to explain herself, and when I saw her in class the following week, she simply walked in and sat down, all curls and dimples as she talked to the other students.

As I watched through darting side-glances, it was as if those dimples were winking at me, laughing. Mocking. I wanted to walk over to her and demand an explanation. But I didn't.

Despite her irresponsible actions, Sharice still handed in her third paper promptly. When it came time to grade it, I noticed that her topic was inappropriate and did not meet the requirements in my syllabus. Afraid of being biased because of the earlier incident, I had another TA read the paper and tell me what she thought. We agreed that it was a D paper, so I felt confident and justified in giving her the grade. It was when I went to make the endnote that my anger and annoyance began to resurface. My bias began to steer my scribbling hand like a witch manipulating me through a voodoo doll.

By the time I had finished writing, the endnote said:

This does not meet the requirements of the assignment. Anyone can claim she is an authority on her own family members, which doesn't make it much of a challenge to prove, does it? No one would refute your argument. Your topic should have been one where someone else could possibly be an authority, so that you would have to exert more persuasive rhetoric to hold up your argument of authority. As is, this paper seems more like character sketches of your family members. If you had come to your conference appointment, I would have told you right away to avoid this topic. I don't appreciate having my time wasted like that. I expect better from you.

I returned the papers the following week, expecting Sharice to read the comments and perhaps come by during office hours to discuss her grade. She never did. During the remaining weeks of the semester, we barely said a word to each other. Sharice would participate once in a while, but mostly, she remained quiet during class. Her grades continued to fall. At first, I was worried that she was upset with me, but then I remembered that it wasn't my job to make students like me. Besides, everything I said on her paper was true. Why shouldn't she know it?

The semester ended, and I turned in the sheet with the students' final grades, relieved that I had made it through my first teaching experience without having shoe prints all over my face. The evaluations came back to us at the beginning of the next semester. A group of TAs ran in excitement to retrieve them. We huddled in the graduate lounge, reading the feedback to each other like girls sharing secrets at a slumber party. Most of my students said that they really enjoyed the class and liked having me as a teacher. Then I came to the final evaluation. My smile disappeared as I read the scathing words.

The student wrote: "Teacher was very rude and inconsiderate. She wouldn't accept my doctor's note. She was also sexist, showing favoritism toward the male students. It was a miserable class for me. It seemed the teacher really didn't like teaching."

As soon as I finished reading, I knew that it was Sharice who had submitted that evaluation. I laughed aloud and read the evaluation to my fellow instructors, saying, "Can you believe this girl? Oh yeah, I know who she is. Obviously bitter about her grades." Inwardly, Sharice had poured gasoline all over my insides and hurled a match down the tunnel of my throat. *How dare she say those things about me?* I thought to myself. None of it was true.

But I was wrong. As I thought more about it over the next few days, I realized that Sharice was right about one thing: I was rude to her. I should have been more diplomatic with my comments on her third paper, but I let my issues with my youth, gender, and authority get in the way of appropriate conduct. Sharice's comments on the evaluation were statements spurred from anger, just as mine were. She was simply another student trying to adjust to college life, and she didn't intentionally set out to challenge me. It was my comments that provoked her into doing this very thing in her evaluation.

From then on, I decided to let the grades speak for themselves and have the student come talk to me so we could each explain our perspectives face-to-face. That way, there would be less temptation for a passive-aggressive battle through written words. Incidentally, a strikingly similar situation occurred this semester, when a student, Monique, missed her conference with me. I didn't see her first paper at all before she turned in the final draft. She received a D, and when she came to talk to me about it, I greeted her in a welcoming tone and with a smile on my face. Instead of trying to appear strict, I implemented the tactic of approachability. I calmly explained that her literacy paper was more of a book report than a narrative, and said that since she missed her conference, she also missed the opportunity to prevent this mistake.

It seemed my tactic worked. The student nodded, understanding that the responsibility rested on her, and the whole conversation was amiable and productive. I remained firm and did not change her grade, but I did let go of my stern manner. Monique certainly didn't give me the attitude Sharice had, but nevertheless, I should have conducted myself in the same way with Sharice as I did with Monique. Sharice helped me learn the consequences of being overly sensitive about authority and taking common student behavior too personally.

While I was reconciling my authority issues as a young, female instructor, my roommate, Rebecca, had to deal with a more severe situation this semester than I'd ever had during my entire teaching experience. She was cursed with her first student from hell, and his skepticism of her authority showed from the very first day of the semester. The same evening, we stood outside our apartment and Rebecca told me about Aaron.

"He wants me to call him Sly," she said as she smoked, shaking her head.

"Already sounds like he's going to be a difficult one," I said.

Rebecca pretended to burn her eyes out with her cigarette, and we laughed. "You'll never believe what he said to me," she said. "I go over the course policy and syllabus. Nothing to it, right? When I ask if anyone has any questions, he raises his hand. He asks me how old I am, and I say, 'Why do you ask?' He has the nerve to tell me in front of the whole class, 'Well, you just look a little green.'" Smoke shot out of Rebecca's nostrils like a dragon, and her eyes narrowed as she recollected the moment.

Fortunately, Rebecca bridged the awkward situation with class discussion and rhetorical goals for the course. She told the class that while she appreciated frankness, they needed to be more rhetorically sensitive about the way they communicated and asked the class what would have been a more appropriate way for "Sly" to frame his question. The strategy worked. Aaron's face turned red and he shifted in his seat.

Sadly, this student was not so easily thwarted. Aaron was intent on making Rebecca's semester a sentence of purgatory, constantly pushing the bounds of her authority with his antics. If it wasn't his incessant chatting with his newfound sidekick during class, it was his blatant eyerolls and clownlike expressions that made Rebecca self-conscious and caused her to contemplate resurrecting the wooden teacher's paddle.

One incident caused my roommate to take more drastic measures. As soon as she entered the apartment, she opened her bag and said, "You've got to see this." She pulled out a manila envelope smeared with crayon drawings. It contained a cigarette, a Q-tip, an inebriation test, and other peculiar items along with Aaron's class work. "I've had it," she told me. She decided to call Aaron into a conference.

They met in her office two days later. Rebecca brought forth the issue of his behavior and disrespect toward her as a teacher. She remained calm and unyielding when Adam's attitude turned defensive, maintaining eye contact and a level tone of voice. Eventually, her perseverance won out. Aaron became silent, and by the end, he broke down.

"It almost became a therapy session," Rebecca told Emily, another colleague of ours, and me one day in the office. "It turns out he was having all these emotional problems and was getting way too personal about them. But I kept my distance. I've got plenty of my own problems to deal with and don't want to blur the lines with any of my students."

I agreed. Emily, also young and petite, told us of a slightly different approach. "Actually, I try to act like one of them when I teach," she said.

"Well, my class is so chatty, that if I had a more lenient attitude, nothing would get accomplished," Rebecca said with a shrug. "I guess it really depends on the group dynamic."

Emily nodded. "Definitely. And I'm still conscious about not getting too personal, as every teacher should be. I don't want them to think, *She's my friend*, but I do want them to think, *She understands.*"

"In the beginning, it's all business for me," I said.

Emily looked thoughtful, then said, "I just don't think that I can pull that off, and part of that has to do with age and gender. They'd think, *Who do you think you are?* and probably catch on that I'm overcompensating."

As I listened to Emily, I realized she had a good point. With large, doe eyes, Emily was never without a smile. Pictures of her dog and little nephews covered her desk. I couldn't imagine her taking on a strict façade with her students.

Talking with Rebecca and Emily about our problems with students was helpful, and I was beginning to understand the various tactics offered by my colleagues to maintain authentic authority. With all the student gossip that dominated much of graduate instructors' conversations, I thought it'd be worthwhile to approach the direct source, curious to hear how the students themselves felt. They confirmed most of what I had already learned through my experiences and those of Rebecca and Emily.

When I asked Rosa Miguel, a sophomore I tutored, what types of teachers she'd had better learning experiences with, she told me: "For some reason, I've had better experiences with older males—the ones that are strict, but still have that nice side while getting their point across."

Older males. It was an answer I had expected. "Why do you think that is?" I asked.

She scrunched up her nose and began tapping her pen against the desk. "Well, the teachers I haven't liked are either too young or too old. Either they've been in the game so long that they think they can step all over you, or they're so young and inexperienced that they don't have the power to rule over the class."

"What about female instructors?" I said.

Her nose crinkled again, this time with disdain. "I've had a couple, and haven't had a good lasting impression. Except for you," she assured me with a laugh. "My 101 teacher was too dominating, and the whole class turned on her. I don't think she had a good semester with us."

"But don't you think that because she was young and female, she had to make an extra effort to establish authority?"

"Yeah, I can see that," Rosa said. "Younger female teachers seem weaker and do have to work harder, cuz at first glance, they're not going to get automatic respect from their students. I mean, that's how I would personally react." She paused. "But with my 1101 teacher, it just came across as too fake, like she was trying too hard. And it felt like she didn't care about what we had to say. She didn't want to relate to us or get to know us; she just wanted to have too much power."

I nodded. It seemed the patriarchal system still unconsciously ruled in the minds of the young—assertive men were admirable, while assertive women were power-hungry. However, Rosa's comment did echo Emily's notion that some instructors may not be able to authentically pull off an astringent classroom personality.

So I asked what advice Rosa, as a student, would give to young, female teachers, and she said, "You need to have a good balance between being laid back and strict."

"What about attire? Do clothes matter in any way?"

"That was never brought to my attention. But now that I think about it, the teachers that dress more casually make you feel closer to them. Casual clothes are more inviting."

It was the first I'd heard of this, and thought with a grin, *As long as they aren't too inviting.* Only days ago, Emily had told me she had made the mistake of working out right before class last semester and hadn't had time to change. When she received her evaluations, a student had written: "Teacher looked really hot and sexy in those running shorts."

Another freshman student of mine, Marcus Bae, claimed that attire didn't matter at all to him; it was all about personality and knowledge. When I asked about his previous instructors, he said that in his experience, the better teachers were middle-aged males. However, unlike Rosa, Marcus seemed more aware of gender roles. "My female teachers tended to be more strict. But since they were— you know—women, they had work harder to get the kids' attention. I understood. That's how they thought they had to be."

When asked if he would prefer male to female instructors for future courses, he said, "No, I don't care, as long as they can show the information in a fun way. I do prefer younger teachers, though. It seems like they can communicate with us better. Older equals grumpier and boring. Younger equals more exciting."

"What would your first impression be, seeing a female teacher who looks your age walking into the classroom for the first time?" I said.

Marcus was silent, then said, "Well, don't get mad, but if she looks young, then I'm gonna think that she's less experienced and maybe not so good a teacher. But then, I'd think the same way if it was a young guy." He paused. "I'm sure it's probably much harder for the women, though," he replied with a smile.

I smiled back. "Then, do you have any tips for young female teachers that will help them overcome students' initial impressions?"

"I guess if a problem comes up, be strict about it and don't let people get away with it. Then everyone's gonna think, *She can't handle it* or *She doesn't care*. But be lenient when it's appropriate. Students who like you will respect you."

While I enjoyed Rosa's and Marcus's insights on young, female instructors, it was my own sister, Mimi, who brought everything together with the most impact and enlightened my approach to teaching. Mimi is currently a sophomore at Penn State University; her views coincided with Rosa's and Marcus's on some levels, but not completely on others.

We were on phone for one of our weekly catch-ups. I lay on my bed and complained about my students and their lack of responsibility, calling them a sour batch. "What's with you kids, anyway? Why do you have to make it so tough on us?" I said.

"Ah, shut up," Mimi said. "They must all hate you. I know I would."

"I don't care about that," I said. "I'm not getting paid to be their best friend."

"You shouldn't care," my sister agreed. "That's the one thing that annoyed me about my freshman English teacher. Sarah always seemed a little too concerned about being cool and down with us."

"You didn't like her?" I said.

"Actually, aside from that, she was pretty good. She knew what she was doing, gave good feedback, and was enthusiastic and encouraging. She made class interesting and was more in tune to the way we think. Relaxed, but at the same time, in control. She's one of the only female teachers I've liked," Mimi said.

"What about the others?"

"They were authoritative, condescending, and easily frustrated. Just too sensitive."

"Hey, I'm not about being condescending or any of that, but there is a reason for feeling a little more vulnerable," I said.

"Yeah, yeah. Men get more respect. That traditional male ideology."

I didn't say anything, somewhat startled by my sister's astute observation.

"But don't you see how it backfires?" Mimi asked me. "Younger female teachers feel like they either have to be cool or have a really tight hold on their students. But we'll disrespect you if you come off as a tight-ass, and we'll disrespect you if you're trying way too hard to fit in."

"So what would you suggest, oh wise undergrad?" I said.

"Just don't think about students liking you, but about the teaching. And teach the material well. If you're a young teacher, students will relate to you naturally; you won't have to try. Just because they like you doesn't mean that makes you a good teacher."

When our conversation ended, I felt strangely encouraged by my sister's suggestions and started to think of my youth as an advantage instead of a crutch. She was asserting what we, as young, female instructors, were discovering for ourselves through our mistakes, our challenges, and these very experiences that we shared with each other. As teachers, it's about learning to balance authority with a more approachable side.

Now I know that as long as I'm steadfast with course standards, the natural tendencies of my personality won't affect my authority. I'm less hesitant about laughing along with my students or bantering with them, and while I remain stringent with class rules, I'm willing to hear my students out. Along with a new inward balance, I've also attained a balance with my outward appearance. While most comfortable with looking professional when I first meet my students, I'm no longer self-conscious about wearing more casual clothes once I feel my authority has been established. I don't take everything too seriously or personally, and, as Rebecca has reminded me in the past: I never forget that I have a support system—fellow colleagues I can talk to whenever I begin to doubt my own authority.

8

"What Are You Looking At?"–Teacher as Stand-Up Comedian

KRISTI MARIE STEINMETZ

I am trying to relax. It is summertime at the Jersey Shore but because I am just two weeks away from teaching college students for the first time in my life, I can't relax. And out of all the concerns about being the best teacher possible, the concern that has turned into angst and prevails above all the other anxieties is the concern about how to control the uncontrollable: nipple erection.

I will be relocating from the North to the South. Teaching in Florida means that there will be no hiding my body in big, bulky sweaters. Teaching in Florida means the opposite of layers; the goal will be to wear the least amount of clothing possible in order to stay cool and fresh while still remaining professionally elegant. And I have to admit, there is an insecure part of me that feels the need to dress as hip and carefree as my students.

I want to be cool on all levels.

I do not want my appearance to give them reason to laugh.

I want to be respected.

So it is time to go shopping to lose the anxiety and to gain some control.

I must first let you know that I was not trained to be womanly even though I was the type of girl who was saddened the day my feet no longer fit in black patent-leather Mary Janes. Existing in a girl's body came naturally to me. But once girlhood disappeared and my girlhood body with it, I was at a loss. My mother did not introduce me to make-up or bras or any other type of feminine contraptions. I was on my own when it came to learning how to be responsible to a stick figure that decided to grow curves.

Sometimes I would garner information via indirect sources. At sleepovers and during impromptu meetings in cabañas at pool parties, girlfriends passed on their mothers' secrets to each other. We were taught by one girlfriend in her van, of all places—we had smuggled her mother's make-up bag out of her vanity drawer—that the way her mother showed her how to put on mascara was to first coat the eyelashes of the top lid with the wand and then to lightly—ever so gently yet quickly—flutter shut the eyes in order to coat the lashes of the bottom lid. Another girlfriend told us that her mother taught her that the way to wear eyeliner was to encircle the iris.

I am proud to say that I have since learned how to use eye make-up properly. My guess is that my girlfriends were covering up the fact that their mothers did not let them in on feminine beauty secrets either.

So there I was at thirty-some years old going shopping to find a way to control N.E. (as my middle school girlfriends and I liked to refer to nipple erection), and I was as embarrassed and clueless as I had been at twelve. I decided to invest. Since you get what you pay for, I traveled north on the Garden State Parkway to the highest-end shopping mall New Jersey had to offer: The Mall at Short Hills. I pushed my self-consciousness aside and marched into Nordstrom's lingerie department with head held high. When the saleswoman asked if I needed assistance, I leaned over the counter and whispered, "I am going to be a college teacher and I need help. How does one deal with nipple erection when standing in front of the public?" Rather than responding with "And you call yourself a woman?" the saleswoman came out from behind the counter nonplussed, headed toward the back wall, and shared information that I should have been privy to years ago: "What you need is the molded-cup bra."

And that is the story of how I was introduced to one of the greatest female secrets of all time.

I purchased one in nude, one in black, and one in baby blue. I left the lingerie department at Nordstrom with the confidence equipment I believed that I needed to make it in this world as an effective teacher. I was certain that if my body was in control, then I would be in control standing in front of twenty-five students for fifty minutes twice a day three times a week.

It's the first day of my teaching career. I decide to begin class with having the freshman students respond to the question, What are your goals in college?

I give them ten minutes to freewrite.

I am nervous but in control.

I ask for a volunteer to read his or her freewrite aloud, and a student by the middle window raises his hand.

"One of my goals is to seduce my English teacher."

The class laughs.

So I laugh.

Then I go home and look at this kid's picture on the class photo roster. Thinking back to the other times during the summer when I had looked at the roster, I could kick myself for missing the fact that this kid, let's call him Jeremy, was psycho. Definite stalker material. Unsmiling. Crazy stick-out-all-over ultralight hair. And cold-looking eyes. Oh, and his head was tilted to the side, you know the pose, the one with the jaw turned slightly up. Threateningly. Or, as if to say, *I dare you. I dare you to stop me from making your life hell.*

Later that same week, I began class with another freewrite: How has college failed your expectations so far? Wouldn't you know that Jeremy was the first hand-raising volunteer who wanted to read his response aloud.

Should I risk it? Why not, I decided, learning is all about taking risks, right? I'm not scared of him.

So I do it, I let him express himself.

He reads about how his teacher has failed his expectations.

He reads, "I never thought a college English teacher could be so hot."

The class laughs.

So I laugh.

Then I go home and start to panic. I have no idea how to handle this behavior. But I must admit that I was still grateful for my molded cups—imagine what he would be writing about without their protection.

And then I receive e-mail from him that evening: "How's this for a story? 1101 student falls in love with 1101 teacher."

That's it. No more. I want this kid out of my class. I want to eliminate the problem from my life. He is ruining my sense of control.

And I run to the phone book to make sure that my home phone number and address are not listed so that he will be unable to move into psycho stalker phase—I yelp when I see that my home contact info is completely available to his desires. And then I decide to meet with the director of the first-year writing program, to see what I can do about getting this crazed student out of my life.

The director of the program is that rare type of boss that you could imagine working with for the rest of your life even if the academic institution continued to pay you the same measly slave-labor stipend that they paid you from day one. So after she met with the student and he bawled his eyes out and apologized profusely and claimed that he was just trying to be funny and begged to not be taken out of my class because he truly felt he needed me for his comic writing ambitions, the director recommended that I keep Jeremy as one of my students. She believed that he was harmless. My trust in her sense and wisdom combined with the flattery of his begging to stay in my class because he was sure he was going to learn something finally persuaded me—after many undignified discussions with peers—to keep him. So I e-mailed Jeremy a letter in which I told him that he had absolute freedom to write about anything he wanted to as long as that subject or object was not me and to remember that along with writing freedom comes the awareness and willingness to accept the consequences of free expression. Jeremy agreed to the terms, apologized in an e-mailed reply, and then apologized in my office during a one-on-one conference.

As the semester went on, not only did he become one of the best writers in the class and a favorite hard-working student, but he also became the class spirit. The entire class could not wait to hear what he was going to read and say next. Jeremy's humor and intelligence and openness and willingness to put himself on the line made the first class I ever taught an amazing class. In creatively turning himself into animal characters or using his weekend foibles for plot development, he set the stage of possibility for the other students. Jeremy taught us how to turn truth into art, how to spin failure into comedy. He was also the best workshop participant in the class in that he offered close readings and inspired suggestions. He shared his skill of intuiting the truth that needed to be revealed and then offered how to go about taking that risk via writing. Jeremy earned a final grade of A, and I do believe that he has what it takes to be both a comic actor and a comic writer.

Audre Lorde's epistemology begins with the idea that you learn as you go by "asking the hard questions, not knowing what [is] coming next" (98). Teaching is about getting the process of awareness and consciousness going in a person's mind. As she explains in an interview with Adrienne Rich, "The learning process is something that you incite, literally incite, like a riot. And then, just possibly, hopefully, it goes home, or on" (98). In a writing class, I find that the course material that is most inspirational to advancing writing, thinking, and discussion is material that deals with controversial subjects—issues of race, class, sexual identity, biases, tradition, nationalism, gender, society, rites of passage. As my mother says, I should wear a T-shirt that reads: I'M THE TEACHER YOUR PARENTS WARNED YOU ABOUT. I try to find material to present to students that will help them grow as open-minded and compassionate human beings. I love witnessing the learning curve that arises from their discomfort and resistance when considering thoughts they never before entertained. I express to them my philosophy that being in college means that they now have the opportunity to learn that there is a bigger world out there beyond their lives and inherited values, that their views are not the be-all and end-all. I try to help them relax about the idea of education and share with them my idea that being an educated person has nothing to do with how many degrees a person has or how many books one has read; it has to do with how open one's mind can be to otherness.

And this idea of openness to otherness is medicine I need to take for my teaching mind as well. I need to learn from students like Jeremy who push me past where I am comfortable; I need to accept that I may not always have a say in what comes next; I need to remember that if I want to be a teacher who truly wants to offer freedom to her students, then I need to be open to the consequences. For isn't that the deal I made with Jeremy? Isn't that the teacher-test Jeremy provided for me? I do not want to be a hypocritical teacher. I want my philosophies and intentions to match my actions. Isn't that how I end up defining integrity to my students? There are times when the only thing I can do is use myself—my answerless questions, my vulnerability, my self-consciousness—to respond in a way that incites the learning process. So how do I use my flaws—my humanness—to shed some light?

I have learned that to be an effective teacher, Audre Lorde style, I need to use humor. Humor is the best technique to teach controversy. Humor relaxes and establishes honesty and therefore creates an environment of mutual trust. And the best way to use humor is for me as teacher to play like the Shakespearean fool: put yourself on the line, sacrifice your image, and perhaps you may be the one to have the honor of delivering the wise lines.

Just like Jeremy.

And if I am going to try to wrangle students out of their comfort zones, then I should at least make it fun, right?

Every time I open up that door to enter into the classroom to teach, a little voice yells out, Showtime!

My oldest brother is a middle school science teacher in Bricktown, New Jersey. He recently shared one of his teaching philosophies: State the obvious. He then went on to give examples of how to handle embarrassing moments. If he is talking fast and on a roll and he accidentally spits and his spittle lands on a student's desk, he acknowledges it by wiping the spittle off and cracking a joke. If he is wearing a tie that may be a little too short for his 6-foot 7-inch frame, he will walk into the room saying, "Think this tie is too short?" And then he welcomes a few minutes of open-fire commentary rather than having his students whispering behind his back.

Winter break and I'm visiting the family in Jersey. I go to get into my brother's car. On the passenger seat are numerous pairs of black dress socks and torn wrapping paper.

"What's up with the socks?"

"They're from my students."

"Why are your students buying you socks?"

And then he goes into the story of how one morning he had no socks to wear so he had to wear his wife's tiny white ankle socks. He walked into class and said, "No one make fun of my socks. My grandmother always said to always wear your best and my wife's socks were my best today. I opened my drawer—nothing. I opened hers—tons of fresh, clean socks. So I'm wearing hers. Anyone got a problem with that?"

My brother's stories teach me how to, as he says, "Keep it real." He believes that no true learning can occur if you are trying to ignore the obvious because then the obvious becomes the invisible. The students' trust in you will not develop, because you are ignoring what is true, and the classroom environment will become tense; tense means no movement, which means no growth, which means no learning.

I've come to believe that I should admit I'm human rather than try to maintain control. When I do, my students are granted permission to admit that they are human too. They're relaxed and trying to do their best from a place of vulnerability because they know it is okay to fail. It's true for teachers too. Vulnerability is the opposite of control. When I do not have control, strangely enough, I earn respect by the way I handle being a spazz. If I can handle myself in those moments as a comedian would, if I can make light of the failure and make fun in the process, then I may be able to help my students feel safe, to take risks in their writing, thinking, and discussing that they may not have ever attempted before. In my personal and teaching experience, I have seen evidence that it is risk taking that yields the most profound results.

So how do I relax when it comes to those undignified moments so that I can become brave enough to state the obvious and to keep it real? My two brothers are the masters of stating the obvious and keeping it real. I was fortunate to grow up having feedback about my appearance and behaviors whenever they felt it was necessary. If I could get an outfit past my brothers' scrutiny, then I believed that there was nothing about how I looked that the world could pick apart. I knew it was time to cut back on double-desserting when they started calling me goat belly. I switched the style of underwear I wore because one brother told me flat out, "You can see your underwear lines in those pants." One evening when I walked into my oldest brother's house in too-tight jeans, he looked at me, looked down at my waistline, paused, and then said, "You are going kill someone with that button. God only knows where it is going to ricochet when it pops off." It is because of my brothers that I have been able to modify my obnoxious laugh and to accept the fact that I have a larger-than-normal head. Because of my brothers, I have learned the beauty in the humor of the body's many ways of betrayal. I have to constantly get over myself and accept the fact that no matter how cool and graceful I try to be, I always end up behaving like Chevy Chase in a National Lampoon movie.

But it is also because of my brothers that I have learned the beauty of the quick comeback and the proper usage of our inherited Jersey wit. I know how to play the class clown, and I know how to play the straight man to the class clown.

Who was I kidding when I thought that the molded-cup bra would give me all the control I needed to conceal what a spazz I can be? Body humor happens constantly when I teach. I am probably the most disruptive class clown in the room. One time my skirt got caught on the desk as I got up and tried to walk away. If that particular skirt wasn't made of stretchy fabric and if it didn't have an elastic waistband, that skirt would have been ripped off and I would have been standing front and center in my underwear. Another time, I walked into the classroom trying to be all serious and determined, and as I announced, "We've got a lot to do today so listen up!" I bulldozed right into a desk and knocked it over. I have noticed while teaching that one sock was on inside out. A number of pre-class food stains have been sighted on my clothes too late to do anything about. I have taught class after having minor facial surgery with a big spot on my face. Early in my teaching career, I have had to give up the appearance of having it all together, of being hip and cool, of being dignified and well above the conditions and the betrayals of the human body.

I hear my brother's voice: State the obvious, keep it real.

The show must go on.

So I did it. I made it through my first year of teaching to the second year. What a miracle. And here I am alive and well and confident, but nervous, on my first day of class, fall semester.

I spot the class clown right away sitting in the desk positioned closest to the door. He has already started up a disruptive conversation while I am trying to go over the course policies. He is even getting this one guy to laugh . . . of course I get tense wondering if they are laughing at me. And then the kid raises his hand and asks, "When can we leave since it is the first day?"

I end class that day scheming: How can I get this troublemaker to switch out of my class? He is definite rotten-apple potential.

And then I think back to last year's first day. And the surfacing of the class clown. And how reactive I was, how overreactive I was, and how the lesson learned was not about getting rid of the problem but figuring out how to use my personality to deal with the student in such a way that the entire class benefited. Once I figured out how to handle Jeremy, he transformed himself from the class clown into the class spirit.

So I decided to embrace this term's class clown and to handle him in much the same way that I handle my brothers: I class-clown right back at them; I take their lines as setups for an even wittier joke. I get over myself. I demonstrate my quick wit and East Coast humor—rather than my authority—to earn some respect.

The first paper this class clown wrote, let's call him Dennis, was about his third-grade teacher and how she shut him down ruthlessly. How she embarrassed and threatened him and yelled at him constantly. How she set him up for failure. Eventually this teacher's need for control shut Dennis down to the point that he could barely function in class, on the playground, and then eventually at home. This teacher was trying to conquer him. This teacher made him not ever want to express himself. And Dennis at the age of nine came to understand the urge to end his life. She nearly did conquer him, she nearly killed his spirit, she nearly brought him to the point where he took his own life because she held no regard for his life.

Imagine reading that essay and the relief that I felt knowing that Dennis had come to be my student after Jeremy, after my program director's guidance, after my realization that the class clown is not a threat but a wake-up call to those of us who feel that to be the best teacher we can be, we need to be in control. I took a vow that I would always welcome class clowns into my classroom and I would not only try to see them as the class spirit but also understand them as reminders to relax and to be my truest self, to be the most real teacher I could be, to clean up my act, to walk my talk.

This semester has been the most body-conscious semester of them all, the semester where I feel like a bigger oaf than ever. The molded-cup bra can't help me now because I am beyond its range of salvation: I am pregnant. I walk into class hearing students whisper, "She's getting bigger." Now the obvious has no choice but to be stated. And questioned. So I have to keep it real. And it is not just my belly that is growing rounder and larger. It's my breasts, it's everything about my body that is woman. I feel like a teaching fertility statue. I should have my students address me as Ms. Venus of Willendorf. The distance between my body and the first row of students is getting smaller as I get bigger. And you should see the maternity clothes that I am forced to wear because there is no high-end shopping mall here in town like Jersey's Mall at Short Hills! All of my pants are held up by some kind of elastic waistband—well, not exactly waist because my waist no longer exists. Which means that as the minutes tick by, my pants slide down right over my belly like a sled down a hill. I stand there in front of my twenty-five students wondering if I should hike them up constantly or just let them keep sliding as low as they want to go? By the end of class, while I'm writing last-minute reminders on the board, I feel that the end is in sight. Yet what end will appear first? My pregnant rear end? Or the class's end?

It is as close to a fall day as you can get in early November in north Florida. It is an early Sunday morning and I am driving through campus. I have all the windows down, the sunroof open, and I am playing my music as loud as I can stand it. I am relatively happy, considering. Considering that the only reason I am up this early on a Sunday while the rest of the academic world is sleeping is that I am pregnant and lonely, and my nights are no longer anywhere near as much fun as they used to be. The campus is quiet except for me, my car, and my music. Ahead I see a person with crazy stick-out-all-over ultralight hair walking with his head down. His white T-shirt is a mess—wait! It's Jeremy! And he's doing the walk of shame! I have the urge to beep and wave and pull over to talk to him. But something teacherly inside of me does not feel it would be appropriate to interact with him right at this moment of our paths' crossing. After all, he is doing the walk of shame and he is a wreck and he looks like he feels absolutely awful. I laugh thinking back to his freewrite about goals: *I just don't want to wake up dead on a toilet face surrounded by girls in white cotton panties, me bloded* [sic] *and missing my wallet.* Ah, look how college has failed his goals, his expectations, and how teaching has failed mine. You can make a teacher out of a class clown, but don't take the class clown—or the Jersey humor—out of the teacher. I drive by recognizing and accepting that I am a teacher and a class clown, but at this moment I am a teacher first.

I am happy that I have learned a most valuable lesson: I can appreciate spirit when I see it and I can leave it be.

Being a good teacher is not about control.

Work Cited

Lorde, Audre. *Sister Outsider*. "An Interview: Audre Lorde and Adrienne Rich." New York: Crossing Press, 1984.

9

Reasonable Relationships: Gay Teachers and Straight Classrooms

Jay Szczepanski

Who I'm Writing for and What It Is, Exactly, That I'm Going to Tell You

Mainly, this discussion is for gay teachers. But I think it's useful for heterosexual ones as well. With that in mind, I've certainly overexplained some notions to my gay audience, and for that, I beg your pardon. But, for the straight ones among us, I think it's important to have a little context. And for that, I do not beg your pardon.

My experience as a teacher is incomplete; I think most of our experiences as teachers are incomplete, too, and that's what I like most about my job—it won't *really* be finished until I retire. That said, I can only relate in the following essay those situations which I've experienced myself. I haven't had a student of the same sex hit on me, and I haven't had one try to beat me to death; it may happen someday, or it may not, and I'm prepared for it. So, I can't speak with any authority on these matters, and I won't. All I can tell you is what I know, in the hope that it alleviates any fears, and, most hopefully of all, encourages you as a gay teacher. It's easier than you might think.

Who I Am?

It's interesting to write publicly about a seemingly private part of my life. Sometimes I think, "No one would be interested in a straight teacher writing about what it's like to be straight." Then I think, "Well, I am a minority, after all."

And I am—but much of the time I don't feel like it—I can hide my homosexuality, if I choose. Or, I can use it to manipulate situations (i.e., when I'm teaching). I view minorities as less powerful, or powerless, even, and that's not something I've ever considered myself to be.

I grew up in a village in northern Ohio, five miles from Oberlin (home of Oberlin College) and outside Cleveland. The close-mindedness of small-town life juxtaposed with the far-left liberality of one of this country's finest performing arts colleges created an interesting duality. Being so near Oberlin, I didn't find it difficult to embrace my sexuality—I knew I was gay, and I was often involved in gay society. I had few coming-out issues.

When I left for college in Florida, I chose Flagler College in St. Augustine. I'll admit that I didn't do my homework, and northeastern Florida is Republican, Old South style. Even at my college (which was roughly the size of my hometown, 1,800 people), the close-mindedness of the administration about matters of diversity was an interesting opposition. For the first time, I had to be a little more careful about the way I presented myself to others. And, for the first time, I encountered masculinity like I had never seen: guarded and macho. Oberlin this was not.

In a sense, I was forced to "do the gay thing" backward. After being open for so long, I found that being closed was a more difficult problem for me to deal with. But, I made it, and I eventually came out of the closet again. And now, here I am teaching at a burgeoning Research I university in one of the most liberal counties in Florida. The process starts all over again, and this time I'm not sure if it's in reverse or not. Out of the closet, once again.

A Story

The first class that I ever taught was a homogeneous group: white, middle-class, unaware. Now, I do love my students, but I love them enough to realize also that they are sometimes extremely sheltered. Among the white students I taught, I also encountered four minority students (three African American females and one Hispanic female). I like to make my students think about social issues. I think that confronting students with uncomfortable subjects can spark passionate writing, and if I have one complaint about student writing, it's that it's done merely to fulfill the assignment or to give "the teacher what he wants." By challenging them to respond to dicey and political issues, I usually end up with heated conversations. So, one day I planned a discussion on race in which I posed the question, "Does American society still racially discriminate?" The conversation was heated but disappointing.

My white students insisted that discrimination was no more—and they moaned bitterly about "reverse discrimination." They complained about being passed over for scholarships, denied admission to universities where the infamous "they" had to fill quotas, and the taking away of their fair chance in life, all for the sake of affirmative action. They contended that affirmative action should not exist because racism and discrimination are no longer practiced in this country.

My majority students were selfish and nearsighted, and I can say this because I care about their future.

Dave's Response

Jay—

I am on the fence about you. On one side, you have helped me to realize a talent that I never knew I had. Through a year of hard work, and revision, you gave me a boost that is still providing me with momentum in this English major. You are an editor, advisor, and friend. On the flip side however, I don't think I will ever be rid of these damn journal reflections.

After my first week of classes as a freshman last year, a friend asked me how I was getting along. I bitched about the homework load, explained my concern with the use of computers in the class, and bemoaned the price of textbooks. One thing stands out about my first week of school, more boldly than my first keg stand. I was waiting outside my English class on the first day with someone I thought was another student. You buried that assumption when you guessed my name out of nowhere like a magician, as you would do to many of my ideas and opinions. You provided plenty of room to move about in, but made us defend our every position. I set my expectation for you high after that; more than just a course syllabus and class calendar, but the attention, guidance, and responsibility that a freshman needs. Your hard-ass attitude that I met in the next few class meetings didn't intimidate me, but from day one made me want to impress you.

I had speculations about you being gay as anyone would, especially after seeing you in the mall with another guy, but I was still caught off guard on judgment day. When Dee, with her homosexual experiences, made her arguments, and you comforted her loud enough for us all to hear, I was still unable to keep my breath from being cut short. On the day we debated about language, race, sexual-orientation prejudice, almost every argument I made attempting to defend my position on the awkwardness of gays in society was rammed, head-on, with a counterargument that crushed mine. Thinking about it today, I'm almost glad that my assumptions were not confirmed until my arguments were put to rest. I realize that it isn't fair, but I think that I would have not put as much faith in you as I was able to after I better understood you. I was blind to the perspective that minorities experience, and for the most part I still cannot claim to understand. At least now I have more of an open mind. You hadn't allowed me to keep any secrets in my writing, and at first I felt slightly betrayed somehow. I filtered my writings in my literature journal about the gay character trying not to let my politically incorrect attitude show through for the next two weeks. I don't have a great "awakening" story that should fit here. All I can really say is fuck it. I don't care if you are gay. I'm not scared of you, and if nothing else, it's forced my eyes open wider about a lot of issues, a view that will help my writing.

I laugh when I hear people say that they don't see skin color or care at all about two guys holding hands. Of course they care; it's impossible not to notice. A more honest statement would be that I don't let these petty differences bother me. What difference does it make what pictures you have in your cubicle, or who you go to the mall with? The difference came about when you were able to convince an already tainted opinion to view society in a new perspective; when you coached an amateur who's never written anything worth reading into a writer who's proud of his work. Thank you for your inspiration.

Yours truly,
Dave

My minority students were uneasy, and I, this bland and white teacher who facilitated this discussion would, of course, side with the majority (though I don't and didn't, of course). I decided the next day to tell them that I am gay, maybe to prove that I know what discrimination is. Or, maybe to try to connect with my nonwhite students. Or, maybe to get it out in the open. I'd never hidden it before—why start now?

So, the next class session, I posed this question: "If your best friend told you that he was gay, what would you do?"

"I'd still love him, but he would have to change."

"He'd still be my friend, but he better not hit on me."

"What's the big deal? So she's gay."

"My best friend would never be gay—he just wouldn't."

"That's just disgusting."

One student said, "Well, I'd have a talk with him and try to get him to change." Another said, "It's a choice anyway. They're probably only doing it for attention." And yet another student said, "They should be careful about AIDS. Gay people are really promiscuous."

Though I wasn't surprised, it still hurt me, as comments like these regularly do. I asked them, "What if a gay person were in this room right now listening to this conversation? How do you think he or she would feel?"

A very religious student said, "I'd still say the same things. It's all true."

I relented. "Well, I'm gay. I don't have AIDS. I'm not promiscuous and I've been in a relationship for three years." Then I left the room. I watched the door from my office, and they stayed in there a good five minutes. Later, one of my students told me that what they said wasn't kind.

Ideally, I had hoped that my coming out to my students would prompt and promote better writing. I've always believed that controversy sparks imagination and argument, especially in a composition classroom; however, what I found was the opposite of what I expected. Many of my students lead privileged lives—their attendance in college is partly proof of this—and when "difference" confronts them, they usually aren't happy to be removed from their comfortable positions. My sexual orientation made several of my students uncomfortable, and I can't blame them, really. I don't think they were used to pushing the issue aside. After all, they have to look at and speak to me. There's no ignoring the teacher.

The next class, my religious student wanted to show me the way to God and redemption from my sinful life. Another told me that he didn't want to have one-on-one conferences with me anymore. One student refused to look at me.

And one student told me "Thank you."

Reasons to Keep It to Yourself

You're a gay teacher. These are three reasons why you shouldn't come out to your students:

1. Some students will become incredibly uncomfortable—especially ones who are the same sex as you are. You may lose class cohesion and community.

2. A student or two, beyond being initially uncomfortable, may withdraw and distance himself—then he performs poorly for the rest of the semester.
3. A few students may approach you in order to ask how they can help make you straight. Result: *you* become uncomfortable and withdraw.

And four, though I didn't list it: some students will seek you out for advice about their own sexuality. Depending on your comfort level with this situation, this might be a positive or a negative.

So, which route do you choose? Obviously, that depends on you and what you value in a classroom. I have some gay colleagues who feel that their sexuality isn't relevant to the subjects that they teach—and that's fair. It's no one's business but your own.

Let me wax philosophical for a moment: I've had students dislike me. They dislike me because of the grades that I give them. They dislike me because I won't accept their late work. They dislike me because I tell them to rewrite their papers entirely. I can deal with these situations.

What I can't deal with is having student dislike (or even hate) me because I'm *me.*

Reasons to Let It All Hang Out

You're a gay teacher. These are the three reasons why you should come out to your students:

1. I think that it makes a better learning environment. Diversity challenges students' ideas of what they know and what they *assume* they know about others. It's good to bring students out of their comfort zones—and perhaps some of the best learning comes from situations like these.
2. You will have gay and lesbian students. If you have any discussions about social problems, eventually students bring up homosexuality, and they often joke and make ill-considered remarks—not that your students want to intentionally be offensive, but we all like a good joke. Jibes like these destabilize a classroom community, often putting your gay students (and, often other minorities) on opposing sides. Coming out to your students sets the tone, and it implicitly tells them that your classroom isn't receptive to distasteful comments.
3. Who knows? You might change a few minds.

Of course, you can teach writing to your students without any declaration of your sexuality, and, when I think about it, most teachers remain mute on the subject. Naturally, our straight colleagues don't make it a point to tell their classes that they are straight. We live in a culture that assumes heterosexuality. This is an area where I think we are advantaged as compositionists.

I believe that college is a whole-life experience: students are here to broaden their minds. One paper that I regularly assign is a "position shift," wherein students take an experience about which they felt strongly in one way, and then reverse their situation completely (or very nearly completely). This is an opportunity to use your sexuality as a springboard for student inventiveness and introspection, two achingly necessary elements in writing. I'm not suggesting that you whore yourself for the sake of intellectual stimulation, but, if you're comfortable, there's mileage to be had in it.

Dee's Response

When I first saw Jay walk in the room, I knew he was gay. It was the hot topic the whole semester. Everyone watched him with a hawk's eye, making sure to notice the way he dressed, walked, acted, and noticed the picture in his office of a man or maybe that was just me. One night several peers and I sat down to a meeting with Jay and he received a call. Everyone began to whisper about how it was his boyfriend and how they had seen him somewhere with a guy outside of school. It even fueled the fire when he said I love you to the mystery caller who was waiting at home for him. While others cringed, I secretly said my awww's and smiled. I must admit I was caught up in the gossip too but only because if I took up for him I would have been the *only* one.

I was taught that growing up being gay was wrong. That was until I figured out it is not about who you love but the fact you love them. I found Jay to be a very interesting person before he ever officially "came out." Even when he did, I did not let my ideologies affect how I saw him. It wasn't surprising—after all, I knew it the whole time—but rather I found it encouraging. I can identify with the realities of being gay and how hard it is to live today's society. That semester in his class, my outlook about gay people changed and not because of my own experience, but because I still realized my own prejudices against gay people. Jay's assignment—about what we would do if our best friend was gay and the class discussion—made me realize things I hadn't thought about. I never thought about anyone being born gay (a topic we discussed), and thought it was something that was not possible until he brought it up, even though he talked about gay dogs and not humans. Also that day in class I "came out" to my classmates also. It was difficult, but it also opened my eyes in many ways about being happy with who I am. After this discussion and some soul-searching, I then began to ask myself why from the beginning of the semester I made an assumption he was gay. Also, I thought about what it must be like to go about every day surrounded by people who are overwhelmingly disapproving of the gay lifestyle, something I had not yet experienced, being "in the closet." That day in class I respected him even more than I had before because he was gay, he was a good teacher, and he managed to survive the lion's den known as our classroom (my peers were quite close-minded).

As far as my impression of Jay, even though I "knew" he was gay, I made a mistake of judging him. He could have just been really neat and sometimes in touch with his feminine side. I respected his way of teaching (when it benefited me, of course) and also I think highly of him. He is no longer an old teacher but a friend. His sexuality is not relevant, and he is no less of a man because of his sexual preference. He inspired me as a teacher, and his sexual orientation is not important, because it is just a small aspect of who he is. After all, he is not really gay, he is Jay, and he is really happy.

Relating to Your Gay Students

Some of your gay students will be perfectly secure and happy with their sexuality, and this is so much the better for them. On the other hand, some of your gay students are going to look to you for advice and support while they struggle with their own identity issues. Some of them may have come from a background like mine—being gay has never been an issue for them, and hopefully it never will be. Likewise, some students will come from rural-centered lives into the new and often startling liberality of university life. They'll want to break free and scream their identity from the tops of the dorms. It takes all kinds, and for that I am thankful.

Whether you want to assume the burden of counseling your students or not is, of course, up to you. You may feel that you owe it to your students to listen to their coming-out issues and anxieties. You may send them by way of the GLBT student union (if your university has one—my college didn't and actually quashed several plans to form one). Or, you may not want to be involved in any way, and this last option is probably the safest. But, I'm the kind of teacher who wants to listen to the problems that my gay students face, and so all I can tell you is what I do.

I've had male students come to my not-so-private cubicle and cry. They tell me how hard it is to be gay—their parents will disown them, they are certain (and this has happened, and will probably happen again, to countless other gay young adults). I hear stories of banishment and the cutting off of college money. Romantic flings that they have interpreted as love and that the other party has interpreted as a one-night stand. It's all very heart-rending, and sometimes I tear up, too. But, what do I tell them beyond a pat on the back and a promise that life will improve, that they need to "hang in there"?

I'm honest. "I know. I've been there, too. You're entering a whole new level of disappointment—you'll be disappointed with your friends (and disgusted with your ex-friends), your family, others in the gay community. You'll enter a new world that absolutely hates you for nothing other than the simple fact that you are you. It's a new kind of hurt, and it takes some getting used to. You'll tell the world to fuck off, and it won't. And so, you'll deal with it. You'll cry often, and that's the only way you'll get through it. But you will, of course, get through it, of that I am certain. But never stop talking about it, and don't close yourself off. Too many students like you do, and the results are psychologically damaging, and sometimes life-threatening. Believe me that it hurts only for a while, and afterward, you'll wonder why you were ever so upset in the first place. And I'll listen, for whatever that's worth."

Usually, I get a nod and a smile, and it feels good to know that I've helped a little. And I'll admit that this sort of scenario crosses many, many borders (privacy, student-teacher professionalism, hearing stories that you don't want to hear or that are too painful to remember). But I do, and I stress this, I do point out to my students who need a shoulder to cry on that although I'll listen and offer advice if they want it, these conversations are an entirely different issue from our composition classroom. To give them credit, however, they know this, and are a little put off when you actually verbalize the division. All in all, it's never been a problem for me, and it probably won't be for you, either.

Yet, as I've said, however you choose to handle the situation is up to you. But remember this: the highest suicide rates for teenagers and young adults are among homosexuals. I could no longer be a teacher (or a human) if I could have helped but didn't.

Relating to Your Male Students

If I want to be honest (and I do), a gay teacher, female or male, will face more resistance, hostility, and uncooperativeness from male students. Our culture asks that young men nurture their manliness. Guys don't cry, and they certainly (and naturally) love women. It's a culture of almost hypermasculinity, and I see it every day with more than a few of my male students. Add this pressure to be "a man" to an often hostile or unfamiliar college environment, a predatory or unhealthy desire for sex and scoring, and then the posing that goes on becomes unpleasant and sometimes dangerous.

The student who told me that he believed all gay people who have AIDS should be jailed or put to death was certainly a shock to me. Vehemence that violent and unstable challenges all teachers. Students don't use the N-word, but they certainly love fag, homo, and queer (and, of course, many others that I won't relate in mixed company)—and they'll use them with frequency in a classroom.

What do you say to these usually male students? My course policy sheet contains a statement on civility that expressly addresses this type of language and intimidation—I won't tolerate it, and if a student crosses the line, out he goes. And it also sends a message to my gay students—my classroom is a safe zone.

But what, in actuality, do I *do* when a recalcitrant or hostile male student confronts or challenges me because of my sexuality? The answer is: not much. Thankfully, I've never been called to task publicly. If I were, I'm sure I would invoke my civility clause. I'll let a case speak for itself.

After I told my first class that I was gay, and a male student approached me afterward and insisted that he didn't want to conference with me in private, I simply told him "too bad—you will." I pointed out to him that, in fact, he and I were standing alone in the hallway at that moment, and he was the one who sought a private encounter. I told him that I was offended by his remark. I told him that he would encounter many, many more gay people in his lifetime, indeed, that he knows other gay people right now, and that he had better get used to it. I said, "You will come to class, You will conference with me, you will do your work, and you will personally deal with this situation in whatever way you like, so long as you remain a member of this classroom. My being gay doesn't disqualify me from being a composition teacher, and my being gay doesn't disqualify you from being a student."

I had planned out such a response in my mind, anticipating that a situation like this would eventually arise. I played the hypermasculine card myself. It's an aggressive, forceful, male response. And it worked.

Much as your male students put on a show, they respect the authority that a teacher has, and I find that this overrides any serious problems. When they're reassured that it's a professional environment, they're fine.

Manda's Response

Oi—the pressure of actually writing down my reaction to someone's sexuality. In all honesty, I knew before the rest of the class—and didn't particularly care. Jay seemed to be a pretty cool teacher—kind of scary for the younger students, but all right for us geezers over 21. Two thoughts came to mind when Jay's former student told me he was gay . . . "Figures (the best guys are gay, right?)" and "I hope the guys in the class don't offend him too much."

But I figured he knew what he was doing, in any case. As for the offensive language, you know what they say—"Sticks and stones. . . ." I never thought the softies in the class would physically attack him or anything, but sometimes those verbal attacks hurt more than physical ones.

So what did happen? When the reading assignment and on-line response came due for an article about a lesbian, so many people in the class made all sorts of inappropriate jokes and too many crude statements—I'm straight and I was offended by most of those statements, so I can only imagine how Jay felt—or even worse, if someone else in the class was gay and wasn't prepared for those awful things.

Of course, Jay read the on-line responses before the discussion so he'd know the spectrum of attitudes within the class. One guy really whaled on gay people in general, voicing every prejudice and stereotype known to modern society. He conveniently forgot his position when we started the class discussion. One girl said to me after class, "He (the trash-talking amnesiac) didn't even know what was coming—everyone in the class just attacked him." I just raised my eyebrows at her and struggled not to say "With good reason." To tell the truth, I was pissed that he even showed his face after saying such awful things—even in what he thought was an all-hetero setting. I'm the kind of person to watch everything I say, and I don't entirely understand people that don't. It's like they have a screw loose or something.

In any case, Jay handled the situation well. He and I share a philosophy on college—part of the college experience should be about learning more about the world around you—and the people in it. One of the most effective ways to force someone to open his eyes is to startle him by providing an example he can relate to. That's all Jay did. He startled the class out of its stereotypes using himself as the example. And for some of them, let me tell you, it's about damn time they were startled!

While some of us got our money's worth out of the class for the improvement in our writing skills, almost all of us got something extra from the discussion that day. I suppose some of them didn't learn anything at all, but it wasn't for a lack of opportunity. Jay used every resource available, including his personal life, to make sure that everyone had something to take from that class. Talk about dedication to teaching.

Maybe part of my attitude about Jay's preference stems from my political views, maybe from how my gay friends in high school treated me—I'd like to think that my attitude toward him comes from getting to know him. I found Jay to be a devoted instructor, an excellent conversationalist, and an all-round groovy person—outside class and class-related discussions, he treated me like an equal. That's more than I could ever ask of anyone.

As for all of the marginalization stuff he wrote about . . . hmmm . . . That's a discussion he and I will have to have another day. I guess I'm just one of those hated, close-minded Republicans (Old South Style, no less) from the north Florida area.

Concluding Thoughts

Hopefully, life gets better. Being gay can be political, and as politicians, we run our classrooms hands-on or hands-off. I can only tell you what works for me, and thankfully, it all *has* worked for me. I'm comfortable letting my students know that I'm gay, and I usually find that ninety percent of them are happy to know it. If I'm guarded, then I can't relate to my students. Some would argue that it's no one's business but your own, and normally I would agree. But, when you're the head of a composition classroom that asks its students to tap into their thoughts and feelings, to express themselves for the first time without high school restraints, it's a different matter altogether. You want them to be honest and raw, and I would feel like a fraud if I weren't just as honest and raw right alongside them. Writing breaks rules and breaks down boundaries; community matters in a writing classroom. But, don't forget that you're a member of the community, too.

10

We Teach Alone: The Lesbian Instructor in Academia's Lonely Groves

RITA MAE REESE AND BRANDY T. WILSON

Among the classic lesbian pulp novels of the 1950s was one titled *We Walk Alone*, subtitled "Through Lesbos' Lonely Groves." We—Rita and Brandy, two new instructors of first-year writing and out lesbians—certainly felt alone the first time we stepped into our respective classrooms to teach. We felt alone because we had left our colleagues behind in the pedagogy classroom or in the hallways and were each about to face twenty-five or so young strangers, who expected us to be college professors or some reasonable facsimile thereof. But, at least at first, the fact that we are lesbians is not what made us feel alone or nervous.

As first-year writing instructors, we assumed that getting used to being the lone authority in the classroom would be challenging. We made other assumptions about our roles in the classroom. We felt that our teaching personas would incorporate and benefit from the way we are treated as minorities in the larger society—as women and as lesbians. Because we are both out in our daily lives, we assumed we would naturally be out as lesbians in our classrooms. We assumed our students would naturally question or address this on their own. We assumed that with all the recent representations of lesbians in the media our students would be able to identify one when they stared at her for three hours every week. But, our students assumed their teachers would be straight. Our assumptions and their assumptions remained at odds.

We were talking with a straight friend of ours the other day about coming out in the classroom. She laughed and said she never told her students that she was straight—in other words, no one should disclose her sexuality to her students. We agreed with her, though only partially. Her students assumed she is straight, most likely, and they were correct; most of our students assumed that we are straight, but they were wrong. Do we need to set them straight?

There is a lot of strong emotion surrounding coming out in the classroom, and it is a delicate topic to address even with our closest friends. We might suspect that we are being judged no matter what stance we take: if we are explicitly out to our students, we might be seen as being narcissistic, touchy-feely, or overly political at the expense of being effective English instructors; if we aren't out, we might be seen as cowards, failing to be good role models for impressionable young minds.

We met in the pedagogy training program and interned in the same freshman composition summer class. Even after we came out to each other and agonized over syllabi and first-day wardrobes, we didn't talk about coming out to our students. We talked about grading and daily challenges, and pretended our sexuality wasn't an issue in the classroom—we pretended that we were comfortable with the ways we were being perceived. Many weeks into our first semester of teaching, we had each forgotten that our students might not know and we had ceased to question whether we should tell them. But as the students became more relaxed in the classroom, they started making homophobic remarks like "that is so gay." We did not want to tell them that was offensive because we were gay but that the phrase was inaccurate and offensive; gay is not synonymous with weak, bad, uncool, sissified, or stupid. By coming out in response to such a comment, we felt the students would believe that homophobic remarks were fine except around homosexuals, and that is not what we wanted to say. We were forced to realize that they didn't know or weren't as aware as we had hoped and that homosexuality might come up in ways that would further complicate coming out to our students.

Then, one day, one of Brandy's students sent her an e-mail flat-out asking whether or not she is a lesbian. With years of being out and always vowing that she wouldn't lie if anyone asked, she was caught off guard. Did a student really have the right to ask that question? Did this blur the teacher-student boundaries? Why would she ask in an e-mail? Why wouldn't she ask in person? Did any or all of this imply disrespect? It did not seem advisable to either one of us to come out via the Internet. Brandy suggested they meet in her office, a large public room that was always occupied by several other students at any given time, to discuss it. This would ensure that the student understood that Brandy's orientation wasn't a shameful secret and that the conversation was kept at a professional distance. When the student finally did drop by Brandy's office, she was seemingly unable to bring the issue up again and the matter remained unresolved.

This did, however, provide us with an opportunity to finally talk about issues of sexuality in the classroom in a very real and immediate way. We had to face the fact that we weren't out to our students, that we didn't know how to come out to them, and, most of all, that it did matter to us. We hadn't gone into the closet but somehow found ourselves there. We had to admit that we weren't as open or confident as we wanted to believe, and desperately wanted everyone else to believe, we were. We had to drop this stance and admit we had more questions than answers. But three semesters went by before we made any sort of concrete decision about coming out in the classroom.

As graduate students, we had no difficulty being out with our peers and even with our professors. We spoke openly in our offices with our colleagues and as students in our classrooms about our lives and experiences. For example, we focused on queer theory and did presentations on Ma Rainey's lesbianism and African American lesbians in movies for an African American Women in Folklore class. We weren't painting every woman we studied with a rainbow brush (though Brandy did try to hand Katherine Mansfield a labrys). Often lesbian experience was ignored or invisible in the topics we were studying, and we simply wanted to reinstate it. We even came out over the English department Listserv to people we'd never met. The only place we weren't out was in our own classrooms.

We always try to base our decisions on the good of the students. We began to ask ourselves, What would it benefit them to know that Ms. Reese or Ms. Wilson is a lesbian? Could the information do more harm than good? Is it our responsibility to come out, to be role models? Part of combating homophobia involves letting straight people know that people they interact with are or could be gay. Many of our students will be figuring out their sexual identities while navigating the complexities of dangling modifiers and MLA citations. Some of them will come up with answers that surprise them. Some might even be devastated; it is important to remember that gay and lesbian teenagers are still at greater risk for suicide than their straight counterparts.

We began to talk to other lesbians about their decisions and behavior surrounding sexual politics and teaching. Some lesbian teachers that we've talked with said that they also assumed students would figure it out. They assumed that their appearance or behavior or classroom politics would be clear signals of their sexual orientation. However, few reported that they believed students actually did figure it out. The sobering and relieving fact is that our students didn't give us as much thought as we believed they did. We wish we'd known from the beginning that it really doesn't matter to them.

Some of our colleagues shared with us their experiences with coming out or staying in the closet. Roughly half of these instructors felt that coming out wasn't an issue because they felt they were obviously lesbian. However, these women were less traditionally feminine and assumed their comfortable shoes told everything that needed to be said. They felt everything else was simply none of their students' business.

Only one of these women had a negative reaction about her sexual orientation from a student, a reaction that actually contributed to her decision not to continue teaching. She told us,

> A student in one of my 1102 classes wrote on my end-of-semester evaluation that all I talked about was homosexuality. (I knew it was him because I knew his handwriting well.) He was an older student, a transfer ROTC cadet. So he pretty much figured out that I was a lesbian by my appearance, I guess. He was always a troublemaker in discussions—not in disrupting class, but in always trying to get students (and me, I suppose) riled up by stating extremely conservative views. I never responded to his views, other than to get him to talk more about why he thought the way he did. I really liked him as a student—he was smart. . . . There were other problems that I had that semester, but this single student created most of my difficulties. I think I spent so much time trying to like him and respect him, only then to blow up in my

face—I think I somehow made him a gauge of my success or failure as a lesbian in the classroom. And, of course, he was just a jerk that I couldn't do anything about. So when he rejected me completely in the end, I felt really hurt. And I let that hurt become a major influence in my decision not to teach anymore.

The issue of our status as a frequently derided minority might be present in the classroom whether we choose to name it or not. This incident makes clear that we cannot control the way our students (or anyone) perceive us, and by not addressing our status we might be postponing, rather than avoiding, a hostile reception without the opportunity to respond.

The other half of the instructors we spoke with felt that it was not only an issue but also an obligation to come out. One instructor had her students do a freewrite in which they discussed what their response would be should their future child come home one day and tell them she was gay. Even with overwhelmingly negative responses such as "I would start taking drugs" or "I would kick them out of the house" or even "I would cry and tell her she was not a good Christian," this instructor shared her story of growing up and into the American dream of heterosexual bliss and then waking up one day to find that she had fallen in love with a woman. This, she says, helps them reconsider their views against homosexuality, since it makes them realize that sexuality is not always predetermined and how fluid it actually is. She says,

> I feel like it is my responsibility to come out/share my story—I look at coming out and being a teacher as a gift set. The personal is political, and I believe coming out to fifty students who seemingly look up to you each semester can actually raise awareness in this world. Think of the ripple effect! Perhaps it will save their child's life! I also think that it is important to get the message across that it is not just about tolerance or acceptance: it is about celebration—the same way heterosexual love is celebrated. AND when you teach in a VERY Christian environment it is even more important to come out.

As first-year writing instructors, we might be the first teachers to treat our students as adults. They have just come from high school and are in transition, unsure of who they are and changing at an incredible rate. In many of their other classes, they may be one of hundreds. They are away from family and friends, and chances are that you are one of the few adults who see them on a regular basis and actually know their names. However, while we treat our students as adults, they may not always be capable of acting that way. Since this is new territory for them, they frequently will slip into behavior that feels safer and more familiar. Sometimes that means acting out to get attention or finding an "other" to deride so that they can bond with their peers. Their connections to each other are always more tenuous than they appear to us on our first day.

Coming out can raise many issues, among them having your students treat you as a sexual being. In our society, being treated as a sexual woman frequently undermines your authority. All the instructors who are not out in the classroom indicated that they thought coming out would sexualize them and undermine their authority. Dr. Sheila Ortiz Taylor, a professor with twenty-six years' teaching experience, said she felt that coming out was like saying, "OK, take five minutes to think about Sheila's sexuality." Despite that discomfort, we have come to understand that we have to be authentic—students can sense when someone isn't being upfront with them. The first semester, they are generally compliant if not always eager, but after a while they wonder what the relevance is, why they should have to take English as a class. Coming out is one of the ways that we make the class relevant; it connects words like "gay," which many students use casually to mean things they have not examined very closely, with a physical presence. This shows students why we are offended, not just as lesbians, but also as English teachers, by their thoughtless use of such words. Coming out shows the power of words and how difficult and sometimes dangerous telling the truth can be. The class is about telling the truth about real people, naming things accurately. There is power in naming, and we have to claim that for ourselves.

All our students, with that one exception, made it clear that we could "pass" as straight women, and probably did more often than we realized. We had been coasting along mostly accepting this fact until we were asked to write this essay. At the same time, we were also taking the first lesbian literature class at our university, a conservative university in the South with a predominantly Christian student body. Finally, in our fourth semester of teaching, we both decided that it was time we came out to our students in the classroom.

Each semester, we conduct an exercise with our students addressing assumptions. This exercise mostly concerns the assumptions they make about their audiences. Since we are primary members of that audience, we ask them to give us their assumptions of us. They ask the questions and also call out the answers, which we then write on the board; at the end, we erase all the incorrect guesses. The questions range from where you were born to whom you date. Usually the students skirt around the issue of sexuality, either by giving such vague questions and answers that it is never addressed or by ignoring the implications altogether.

This semester when one of Brandy's students asked what actor she would most want to date, the class seemed to catch on more readily that the questions and all their answers were being too assumptive (the goal of the exercise). They began to include female actresses with their male guesses and added the question of her sexual orientation. When the truth was finally revealed, the students were confused and inquisitive: how could she have been married before and then become a lesbian? Did she just wake up one morning and decide to date women? Brandy explained her experiences, and the students even began to talk about those experiences like any other relationships, heterosexual or otherwise.

Rita's students guessed that she dated thirty-year-old black men or twenty-year-old white men; then one student yelled out, "Thirty-year-old women." That was the only answer she did not erase. The students all began talking at once, and one even pulled out his cell phone to call an absent student to tell her that she had picked the wrong day to miss. The moment of humor was a nice relief for the class, and many of the students seemed more comfortable with her and more respectful after that.

We are happy and proud to say that our experiences were positive. We trusted our students and they appreciated it.

We daily make decisions that affect whether we are truly alone in the classroom. Coming out can build bridges between you and your students, or can create distance. Each class and each instructor are different, so no one answer will fit everyone. But if you are a lesbian teaching first-year writing, you should know that you are not alone, that teaching, like writing, is always a work in progress, and that you will always be learning to trust yourself and your students. As Dr. Sheila Ortiz Taylor says, "Coming out is a process," so while we assumed the information would be obvious, each class will bring with it its own decisions and challenges, and coming out or not will be one of those each time. Don't get frustrated that it never seems finished: as one lesbian author has noted, the important things need to be done every day.

11

"Leave the Office Door Open, Please": The Young, the Restless, and the Teaching Assistant

EDWARD TARKINGTON

"Dude, Emily[1] is hot, and *you know that*, too!! I mean, her face is so beautiful and she's got a great body—oh, to tag that would be *awesome*!!"

Three guesses where this ribald declaration of lust appears: (a) on the most recent episode of MTV's The Real World; (b) on the wall of the men's locker room of a high school gymnasium; or (c) in a journal entry presented as part of a "reading, writing, and self-exploration" assignment to a first-year composition teacher at a major American state university. Give up? I don't blame you.

But wait—it gets better: the author of this lovely lyric—whom I'll refer to as Joe (as in Joe College)—was only getting started. Joe went on to explain how, after he "used his magic; worked his mojo" to get closer to Emily, he faced a dilemma: "I found myself becoming attracted to Susan (another classmate), also. Who to choose?" The question might have seemed more appropriate if Joe were discussing which dolly he wanted to buy for his little sister at the local toy store, but even then I would have felt a bit concerned.

But Joe wasn't finished—by the end of the journal entry, in addition to discovering what it means to "tag" someone or to "work" one's "mojo," I learned the following: the best part of college is orientation week—before classes start—when Joe and friends were able to "go out every night, get drunk every night, and find a new girl—every night"; the majority of his female classmates smoked and were "cock-teases"; and that "since woman is the cause of much trouble in the world, she should go back to her old role—she should be in the kitchen, cooking

---

[1] All names in this essay are pseudonymous.

and cleaning." I wonder how well those suggestions and observations would have gone over with Emily and Susan had it been they and not I who was exposed to Joe College's illuminating perspectives.

Indeed, dear reader, young Joe's observations were in fact made in an assignment for one of my sections of English 101 during my tenure as a graduate student–teaching assistant in the fall of 2001. Coming across this journal entry, along with numerous other journals by Joe's classmates that made alarmingly frequent references to sexual conquests and experiences, as well as other matters one does not normally associate with 101 (was God punishing me for praying never to see another "going fishing with grandpa" essay?), I was forced to wonder: was this the new norm of conduct and frankness among undergraduates, or had I done something to solicit this sort of subject matter? In trying to foster an open, communicative, liberal classroom environment—encouraging students to draw on their most profound and meaningful personal experiences for their essays, engaging new and sometimes controversial ideas, trying to treat them as equals and acknowledge their adulthood—had I given the impression that Mr. Tarkington was interested in hearing about what went on in their lives "behind closed doors"? Had I tried too hard to be friendly and accessible—to be cool—and, in doing so, allowed my students to presume that I was, despite my authority, just another one of the guys, and that their journals and paper assignments were an appropriate forum for discussion of their raciest experiences?

Reading Joe's journal was a turning point in my life as a teacher. My first section of college composition was not my first teaching experience—I had taught previously at another university, served as a teaching assistant for a lecture class there as well, and spent a year as a secondary teacher of English literature and composition at a small private day school. I was not oblivious to the changing styles and attitudes of youth, nor was I unaware of the complicated nature of student-teacher relations, the sexual dynamic of which is always at issue, even when it is unspoken or subconscious. What distinguished that particular teaching experience was that never before had such issues been so openly engaged by my students. Had I inadvertently invited them to do so?

As a young male teacher, I had been made plentifully aware by mentors and superiors of the possibility—nay, the inevitability—of schoolgirl crushes. After all, any male teacher, whether he resembles Brad Pitt or Quasimodo the Hunchback, will occasionally enamor a curious young woman whose intellectual growth is defined by the authority figures in her life. And, therefore, I had trained myself to keep up certain boundaries.

Nevertheless, I saw it as imperative to my role as a teacher that I be easygoing and accessible, the kind of teacher a student would feel comfortable coming to for advice on anything. I was even aware on a certain level that the admiration of my students fed my vanity, and that, within the bounds of ethics and good taste, I was probably guilty of soliciting their affection and their confidence. I admit it—I wanted to be "the cool teacher." But before my encounter with Joe and his classmates, it had never occurred to me how my classroom demeanor—particularly relating to how the sexual dynamic unfolded in my classes—might have significant bearing not only on my pedagogical effectiveness but also on my professional future.

Futures in English education at the college level are not things to be tampered with. Largely because of the mid-twentieth century baby boom and the recession in college admissions as the last generation of baby boomers' kids graduate, the academic job market is tough to say the least. Mandatory retirement ages are being extended, and many tenure-track positions are being eradicated, the courses formerly carried by retired faculty being taught by less expensive adjuncts or teaching assistants—meaning that we, as TAs, are indirectly threatening our own job prospects.

Simultaneously, in order to keep their universities alive and their faculty and staff employed, admissions departments nationwide have begun to resemble corporate marketing departments, selling good times, championship football and basketball teams, immaculate, top-of-the-line exercise facilities, student centers out-fitted with fast-food restaurants, video arcades, bowling alleys; and—most of all—freedom from authority. All but the most elite of US colleges and universities actively recruit students, not just to get the best and brightest, but also to make sure there are enough butts in the chairs when fall semester rolls around. As a result, students are naturally left with the impression that what the advertise-ments have offered is the reality of higher education in contemporary America: everything is fun, nothing is risky or consequential, failure does not exist, rules are made to be broken—the world is your oyster, come slurp it out of the shell.

I've found this condition to be especially apropos where I currently teach composition and study creative writing, a large state university in the South which enrolls over 35,000 students annually. Its undergraduate college is consistently ranked by such periodicals as *Rolling Stone*, *Playboy*, and *Maxim* among the top "party" schools in the nation. The weather during the school year tends to be tropical save for the last few weeks of the fall semester and the first month or so of spring. It is not uncommon for female students to attend classes wearing their bikinis beneath a T-shirt or halter top and shorts so that they can immediately pro-ceed from first-year comp or chem lab to Sun-Worship 101 on the university quad, where bare-chested boys can also be found, tossing Frisbees and footballs and, as our friend Joe College would put it, "checking out the talent." At the beginning of each of my four semesters here, I have submitted a questionnaire asking for basic personal information so that I can get to know my students better—that is, what's your major/prospective major, where are you from, what are your interests—and on over ninety percent of these questionnaires from a pool of about one hundred seventy-five students, "working out," "fitness," "body-building," or the like has been the most highly ranked avocation. With the exception of exam week, if I were to see more students in the library than in the fitness center, I'd worry that the apocalypse was looming large. Body image and sexual attractiveness hold a higher premium with each passing year, and just as today's university students must compete for grades and internships, also must they vie with each other and with themselves to look as thin, fit, and sexy as possible. The world we live in does little to discourage the impression that beauty and sexuality hold roles of enormous importance in all facets of life.

This is not to say that my students are not bright, talented, and, as often as not, driven to succeed. For every Joe College I've had to suffer through, there has been a future doctor or research scientist, a federal agent or veterinarian—perhaps even an English teacher or two. But regardless of talent or motivation, my students have consistently presented a level of frankness regarding their private lives—especially related to sex and sexuality—that challenges me daily on how best to serve their needs and interests without compromising myself in word, thought, or deed.

Sex and sexual concerns are a big part of being young, and, for whatever reason, among contemporary American young people, it's out there on the table at all times. Maybe it was the sexual revolution of the late sixties and seventies, maybe it's MTV, maybe it was *Vogue* and *Cosmopolitan* and *Playboy* and *Penthouse*—where it came from is almost as irrelevant as whether we celebrate or condemn it. We have to live with it, and we have to face its presence in the classroom, particularly if we hope on any level to be able to facilitate our students' growth as human beings along with their competence as writers.

Of course, ethical concerns regarding sex and the college classroom are nothing new. Any graduate student in English should have gathered somewhere between Plato, Shakespeare, Hawthorne, and Foucault that sexual tension between teacher and student—whether it be open, subconscious, or subversive—is ever-present in any teacher-student/mentor-protégé relationship. Ironically, for previous generations of university-level teachers and professors, students were considered an appropriate dating pool. My mother, who taught Spanish at a women's college in Virginia before retiring to raise children, even suggested to me when discussing my career ambition that I might find my future spouse among my students. At least three of my own undergraduate college professors married women who had once sat in front of them being lectured on Shakespeare, the Victorian era, or the Romantic period.

But, somewhere between the sexual revolution and the advent of sexual harassment litigation, university administrations' attitudes and regulations regarding fraternization between students and faculty or teaching staff have become decidedly rigid—and rightly so. Today's average college student is less mature than she or he would have been in previous years—psychologists now generally agree that adolescence for the average American young person extends to age twenty-five, placing the age of legal adulthood just past the midpoint of intellectual and emotional development. At the very moment in which students are becoming more and more comfortable projecting themselves as adult sexual beings, some of whom are far more sexually experienced than their teachers, the average students' maturity level renders them far less capable of handling the complications of an adult relationship, particularly with an authority figure. Furthermore, the days of "courting"—catching a movie, sharing a milkshake with two straws at the soda fountain and then a peck on the cheek at the door—passed definitively around the time the Rolling Stones first complained about not getting satisfaction.

Of course, it would be naïve to suggest that teenage hormones weren't raging back before Woodstock and the pill, but it seems reasonable to argue that sexual issues—and sexual tension—have only recently become a constant, visible presence in the classroom. The challenge of sexuality seems particularly relevant for teachers of first-year composition, because our courses tend to be geared toward allowing students to engage issues and experiences of personal concern in improving their abilities as writers. At my university, first-year writing teachers are encouraged to give their students the freedom to write about the things that matter most to them. Being someone who believes firmly that one writes most skillfully when one writes with passion and inspiration, I couldn't be more grateful for the right to push my students to write freely, and the results have frequently been extremely rewarding. During my first semester, one of my students wrote a thoughtful and complex essay about her experiences with the drugs LSD and MDMA (better known as Ecstasy). As a result of writing the essay, the student later informed me, she was able to confront the increasing control drugs were exerting over her life and seemed sincerely improved by the experience. Other students have written on similar issues and concerns, and more than one has claimed the experience had been as valuable to their maturation as young adults as to the improvement of their writing skills. Nevertheless, I had to take pause when one of my female students approached me after class and asked, "Can we write about our sex lives?"

Even if you choose not to open up that Pandora's box, you had best be prepared to face both confrontation and temptation when you step in front of a room full of hot-blooded young people. Students will often flirt without even knowing that they're flirting; others will make outright advances: one close friend and fellow TA had to have a student removed from her class who had been writing inappropriate remarks about her in his in-class writing assignments; others have mentioned similar experiences—tales of temptation, instances of discomfort that they had neither expected nor prepared for.

So how does one remain safe from sexual harassment disaster without shutting down or shutting out one's students? It seems to me that the first and most important means of doing this is to be honest with yourself about who you are and what your needs might be. Graduate students are notoriously needy. Need is almost the fundamental condition of existence in graduate-school life: We need more money, more scholarships, a longer, more impressive curriculum vitae. We need letters of recommendation, an A in History of the English Language, job interviews in a market glutted with competition. We need more time, a greater sense of hope, a lighter workload, and most of all, love. We need to feel that what we do is important, that we wouldn't have been wiser to go to law school or sell real estate—that we matter in a world that trains our students to value image over substance, simple pleasures over the satisfaction of hard work well done. These things are hard to come by in most US universities, where graduate students who are fortunate enough to be afforded the opportunity to teach are almost universally underpaid and where, in all honesty, the nineteen-year-old football or basketball star is unquestionably more important not only to the student body but also to the university itself than the person who teaches him. After all, when was the last time seventy-five thousand tickets were sold to watch a first-year comp teacher in action?

Know your needs. Know that, even if you are lucky and have a spouse or companion to turn to for emotional support, there will be times when the demands of your work and your study will leave you feeling lonely and alone. Know that, as a teacher, you are dependent on your students, that winning their confidence and approval is almost always necessary to motivating them to do their best work, and that a considerable portion of your self-worth will be tied up in how successfully you are able to facilitate their learning. Know that you are a human being, and that, even when acting with the best intentions, you are fallible, and that what you say or do may come back to haunt you.

Know that, whether you sense it or not, you have power and influence over your students by the very nature of your position. They may look like grownups, and they may act like they know what they're doing, but they will always be looking to you to set the tone of conduct and rigor. Know that, no matter how mature and experienced your students may seem, they are college freshmen and you are their teacher and authority figure. You can be as open and accessible as your temper and schedule permit, but the more open you choose to be, the greater is your responsibility to maintain control, over your classroom and over yourself. You are invested with a tremendous degree of trust—from your students, from their parents, and from your university and your immediate supervisors. Trust is a precious thing and is difficult to regain, in almost any circumstance. Being aware of who you are and what you are capable of on your worst possible day will go a long way toward guaranteeing that you maintain the confidence you've been granted.

Keep yourself honest, and avoid compromising situations. Leave the office door open! Avoid circumstances where your actions might be called into question: meet with students only in public, professional environments like offices or libraries. While it's probably wisest to avoid fraternization of any kind outside the office or classroom, if the opportunity comes up to get lunch or coffee with a student, at the very least, never do it alone—bring someone along, preferably another TA. It's unpleasant to have to feel paranoid or overcautious about interacting with young people who may want your mentorship or guidance, but the best way to avoid finding yourself in a discomfiting situation or being accused of inappropriate action is to avoid circumstances where such behavior could take place.

Remember what you're trained for and what you're paid to do. Tempting as it may be to mentor or befriend certain students, few first-year writing teachers have counseling experience. Many if not most FYW teachers only a year or two prior to becoming TAs were still undergraduates themselves. Pure as your intentions may be, you are simply not being paid to be their friend, nor are you qualified. Callous as it may feel, it is always in your and your students' best interests to confine your relationship with them to the office and the classroom. This isn't always an easy thing to do, particularly if you feel, as I do, that many of the most important learning experiences in college life are not part of the core curriculum. But, as a graduate student, you should have more than enough on your plate without being big brother or sister to undergraduates. With experiences, your preparation and aptitude for mentorship will increase, and by the time you take your first tenure-track university position, you'll be better prepared to guide and befriend your students in a manner that won't leave you overextended or professionally compromised.

But what about love? As I've mentioned before, it happens, and it is usually the nature of love to foster recklessness and irresponsibility. Though it's highly unethical, inappropriate, and, in some cases, illegal to pursue a romance with an undergraduate student, TAs and tenure-track professors do it every day, often with the best of intentions.

During my own college years, one of my best friends secretly dated a favorite professor. Though Sally was still a student, the professor waited until after the semester in which he taught her to approach her—he even gave her a B in the class, negating the suggestion that he might have altered his standard of rigor to curry her favor. Their romance progressed beyond our college years, seemed to be conducted maturely and respectfully, and ended amicably. They still keep in touch, six years after their breakup. Theirs was an extraordinary circumstance, largely attributable to Sally's unusual maturity and, frankly, her willingness and ability to keep a secret. Both student and professor took an enormous risk in seeing each other, and the situation could easily have exploded—all it would have taken was one slip-up and a mild churning of the gossip mill to put the professor in question back on the job market with an inescapable blot on his reputation. It's hard enough to get a job in academe without such a stain, not to mention the potential damage the relationship might have done to Sally had it unfolded differently. Do as thou wilt, but remember that, whether you think the rules apply or not, you are gambling not only with your own future but also with the emotional health of a young person who trusts you *because you are a teacher*.

Remember, of course, that teaching should really be about love: love for learning, for your area of specialty, for young people—love for the challenges of performing every day, adapting your style to your students' interests, staying fresh and keeping the work interesting both to yourself and to your classes. You wouldn't be in it otherwise—lord knows you aren't in it for the money. But love is never easy. There is always a reason to fail, a missed opportunity, a poor choice, and a hard day. Part of what makes teaching interesting is that every year, every semester, every day, something is different. Challenges will appear that may leave you frustrated and wounded as often as they gratify or exhilarate. You'll learn that you are capable of things you would never have thought possible, and that's not always a pleasant realization. But you shouldn't be in it if you don't love it—and the more you love your students, wish to be loved by them, and recognize that love is best defined by sacrifice, deep concern, honest good will, and high regard, the more fulfilling and rewarding your experience as a teacher will be.

Teaching Beyond the Happy Ending?

SHIRLEY K. ROSE

The seven essays in this section address three questions that are of central concern to new teachers of writing and to the writing-program administrators and others who work with them in the ongoing process of professional development:

> What lessons about teaching are the most important for writing teachers?
> What are the processes of learning to teach writing?
> Where, when, and from whom do writing teachers best learn to teach?

As relatively inexperienced teachers of writing, the TAs who have written these essays obviously provide some answers to these questions as they pertain to new teachers. But as a reader who is a relatively experienced teacher of writing, and a long-time writing-program administrator, I recognize that these authors have also helped us to identify processes that never end, contexts that continue to sustain us over the course of our teaching careers, and lessons we learn over and over again.

What Are Some Important Lessons?

All the essays in this section remind readers that though each of us reinvents herself when she takes on the role of teacher, we work with only the basic materials provided by our experience, personality, and knowledge to invent and construct that role. The identities we construct for ourselves inside the classroom are defined by the same constraints as those we construct outside the classroom. Insofar as "teacher" is a new role or a continuously renewed role, we have an opportunity to reinvent ourselves with each new class. It's helpful to remember that our students are doing the same thing, especially our first-year composition students, as they take on new roles as college students, some of them away from home for the first time or going through other critical transitions in their lives.

What Are the Some of the Processes of Learning to Teach Writing?

One of the processes of learning to teach writing that is demonstrated in these essays involves a sequence of describing experience, analyzing experience, and speculating about the significance of that experience for oneself and for others. This reflective process is critically important to developing an initial understanding of how one can play the role of teacher. And it is an essential element of developing a reflective practice of teaching for the long term. Finding or creating communities and opportunities for this reflective practice must be a priority for new teachers and those who work with them.

Where, When, and from Whom Do Writing Teachers Best Learn to Teach?

As the stories in these essays demonstrate, we learn to teach writing from experience. But experience alone is not enough. For experience to teach us, we need opportunities to think and talk about it with colleagues who will listen, who understand our teaching contexts, who care about us. We need a mix of colleagues who are more and less experienced than we are to provide us with perspective. And we need a variety of colleagues who can model for us diverse ways of approaching our work with and relationships to students.

All the authors in this section have used narrative strategies effectively to make their points. There's a danger that the predominance of happy endings in these narratives will suggest that learning to teach writing is a process that has a recognizable endpoint. My own experience, including the experience of reading these essays, has taught me, however, not only that I am still learning to teach writing but also that there is still a lot for me to learn.

RESPONSE

Rereading Experience

BROCK DETHIER

A good story yields new truths each time it is read, as each reader brings different needs, different associations to the reading. We learn not just from the conclusions, not just what the writer has learned, but also from the experiences themselves, from the details that lead to the conclusions and support the arguments.

This section is full of good stories. The writers know their business, as writers and as teachers. They've used their writing to study their experiences, and they present their ideas with such clarity and honesty, such a wealth of personal details, such real and immediate voices that the stories don't need interpretation, summary, or exegesis. So when you look back over the essays in this section, I invite you not just to glean from beginnings and ends, as an efficient reader does, but also to immerse yourself in the experiences, keep track of your own reactions and associations, identify the situations you would find problematic and the strengths you would bring to solving them.

To demonstrate that process, I will use this response not to recapitulate each essay but to look at these seven stories with different eyes—those of a composition veteran with old straight white-guy demographics and almost thirty years of watching and participating in the fascinating dramas of teaching writing. I want to share with you some of the secondary and perhaps unintentional lessons that each story brings me.

I'm fascinated by the scene in Carlyn Maddox's essay in which the "I-HATE-WRITING" student begins to come around. For me, it underlines the mystery of our business. Does he respond because of the personal attention of the conference? Because Maddox has made an effort to value and connect with his interests? Because she has reduced his quota of journal writing, something he may view as touchy-feely or feminine? Because he has found a way to write about his interests? Because he views relationships with teachers as a power struggle and needs to win? Because for the first time he can see the practical value in what he's writing?

I have no quarrel with Maddox's reading of the scene, but I imagine she would agree that we seldom know what combination of factors motivates a student.

That mystery can be frustrating—there are no cure-alls in this business—but it also means that there's always something else to try.

Amy Hodge's essay left me thinking most broadly about what we do and why. A thread that runs through each of the difficult, painful stories in that essay is our tendency to rethink, rehash, relive so many moments in our teaching lives, groping for what we could have done differently. Our readiness to take the blame makes me wince, but of course the only behaviors we can change with certainty are our own. Such obsessing robs us of sleep, but it keeps our jobs from being dull.

Juli Hong's story about her student Sharice also speaks to me, though I DO have a penis and a mustache. Whether our worries are about being too young or too old, too attractive or too square, or maybe about the car in the body shop or the parent in the hospital, they're likely to lead us into our biggest mistakes. Like parents, we have to learn how to avoid taking our frustrations out on our "kids." Luckily, most of the time the little burst of adrenaline that we get when we walk through the classroom door helps us forget the lost wallet, the head cold, last semester's nasty student evaluation. One of the miracles of teaching is that it constantly starts over, fresh—every year, every semester, each day.

My first reaction to Kristi Steinmetz's story is "smart"—smart to identify her own needs and figure out how to meet them (with the right kind of underwear), smart to get a second opinion on her problem student, smart to confront him directly, smart to use his strengths and her own to create a happy outcome rather than throw him out of class, which would have discouraged a gifted writer and produced a duller class.

My second reaction is "lucky"—lucky (or blessed) to have a quick sense of humor, to have a reliable supervisor, and especially to have had her class clown turn out to be talented rather than psychotic. With luck, all your class clowns will turn out that way; certainly the majority of mine have. But then there was Howie. He was one of a gang of four men in a freshman English class who acted as a clown unit, cheered on by a corresponding group of women across the classroom. Taken individually, each of them would have been fine. Except Howie. He scared me. He was a big wrestler, and the only time I made him happy was when I asked him to detail the tricks he'd learned for punishing his opponent in ways the ref couldn't see. I tried everything I could to connect and rein in Howie and his henchmen, including writing a play about the class, "Attitude Problems," which the class read aloud. But the course was a failure, I never felt I dealt adequately with Howie, and the next semester he was expelled for beating up another student so badly he had to be hospitalized.

With twenty more years under my belt, I'm still not sure how I would deal with Howie today. But I tell that story to alert new teachers to the other face they might discover behind the joker's mask. And to try to relieve the guilt that we inevitably feel when we can't turn the frog into a prince the way Steinmetz did, when we have to, in fact, focus on limiting the damage that one student can do to a whole class. We tend to trade success stories more often than failures, but most of us fail to transform at least one problem student per semester, and we need to accept that some things are beyond our control.

I am not part of the target audience for Jay Szczepanski's essay, but while I won't claim to know what it feels like to be a gay teacher in a straight classroom,

I am familiar—and I bet most readers are—with the inner struggle over how much of our real selves to let students see. Someone with left-wing, agnostic politics is almost as strange and threatening to my Utah students as a gay teacher, and while I want my students to get used to the possibility that "liberal" is not always a dirty word, I worry about the whines on my evaluations saying that I talk too much about politics or am biased against Christian students. So I need Szczepanski's words of encouragement even though I share many demographic factors with George W. Bush.

Rita Reese and Brandy Wilson's stories teach me lessons of sameness, although their conclusions highlight the difficult decisions caused by difference. Though not gay myself, I share their sense of inadequacy at not knowing how to deal with the ostensibly sensitive, empathic student who says, "That's so gay," days after the lesbian sitting next to her has come out in class. Or with the fundamentalist pre-service teachers who say they won't tolerate racism or sexism in their classrooms but who won't grant sexual orientation the same respect because they "know" that homosexuality is a sin. Our greatest resource in dealing with such frustrations is obvious but not explicit in "We Teach Alone"—the "we," the importance of finding a kindred soul to tear our hair with. For me, such souls have been older and younger, male and female, straight and gay; we're united not just by such things as sexual orientation but also by our experiences and our reactions to those experiences. No matter how individualistic we are as writers, no matter how isolated we like to be socially, as teachers we have to find ways to share and connect.

My reaction to Edward Tarkington's essay on sex and the TA was colored by my wrong guess about the speaker of the opening lines—I figured this was TA talk, and it easily could have been when I was a TA. Despite Tarkington's story about his friend Sally's relationship with one of her professors, overall his essay leaves me thinking about how far college teachers in general have come in the past thirty years; somehow, as we were casting off the *loco parentis* roles we also managed to stop being such loco predators.

It can be painful to rexamine difficult teaching experiences and engage in second-guessing, but I think a sure sign that you're in the right profession is that you find such cogitations fascinating. Driving home from work, you're thinking of yet another strategy that might bring the problem student around. Trying to forget about one day's disaster, you're simultaneously planning tomorrow's class. We can never with certainty get it RIGHT, and that means it never gets old.

RESPONSE

I'm Looking at You—Now What?

ANDREW COHEN

We don't have a bell here, but the students know when class is over. They stare at their watches, waiting for the last seconds to wind down, and then they look up at me with the can-we-go-now face, and I nod and they're off.

The hallways fill with college freshmen, some walking zombies trying to get back to bed, some nursing hangovers, others spilling food, and the rest on their cell phones catching up from the fifty minutes they lost while in class.

The mass of student bodies is overwhelming when class lets out, like Penn Station during rush hour, or the Enormodome just after a football game—but this crowd is far more heterogeneous, so it's easy to spot the people that don't fit in: my friends and fellow teachers. There's one making his way through the mob, being pushed to its periphery and feeling his way along the wall. And there's another, but she's been cornered into a nook and will have to wait until a spot opens up in the fast-moving rush of freshmen.

Just minutes before, we were in control of our worlds, each of us teaching in our own special way. But it wasn't always like that. We weren't always in control. We had these things, let's call them essays, that we needed to complete before assuming control of our classrooms.

These essays here, in *Part II: Inside Out*, let you into our classrooms and into our lives. My students know my door is always open, but I've never had to leave it open for fear one of them might come on to me. The issue of coming out isn't directly applicable to my situation. And with five o'clock shadow coming regularly by noon, I've never had to deal with looking too young to teach. But all these issues are universal, because gaining confidence (and teaching effectively) is tied into who we are; I can relate to each of the preceding essays as if I were four-eleven or gay or both. For me to find myself in the classroom, I had to drop my guard and embrace what I thought I had to hide: my goofy side. This is why the essay by Kristi Marie Steinmetz, "'What Are You Looking At?'—Teacher as

Stand-Up Comedian," especially speaks to me, and helps me define my teaching philosophy.

If there's a defining moment in my philosophy, it dates back to my first day on the job. I was all ready for my first day of teaching. I had spent the summer in a "boot camp" training program. I had taught classes in my summer internship. And I had devised the perfect syllabus for a first-year writing class. I had integrated tried-and-true exercises into my lesson plan. I had invented assignments that would be exciting, yet personal and instructive. I had every day of the semester planned. I had every minute of each class planned. And I had a new watch, purchased solely as a teacher's timepiece. I was all ready for my first day of teaching . . . but the building wasn't.

The Williams Building was closed for reconstruction throughout the summer. The major components—the air conditioning, furniture, computers—were all ready for the first day of the semester, but there were workmen on every floor performing some sort of reattachment or realignment, and their hammering echoed through the halls.

My class was at 8 a.m., so it was my students' first college class as well. And they filed into the room and sat silent, too excited to be tired and too nervous to be comfortable. Distant hammering and drilling were the only other sounds as I called attendance. I was nervous, too. The room was cold, but I was sweating. My voice stammered with each name and my eyes continually sought my timepiece. And then it happened.

The whining of the drill grew louder and a large shiny spinning drill-bit punctured the wall just beneath an outlet. We all watched as a metal conduit—a silver pole thicker than a garden hose—grew from the wall and inched its way toward the middle of our classroom. I was silent. I had not been trained for this. And my students looked to me for an explanation.

I didn't know what to say, but before I could speak, a loud trumpeting issued forth from the now eight-foot-long conduit, heralding childishness from a worker's lips on the other end, the end behind the wall. And everyone laughed, including me. The harder the workman tried to make it sound like a trumpet, the louder we laughed, until finally I took hold of the conduit and pulled the entire thing into the room and dropped it, letting the pole clank on the floor. My students laughed and clapped. They applauded me again when the worker showed up at our door and sheepishly asked for his conduit back.

A summer's worth of planning could never set up an icebreaker like that. I bonded with my students the first day of class, and I credit that incident for providing our semester with an energetic impetus for intellectual and creative growth. Laughter came easy after that first class, and the enthusiasm continued.

I learned on day one that there's more to teaching than a well-planned syllabus and that laughter is an all-powerful tool when used in concert with creative assignments. But what if your classroom is not under attack by mischievous workmen? What if it's one of your own doing the attacking?

When I was in second grade, I was awarded the title and responsibility of "eraser monitor." Every day at one, I'd leave class with a bag of dusty erasers, make my way across the building to the custodian's office, pick up the key to the boiler room, and then spend the better half of the afternoon running erasers through a noisy contraption designed to suck the chalk out. At the time, I felt on top of the world—I stood out; I was the responsible seven-year-old. Last year, when I began to teach, I saw my first job (eraser monitor) in a different light: I had been sent away so that the teacher could teach. I was the disruptive class clown.

Ms. Steinmetz tried to send her "Jeremy" away, attempting to make her first class the perfect class. Ironically, Jeremy turned out to be the ingredient necessary for the class to develop its spirit, and he turned out to be a model student.

In judo, you use your opponent's momentum to your advantage. Ms. Steinmetz pulled a judo maneuver on Jeremy. In figuring out how to handle Jeremy, Ms. Steinmetz created a vibrant class atmosphere, one that creates enthusiasm through humor. This is the power of working *with* your class clowns. Our class clowns are here to help us teach.

So what if you're teaching and you have no conduits or Jeremys? Ms. Steinmetz has her body humor. We all have something. Kicking over the garbage pail is always a hit. I rely on my artistic ability—I have none. My drawings are horrible. So when I use the dry-erase board, I make my drawings as awful as possible, which isn't hard, and my students laugh.

I still plan my syllabi down to the minute. I find that my organization helps my students remain focused. Yet, I rely on humor to keep my students enthusiastic. And if there are any comedians in the class to help me out, I'm thankful.

RESPONSE

Adeeeeeeeeena

DAVID WALLACE

"Adeeeeeeeeena." Adina smiled every time Moesha drew her name out. It was a sign of affection, and I envied the power that Moesha had to make Adina smile and feel good about herself. Adina's demeanor and body language in my composition course suggested that she did not often feel good about herself, at least not in school settings. She was a shy, heavy, black girl from Des Moines attending Iowa State University the summer after she graduated from high school , and she was on temporary admissions status because of low grades. She was also part of a summer bridge program for students who self-identified as racial minorities. The program gave students a head start on college by getting a required English and-required math course out of the way and by creating a social group that would help them manage the masses of white folks when the regular semester began. In just six weeks, I saw Adina blossom in this setting, largely because more popular students like Moesha made it a point to draw her out. Imagine my surprise and pleasure when Adina wrote in her last journal entry that she believed herself to be a better writer at the end of the course because I'd told her that she had a flair for dialogue. She had many other problems in her writing, but for the first time she had a sense that she could accomplish something with writing because I convinced her that she could do something well.

I remembered Adina as I read Carlyn C. Maddox's description of how Mr. B encouraged her and as she counsels us to remember: "We may be the first teacher ever to tell a student that we think he or she is a good writer—or a great writer." Indeed, I remembered a number of other basic lessons about teaching writing that have become automatic in the many years that have passed since I first set foot in a writing classroom as a teaching assistant.

Get Them to Write about Things
They Care About

Maddox's description of the conference in which she persuaded her "I-HATE-WRITING" student to be excited about writing his Marching Chiefs paper reminded me of the look of amazement on the face of one of my students when I suggested to her that she should draw on her extensive 4H experience and write a paper about why a teenage girl would choose to spend her weekends driving her prize Hereford around to competitions and spending more time brushing its hair than her own. I was also reminded of Richard Whately, who gave similar counsel over 150 years ago; he wrote that the subjects for students' compositions should "be *interesting* to the student, and on which he has (or may, with pleasure, and without much toil, acquire) sufficient information" or we risk the sort of writing that induces a student to "string together vague general expressions, conveying no distinct ideas of his own mind, and second-hand sentiments which he does not feel" (1013).

Don't Take Yourself Too Seriously

Amy Hodges's and Edward Tarkington's essays reminded me that getting too hung up on whether or not students like or respect your authority is a losing game. As Tarkington points out, graduate students (and just about all English teachers) are notoriously needy, but looking for validation from your students is the wrong game to play. Better to be surprised and pleased to get any recognition at all. Oddly, coming out in my life and my teaching has made me care less about what my students think of me, as has becoming more aware of race, class, and gender issues. I have a new definition of cool that refuses to pay homage to the usual jock/homecoming queen/big-chested/pretty-faced, Abercombie-and-Fitch-wearing hierarchy. Somehow I've manage to convince myself that my insight into how culture works makes me far cooler than most of my students will ever be.

Be Firm but Generous

The story Kristi Marie Steinmetz tells about Jeremy's inappropriate comments toward her reminded me that some students are always pushing on boundaries. Steinmetz was right to be firm; we should expect our students to act like adults and accept the consequences of their actions. In Jeremy's case, Steinmetz was also right to be generous, to offer a second chance. I've found this to be a good policy as well, on the few occasions when I've had to call students on the carpet for inappropriate actions or comments. However, I want to say very clearly to women who read this book that you are NOT required to be generous when students make sexist comments that are directed at you or make inappropriate sexual advances. If your composition program, department, or university does not have a policy regarding such incidents, insist that they get one.

Sexuality Is Never Absent in the Classroom

Students look at our nipples and lips and hair and legs. They make assumptions about our sexual identity from the clothes we wear, how we walk, and what we say (or don't say). Some of them find us attractive. We find some of them attractive.

This is normal. However, as teachers, we bear a heavier responsibility in managing the tensions that can arise from such attractions. Because we are in a relationship of institutional power with our students, we cannot risk having an intimate relationship with a student while we are in a teacher-student relationship. However, it is also important to realize that institutional relationships are not the only relationships of power that exist between students and teachers. Even in situations where a student is clearly putting you in an uncomfortable position, your institution may hold you responsible for mismanaging the situation.

Having a Mustache and a Penis Matters

Juli Hong reminds me of the gratuitous authority most of my students afford me the moment I walk into class as a tall, thin, white man. I can afford to dress sloppily sometimes; indeed, I often have to burn off some of my authority just to get my students to feel comfortable challenging me. This is not the case for others; a small, young-appearing woman will have to work out authority issues in different ways than I do.

Being Out in the Classroom Is Never Easy

Rita Mae Reese and Brandy T. Wilson raise the interesting issue that many of us gay and lesbian teachers face: should we be out in our classes or not? Students often whisper behind our backs and speculate to each other anyway, but making your alternative sexual identity explicit to the class is never a neutral choice. For the last four or five years, I've come out to each class that I've taught usually by sharing something I've written. I've been called brave by students, I've been prayed for by others, and I've been despised by a few. Lesbian, gay, bisexual, or transgendered teachers need to make this decision for themselves. However, I will offer three pieces of advice. (1) Don't be out only as LGBT; share some other aspect of your life as well. (2) Be prepared for a variety of responses to your decision to be out, including your own. I'm always caught a little off guard that the act of being out in the class for the first time leaves me a little shaky. (3) Don't feel responsible for students' negative reactions to your decision to be out. Students who participate in homophobia and heterosexism are part of the problem. I'm over the pseudoguilt of feeling that my being out in the classroom means some of my students won't feel free to blurt out homophobic or heterosexist things. I'm cool with that. I'm also "out" as someone sensitive to gender and race issues, and I consider it an important part of my job to give my students pause to think about how they are representing others in their speech and writing.

Teaching Is a Journey

Jay Szcepanski reminded me that the surest way to become a bad teacher is to assume that you've arrived, that you've got it all together. A good teacher often leaves class dissatisfied, mulling over why things did not work the way they were supposed to, plotting how to change things the next time the class meets. An important corollary to this point is that learning is also a journey: important things can happen in three hours a week for nine or fifteen weeks, but students are on learning journeys of their own. Freeing yourself from the need to be a perfect teacher will likely make you a much better teacher.

Work Cited

Whately, Richard. "From *Elements of Rhetoric.*" *The Rhetorical Tradition: Readings from Classical times to the Present.* Ed. Patrica Bizzell and Bruce Herzberg. 2nd ed. Boston: Bedford/St. Martins, 2001. 1003–1030.

On Teaching and Its Contentments, or Teaching as Process, After All

KATHLEEN BLAKE YANCEY

I had forgotten.

It was thirty-one years ago—and where did those teaching years go?—that I first taught. Prompted, I find that remembering isn't difficult. I had just graduated from college; I wasn't even twenty-two. I was teaching summer school in order to gain a high school teaching license. I was assigned two classes: one a group of students who were trying to accelerate their high school career by taking a junior class in American literature, a second class that had failed ninth-grade English and needed to complete it successfully if a high school diploma was to be had.

In that second class, I experienced nearly every dilemma faced by new teachers as well as a few that were unique to that experience. I was young, just out of college, and for the last three years I'd worn jeans on a daily basis, so upgrading to professional attire felt not only odd but also, in its own way, fraudulent. I had little professional support: the university coordinator was unable to meet with me at all and never observed my teaching; the one cooperating teacher seemed to think that I should teach *his* curriculum, the other that I was completely on my own, in a sort of sink-or-swim version of professional initiation. I was heterosexual but disinclined to share sexual orientation, although I think everyone knew I was single, and quite frankly, I was so overwhelmed by the experience that I didn't have a chance to think about being anything other than single. Most of the students came to class stoned, which, admittedly, precludes their acting out but, on the other hand, precludes their acting much at all. One of the students wrote in his journal—not once but consistently—about torturing animals and the pleasures thereof; when I talked to the school-system psychologist about my concerns that animals would give way to humans, he said the only service provided by the school district was testing. And the larger rhetorical situation of the class? On the first day, my cooperating teacher asked me what curriculum we would use, since the students had failed the school-sponsored ("normal") curriculum. And while I took his point, I didn't really want to take his point at that time, given that it would mean that I'd need to invent a ninth-grade curriculum over the weekend.

Which, by the way, I did—and not without making some seriously bad curricular choices. Or: That summer, I Think we all learned a great deal.

* *

Which is what still happens, after all.

I moved to teaching college, as a TA, at the end of that summer of student teaching. The first quarter, I was golden: the students were good, classes went well, and I felt that I was born to teach. The next term, one of my classes was dominated by a young woman who, in her words, didn't like "young" teachers, especially when they were "female," and who challenged me at every turn, muttering under her breath, rolling her eyes, dropping papers and books on the floor, in those early weeks preparing to turn the course into a major contest between her and me. Alas, she was likely to win. I consulted with my mentor, Marjorie Kaiser, who moved immediately to re-place the student into a section meeting at the same time, taught by a middle-aged, professorial, bearded, hairy-chested man. I think she did well; without her, the class did superbly.

I needed that help.

* *

Fourteen years later, a good student—a tad different from the other students, but funny, smart, cooperative, interesting—came to class with red eyes, head drooping, clothes rumpled. Disengaged. I gave the class a task, and we walked into the hall. I tried to talk with him, but he wasn't processing what I was saying, and his replies to me were, well, gibberish. I recognized some of the words, but they weren't strung coherently. He wasn't stoned, I could see that, nor was he drunk. He was disoriented, increasingly frightened, decreasingly aware that I was even within earshot. Intuitively, I sensed that he was moving out of control, and I became afraid—that he couldn't hear me, that he needed help, that I wasn't the right person to help him. Touching his elbow, I walked him to my office, down the hall, talking calmly. I asked him to sit. I called the student health center.

That student needed my help—as it turned out, he was in the midst of a psychotic episode which would bring his parents back from France and institutionalize him for six months—and the help he needed that day was personal, not pedagogical.

Or: Perhaps sometimes the pedagogical is personal.

* *

Fast-forward ten years: I'm teaching a sophomore gen ed lit class. I had taught this class once before, and it had been the highlight of my term: interesting readings, good students, fun for me and them both—and in fact, I had decided to write a book based on the kind of class, that gen ed lit class: *Teaching Literature as Reflective Practice*. I was eager to teach the class again; it's an axiom that it takes us three iterations of a class to get it right, so I was eager to have that second iteration.

That class, as it turned out, wasn't the proverbial class from hell, but it surely was from purgatory. I'm still not sure why. It was a large class: thirty-seven students. They were crammed into a small space. It was at a time in the afternoon when most of the students would have preferred playing Frisbee or preparing for dinner or taking a nap or even, I began to think, eating dead worms. I tried to make changes to accommodate students' needs; I asked them to write and I wrote back; I let them know what they were doing well; I showed them how to do better. I made all the teacherly moves that, for me, typically work. This time, regardless of my experience and my enthusiasm and my efforts to engage the students, they didn't.

I'm not happy about that, and I'm less happy about not knowing why. Now, some twenty months later—when I have taught the class one more time, and this time, by all accounts, successfully—I *still* think about what I could have done better in that prior class, about what I would do differently. At the same time, I accept that teaching—like human beings themselves and like learning, too—is imperfect.

*   *

Which I think is the point of all these narratives, these by new teachers, this by me: Teaching is always a process. It's located in the relationships of teacher and students and materials and goals, in the world of English taking place in sites of reading and writing and, increasingly, the visual and multimedia. Done well, it is an art. But even composed very well, it is an imperfect art.

Which is why artful teaching remains a process that we—novices and experts alike—continue to learn.

RESPONSE

Teaching on Planet Earth: Inside the Classroom, Outside the Vacuum

AMANDA FLEMING

Sure, I am possibly the only instructor on campus who knows the first and last names of her students (as well as their sweethearts' names, their pet peeves, and the details surrounding their first tattoos). I have a better than great advantage when it comes to bonding with my students. However, after several years of teaching, I have only found two categories of students: the teachable and the unreachable. Some students come to class to learn and some don't. It doesn't matter how creatively or enthusiastically I present the material. It's no reflection on me as a human being. The thing is, I earned a degree to teach English, but a degree did not promise a successful classroom experience. For the teachable, I cannot rely on familiarity alone to fuel their interest; they must know me and know I teach writing because I'm passionate. I devise plans to hold the students' attention and to let them know I am human, just like they are, that a classroom does not exist in a vacuum.

Every semester I make a pledge to myself to get tougher, to achieve more in the classroom, to earn a medal for teaching. And each semester I revert to the same technique:

Week 1: I wear a black three-piece suit to assert authority. I hand out a grueling prospectus (always overplanning!). I initiate a timed writing. I remain professional, revealing nothing about myself, maintaining the boundary line between their personal life and mine.

Week 2: Because the rough drafts show signs of severe thesaurus usage, I let down my hair, wear khaki slacks, and explain they should write like they talk—for starters. I try to do stand-up comedy. I use my recent car accident as a means to explain organization. Maybe I don't confess I caused the three-car pile, up.

Week 3: I take up their first graded paper. I pull out some props when I grade: cheerleader pom-poms ("Go, Active Voice, Go!"), the psychiatrist's pad and pen ("How did this make you feel?"), and the grammarian's red ink ("Comma Splice City!"). I make pop-culture references when applicable—to show I'm hip to the current trends. But during lectures, I have to ask students to repeat themselves. I claim I need a hearing aid.

Week 4: I attribute the disorderly atmosphere in the class to my Jimmy Buffett-like style of teaching (outside on the lawn). I feel like a babysitter ("Get on task. Stop pulling up the grass."). I become the lost-and-found ("Did you find my umbrella/math folder/wallet after class?"). Back to the three-piece suit, students quit talking out of turn. I get more volunteers when I wear my reading glasses. If I doodle in my grade book from time to time, students wake up, eyes shiny. I sense resentment. They pack up their book bags way before it's time to leave.

Week 5: I grade paper #2. I become schizophrenic: I want them to like me, so I could grade up; but they need to be challenged, so I might grade down. I've heard that influential teachers emphasize their students' positives and minimize their negatives, but didn't one student actually admit to me that he wrote his essay the night before it was due? I'll bet I spent more time grading his paper than he did writing it. Well, he did come from a long line of English teachers who only graded for grammar and never paid attention to content; no wonder he doesn't like to write. But I distinctly remember him whispering during the fourth week of class, "She needs to get laid."

Week 6: While lecturing on passive voice, I use the "to be" verb unintentionally seventy-five times. I confess I caused that three-car pileup. During conferences, I realize a student has a crush on me. The eighteen-year-old reminds me of my college boyfriend. He has blue eyes that just stare, and he doesn't really have a question. He nods, hangs on every word.

Week 7: I go back to starting class on time, not accepting late excuses. I share examples from student papers that impressed me. I smile and say goodbye to everyone by name. I will remember to ask them next week, "How did your trip/date/history paper turn out?" Despite my act to appear older, one student calls me by my first name.

Week 8: I lighten up. Bring a cup of coffee to class and we sit round-table style. Maybe I start class a few minutes late. Suddenly, they all think I am a computer tech ("My printer won't print."), a weather forecaster ("Is it going to rain today?"), their counselor ("I can't focus. My boyfriend broke up with me."), a cleric ("Do you think I'll get an A in here?"), a nurse ("I have the flu/sinus infection/diarrhea/migraine/a cut that's bleeding."), a tour guide ("Where can I find the foreign-language department?"), and their personal financial planner ("Do I need to buy that book you were talking about? I'm broke."). A student who has personal problems (was raped/is suicidal/is getting divorced) finds my home number. They trust me for some reason. Frustrated students from semesters past who are disgruntled by their current writing instructor contact me for sympathy and help. When did I cross that line between teaching English and teaching life skills? And will I identify the line if I see it again?

I find students looming at my office door who persuade me to accept their late papers and homework assignments. Perhaps I know this fear of failure too well. These students will not even make eye contact with me in an elevator afterward. They feel ashamed. Should I?

I think we remember our favorite writing teachers' names. But great writing teachers—I think we remember their sweethearts' names, their pet peeves, and the circumstances surrounding their first tattoos. They support our crazy ideas. They give us room to take risks. They are honest with us. They may forgive us for turning in a paper late, but we feel awful about it. We work hard for them, knowing they pay attention. They meet us at every rung of the ladder: "Private, strengthen those verbs! Cut out the deadwood! Write! Write! Write! Morning, noon, and night!"

And sometimes, my students do the same thing for me—providing me with encouragement when I want to quit, reminding me why I started teaching in the first place. This past semester I read over my evaluations expecting poor results. A good friend's suicide threw me for a loop, and I took well over a month to return their papers. I apologized profusely, but I still expected criticism. Instead, what I read from one student validated my unchangeable condition: "Don't worry about getting our papers back on time. It shows you are human, like us."

PART III
BEYOND THE CLASSROOM

12

Finding the Twenty-fifth Hour

MAGGIE GERRITY

When I was an undergraduate, friends envied my time-management skills. On the day a professor assigned a paper, I would head off to the library to start tracking down potential sources. On the night before a story was due for my fiction workshop, my roommates would be brewing coffee at midnight and panicking to the point of tears, but I'd be asleep, a copy of my story already tucked inside my backpack. I enjoyed my studies, and even with an active social life, I immersed myself in my work. Graduate school would be nothing new to me, I figured, except that as a graduate teaching assistant I'd get to share my love of writing with students not unlike the ones I'd tutored for four years.

Wrong. Some days it feels as if an angry pack of the flying monkeys from *The Wizard of Oz* has swooped into my classroom, my office, and my apartment and upended everything. Students want feedback to their drafts. Teachers want thesis essays, annotated bibliographies, and revisions to critical essays. Sometimes, friends actually want me to leave my apartment to go somewhere other than campus. No matter how much I try to plan, there's always a lecture or a reading to attend, or another story to read and line-edit for a workshop. During my most stressful times, I've contemplated running away to join the circus, because I'm sure I could juggle better than any other clown.

One important thing to remember about graduate school is that we're here primarily to pursue our degrees. While teaching is often rewarding, it's time-consuming, too; we need to leave enough hours to focus on our own development as scholars and writers. Every semester, I come up with a few more time-saving tricks that help me free up extra hours to write. I'll admit that sometimes I still procrastinate—yes, I've finished more than one paper at four o'clock the morning it was due—but when I follow these time-saving tips, I have plenty of time to devote both to my writing and to my students. It's as if there's a twenty-fifth hour in the day that only I know about. The strategies I've learned over the past few years give me extra hours to get to know my students better without sacrificing attention to my development as a fiction writer and essayist.

Good time-management skills allow you to enjoy graduate school. When you're not burned out, you can go into the classroom with a sense of humor and an enthusiasm you pass on to your students. Whether you're planning your semester, grading your students' work, or simply plugging through the day-to-day events leading to your degree, these tips should help you to find extra hours in the day.

Front-Load Your Class

I think the best thing you can do while planning your class is to front-load. Typically, both you and your students will have less to do at the beginning of the semester. By packing coursework more tightly into the first six or eight weeks, you free up space later in the semester for less stressful work, like group projects or creative writing assignments that students will enjoy. These projects are also a lot easier for you to grade, which is a blessing once you reach the thirteenth or fourteenth week of the semester.

Reward Students

When planning my syllabus, I always try to find ways to recognize the hard work my students are doing. For instance, I've stopped canceling a week of classes for my first round of student conferences. Students gripe about having to come to class when their friends get days off, but when crunch time comes, I can give them a day to catch up on revisions while I can get my own work done. I usually give the other day off at the beginning of Thanksgiving or spring break, because students frequently skip on these days anyway. This tip might be better to hold onto until you've been teaching for a few semesters: most program administrators will encourage TAs to cancel classes during conference weeks, since teaching and having conferences at the same time can be a little strenuous.

I also reward students by lessening the workload to emphasize quality rather than quantity. When I teach research writing, the major research essay or project is the centerpiece for the course. I always ask for a twelve-page essay, though I never really want more than eight to ten. When students have immersed themselves in their work and are starting to panic about the due date, I tell them I'll agree to lower the page count if they work their hardest.

Coordinate Class Plans and Stagger Due Dates

Last fall, I found myself having to teach two different courses. I quickly learned, though, that this doesn't automatically mean double the preparation time. You can sometimes plan for two classes at once. For instance, I showed my classes the movie *Life as a House* last fall. My composition and rhetoric students compared and contrasted their own views of home with those of the movie's main characters; my students in research writing completed a film analysis. Even when you can't have both classes doing the same work at the same time, drawing from similar resources can save you time.

It's also good to stagger due dates when you're teaching different courses. Give yourself a week or two between assignments. You can use that time to get ahead (or catch up) in your own classes, while it also helps you not to confuse assignment requirements for different courses. Last fall, my composition and rhetoric students completed two smaller portfolios and a group project, while my research writing students did one comprehensive portfolio for the midterm and a final research project. Both groups did the same amount of writing, but it was nice not having to lug home forty-five portfolios at once.

In my first semester teaching, it took me half an hour to respond to and evaluate a single essay. An *essay*, not a portfolio. I wanted to offer as much help as I could. I wanted to be strict but not too harsh. I wanted to be Super Teacher. In the semesters since, I've found three ways to cut back on responding and evaluation time while still giving my students the same amount of feedback.

Don't Get Carried Away

The most important thing you need to remember the day you bring that stack of essays home is that you need to be realistic when planning your responding schedule. Ideally, you'd love to go through that stack during a Saturday afternoon, but don't put yourself in the position where you have to evaluate all your students' essays at once. Not only are marathon responding sessions stressful for you, they also aren't good for the students at the bottom of the pile; after reading fifteen or twenty other essays, you just don't care about what you're reading anymore. It's essential that you pace yourself. A stack of portfolios typically takes me a week to ten days to evaluate. I never let myself read all the portfolios from the strongest writers first, or leave the portfolios from my weaker writers for last. By responding to only two or three portfolios in one sitting, I can approach each with the same open mind and good attitude.

Ask for Specifics and Keep Responses Simple

It's also helpful if you require specific process memos and comment very little on final drafts. In every paper cycle, I read students' essays at least twice—once focusing on content, and once examining structure and mechanics, as well as content revisions. I respond thoroughly to these early drafts, when students need the most feedback. By the time I get a paper packet or portfolio, I know the essays well. When I assign the process memo, I ask students to tell me what specific changes they made between drafts, and I focus my written comments largely on the quality of those changes and what they still need to work on in the class. Let's face it: while we want to believe our students care about the writing process, when it comes to final drafts, they care much more about their grades. Why spend time writing extensive comments when we've already given them similar comments earlier in the process?

Keep Students Informed

Near the end of the semester, students always inundate me with e-mails, office visits, and after-class questions about how they're doing in the class. That's why I think it's a good idea to keep ahead of students by routinely informing them of the number of days they were absent and late and offering them a projection of their final grade. The best ways to do this are in conferences and in their portfolios or paper packets. If your university uses an on-line computing system such as Blackboard, through which you can transmit grades and absences to students, learn how to use it.

Students are easier to deal with when they're informed all semester, not just at midterm and finals weeks. I offer students a grade range after every major assignment—*right now, it looks like you'll get a B or a B+ if you keep doing this level of work*—and I never tell students they're capable of getting a grade that isn't realistic. They're much less likely to go over the number of allowed absences if they routinely know how many classes they've missed. Some of my colleagues make students sign a contract when they've reached the limit of allowed absences; the contract reads something along the lines of *I know I have missed the allowed number of classes for the semester and that if I miss one more, it will be grounds for my failure of the course*. This doesn't stop students from failing, but it tends to stop them from arguing when you have to fail them.

Don't be fooled into thinking that time management is important only during the crunch times in the semester. If you slack off during slower weeks, your work will pile up before you can realize it. These day-to-day time-management strategies are the most important ones, because they help you to stay focused all semester.

Use Your Office Hours

Try to schedule office hours during off-peak times and keep them. Nothing is better than a quiet early-morning or late-afternoon office. While I love gossiping and commiserating with my officemates, when I do I have to use my evenings for work instead of relaxing. It's essential for you to connect with your fellow TAs— teaching, like writing, is best learned through doing and watching how others do— but give yourself a few hours a week to get work done, even if it means dragging yourself out of bed early or staying a little late.

Keep a Routine—All Semester

I've started thinking of graduate school as my full-time job; Monday through Friday (or Sunday through Thursday) I make myself get up at the same time, and I try to work an eight-hour day. While I hate getting up early, crawling out of bed at 6:30 five days a week helps me work when I'm most focused. On the days I teach, I'll go to school, but on my days off, I'll go to a coffee shop or a bookstore or to the library to escape the distractions of home. Doing this helps me save evenings for socializing, relaxing, and errands.

Listen To What Mom Always Said

When you're on the go, make sure to eat right and sleep enough. These are two of the most important things I've learned. When you're on the go as much as we are, fruits and veggies are much better fuel than a Big Mac. Gone from my diet are the college-student staples of ramen noodles and Hamburger Helper. I try to cook as much as I can, not only because it's more affordable, but also because it's healthier. Also try going to bed at the same time every night, no matter how busy you are. When you're tired, it takes you longer to do everything, and you also have less patience for teaching.

Be Honest with Your Students

I don't think there's anything wrong with telling students that you're a student, too. Mine have said they think a TA tends to be more accessible and easier to relate to than a tenured professor. They also understand that I'm busy, so they try to solve smaller problems on their own. We use e-mails, phone calls, and appointments for bigger difficulties, meaning I can give them the help they need while also teaching them some independence.

Stick To Your Rules

Whatever you do, don't be a pushover. Have a zero-tolerance policy when it comes to excuses and bad behavior. Why should you work harder keeping track of an irresponsible student than that student is working for you? My sense of humor comes out a lot when I'm teaching, and I prefer a laidback classroom atmosphere, but my students understand my limits. I don't tolerate plagiarism or any kind of offensive writing or comment. I will rarely allow a student to hand an assignment in late or miss more than the allowed number of classes. I realized I was being a bit too harsh when a bright but mischievous student came up to me and said, "I'm sorry I don't have my reading response done, but I spent the night in jail." Don't forget that there can be exceptions to every rule.

Don't Forget about Yourself

Time management is essential to getting your work done in graduate school, but it also gives you time to relax and recuperate. Don't forget that. Even at the most hectic times of the semester, try to take half an hour to do something for yourself. Listen to your favorite CD. Go for a walk. Have coffee with a friend. These little things help to refuel your spirit. Your mind can't be sharp if your spirit isn't in your work.

Most important, *keep a sense of humor*. Students can drive us crazy some-times, but they're almost always goodhearted and entertaining. Laugh with them in class, and at their silly typos or misplaced modifiers when you're responding to drafts. Never forget that we're lucky enough to do what we love every day. When we teach, we make an impact on others' lives. What more could we possibly want?

13

The Art of Academic Diplomacy: How to Finesse Departmental Politics as a Grad Student

DAN MELZER AND PAUL REIFENHEISER

Many discussions of graduate-student life focus on teaching and research, but there's one key area in a burgeoning academic career that's not often discussed but is just as important: departmental politics. To succeed in graduate school, you'll need to learn the art of diplomacy. In this guide to finessing departmental politics, we discuss topics that range from choosing a thesis or dissertation committee to acting diplomatically in your interactions with faculty and peers. The essay will be a conversation between the two of us, and although we don't always agree in our approaches to departmental politics, we do agree that politics plays a bigger role in your graduate career than most would like to admit.

We feel that we can offer you a unique view of these issues, since we've had a variety of experiences. Paul has a PhD in literature, and he's currently a Visiting Instructor. Dan has a PhD in composition and rhetoric, and he's currently finishing up an MA in creative writing. As the Assistant to the Director of First-Year Writing, Dan is both a student and an administrator. Paul, despite working in literature, involved himself in the first-year writing program through committee work, mentoring, and presentations. Since we've seen a lot as graduate students, we hope that we can offer you some valuable advice.

Making Your First Political Impression

> **PAUL:** Your first political move sets up all the rest: impress the hell out of one or more of your professors. Possibly for the first time in your academic career, you will need to do more than read all the

assigned works, pass all the tests, and write excellent papers. You'll
need to cultivate a relationship with a major professor. This person
will guide your work, write your most important letter of
recommendation, and probably affect the way you deal with your
own students. Your major professor is a powerful and important
figure. In the best circumstances, which I feel I had, you'll develop a
vibrant and healthy working relationship and a friendship that will
last beyond your dissertation defense.

That is getting ahead of things a bit though. First, you need to
show your major professor why you are worthy of his or her
investment. (Major professors have to do a lot of work.) Start by going
the extra mile and making yourself stand out from your peers. Prove
your intellect, creativity, work ethic, and tenacity. This effort will pay
political dividends. When in a political jam, seek help from your major
professor. If you fear you will cause problems with another faculty
member, discuss your actions with your key mentor. He or she will
know your department well and will care about your decisions. Let this
person help if he or she can. Bring important decisions to him or her,
but don't make him or her worry over minor details you can handle.
Your mentor is a helping hand, not a crutch for all your problems. Of
course, you'll create your own specific relationship; the circumstances
will differ, but you need to start thinking about it early in your career.

DAN: I agree with Paul that finding a mentor is important. Once I
determined the professors with whom I got along and worked well, I
put extra effort into their classes, tried to visit them during office
hours, and got to know them on a more personal level. But I also
want to point out that your first move, as far as department politics
goes, should also involve getting to know the culture of your
department. Which professors get along, and which don't? Does the
department value service, and what opportunities are there for
service (such as serving on committees or editing departmental
publications)? Which professors are skilled at mentoring graduate
students, and which are more interested in their own research than
in mentoring? Who are the staff members, and what role do they
play in assisting graduate students? What outlets are available for
graduate students to make changes in the political climate? In a
sense, then, your first political move should be not to make a move.
Take time to know the culture of the department before you get
involved with departmental politics.

Dealing with Tensions among Literature, Creative Writing, and Composition and Rhetoric Faculty

DAN: Our department is divided into three tracks: literature, creative
writing, and composition and rhetoric. When I say divided, I mean

that literally: often there are open conflicts among the faculty of the different tracks, and this has a ripple effect for the graduate students as well. One of our creative writing faculty read aloud a poem that criticizes dense literary theory at the department welcoming meeting, where writers of literary theory were present. Some members of the literature faculty have, during faculty meetings, questioned why we even have a composition and rhetoric track, and the composition and rhetoric faculty have the least political power within the department, despite the fact that first-year writing courses bring in more money for the department than literature courses. This power inequality is clear in the requirements for graduate degrees. Although everyone pursuing a PhD in composition and rhetoric is required to take five literature courses, literature track students are not required to take any courses in composition and rhetoric.

Since I pursued a composition and rhetoric degree with a minor in American literature, and then later decided to get an MA in creative writing, I've witnessed some of these conflicts among the three tracks firsthand. Creative writing faculty have asked my why I would bother to pursue a PhD in composition and rhetoric when I was interested in writing creatively, and some creative writing graduate students looked at me skeptically when I began taking fiction workshops. In the first fiction workshop I took, the students in the creative writing program would go out after class to drink at a local bar. Those of us in the class who were not in the creative writing track—including "special students" who had full-time jobs and were taking the class for pleasure and not for a degree—weren't directly invited to these get-togethers. No one officially asked us if we wanted to come, although everyone knew that the "official" creative writers were getting together. After I turned in my first story, which was well received by the workshop, some of the creative writers told me they were surprised that someone in the composition and rhetoric track could write so well, and that night I was invited to the bar with the "real" writers.

I've also had "track tension" with my peers in literature. One of my former officemates, an older gentleman who was returning to school to pursue a PhD in literature, asked me when I first met him if I was in literature or creative writing. When I told him neither, I was in composition and rhetoric, he gave me a skeptical look. "Is that even a real degree?" he said. "What would you write about?" The irony of the situation is that more first-year writing courses are taught by people with literature and creative writing degrees than degrees in composition and rhetoric.

It's important to note that graduate students aren't powerless in the face of these kinds of tensions. Graduate students need to learn how to play the political game, but they also can be catalysts for changes in that game. For example, there are a number of graduate students in the composition track who, like me, take creative workshops, and a number of creative writers who minor in composition. Not only are these graduate students helping to break down divisions between tracks, but they're also models for change within the structure of the department. Although it hasn't come to fruition yet, our department is considering a composition and rhetoric track that has a minor in creative writing built in.

PAUL: I probably wouldn't describe the divisions in our department in the apocalyptic terms Dan likes to use. However, the divisions do exist. I should note that sometimes they are a lot of fun for grad students. With friends, we like to play up the differences. For example, I like to call Dan a "Comp/Rhet Softy" because his solution to every problem involves freewriting about your feelings. Dan, not too subtly, reminds me that jobs are a lot easier to come by in comp/rhet. I, of course, remind him that those jobs are available because you have to teach comp/rhet! Joking with peers helps blow off steam, but it can cause problems if it goes too far. I think the best rule is, Do not take the divisions too seriously, and use them to your advantage. Here, the political advice is simple: Recognize the difference between joking around with friends and interacting with faculty; do not use track divisions as an excuse to show disrespect to faculty or their fields of study; do not use track division as a reason to ignore other disciplines within your department. Ignoring the many opportunities of our composition and rhetoric program would have severely diminished my graduate-student experience.

Advice about Choosing a Thesis or Dissertation Committee

PAUL: When you work with committee members, consider one important rule: Take stands only where they matter the most. Sometimes you have to learn to back off, even when you are correct. For example, I scheduled a few meetings with one of my outside professors during the months leading up to my defense. On more than one occasion, he simply forgot the meetings (even when he had set up the time and date that worked best for him). While I had every right to be angry, confronting this professor on this issue could have only done harm to my work and my defense. There is no need to make a faculty member look bad in front of other faculty members. So I acted as though it were my fault in some way, showed a modicum of deference, and rescheduled the appointments. I saved confrontations for ideas I set forth in my dissertation. I believe my major professor enjoyed working with me partly because, while I was receptive to criticism, I took stands on important issues rather than petty inconveniences. In short, fight for your ideas and your goals, not for petty things that may annoy you and your professors. If you really want to cause change in your department, start by knowing the difference between important causes worthy of defense and petty issues that affect only your own needs. If you are known as the grad student who whines about every inconvenience, then some will not take you seriously if you try to transform your department.

DAN: It's common sense for graduate students to choose thesis and dissertation committee members on the basis of shared personal interests and established working relationships. But what many graduate students fail to consider is whether the committee members they've chosen get along with one another. It's possible that the Marxist theorist whom you've asked to lead your committee is locked in a political power struggle with the lingering formalist in your department, whom you'd also like to have; or the two poets you'd most like on your committee loathe each other and each other's work. Ideally, members of a thesis or dissertation committee would put aside their differences for your sake and for the sake of collegiality, and it's true that most thesis and dissertation committees get along just fine. But I've heard enough horror stories of warring committee members leaving the student behind like a corpse on the battlefield that I would suggest paying careful attention to interdepartmental politics as you choose a committee. Although I had an idea of whom I wanted to ask to serve on my committee before I formed it, I asked my dissertation advisor whom he would like to work with, and I took this into consideration. I also let my advisor know whom I was thinking of asking to be on my committee, just to gauge his reaction and to see if there was anyone he'd prefer not to work with. I was lucky enough to have a committee whose members got along well with one another, but I could easily have been caught between two disputing factions if I'd been unaware of departmental politics.

The Politics of Serving on Departmental Committees

DAN: If you get a chance, as a graduate student, serve on a departmental committee. Service on a committee will look good to future academic employers, it will give you experience with how departments work, and it will give you insight into the politics of your own department. I'm on the job market this year, and I think my experience serving on committees will really help. I've served on textbook selection committees, committees that decided first-year writing policies and created mission statements, and committees that interviewed graduate students for administrative positions. With all of this committee work on my vita, I hope schools to which I'm applying for jobs will see that I'm used to working in groups and being a "team player." Of course, serving on committees can be more than just a line on your vita. It's also a way to have a real effect on the goals and values of your department, since it can involve anything from selecting textbooks to forming policies. In my experiences serving on committees as a graduate student, I've helped select three textbooks for composition courses, participated in the creation of departmental syllabi, and assisted in creating a mission statement for the first-year writing program.

Whether you see it as a boon or a burden, serving on committees will take up a large part of your time when you're a faculty member, so volunteering for committee work while you're a graduate student will give you practice in the art of collaboration. My own experience serving on departmental committees has been positive, and I've found that more often than not committees reach compromise and consensus without squabbling.

PAUL: Of course, committees don't always agree. I served for a while as a graduate-student representative to departmental committees. I watched a committee discussing future hiring needs: a discussion clearly about the future of the department. Members had some major disagreements, but they were civil about the differences. It was an important experience because it showed how the game is played in the major leagues. Of course, faculty have more at stake with their political decisions. The tenure track has handled assistant professors who didn't get tenure despite excellent teaching and publication records. In short, these candidates didn't finesse departmental politics or fell victim to those who used their political clout in aggressive ways. Though the stakes aren't always as high, you can begin to learn how to manage the departmental political arena as a graduate student. Pay attention to faculty's political triumphs and defeats to help your own career. More important, serve on committees, including ones not directly related to your field of study. They will still give you a line on your C.V. for departmental work, and they help prove your seriousness to faculty.

Respecting and Failing to Respect Your Peers

DAN: Graduate school is based on an apprentice model, and although some schools do more to prepare you for becoming a faculty member than others, I think it's good to think of your professional relationships with your peers as practice for your future professional relationships as a faculty member. One thing I've learned as the Assistant to the Director of First-Year Writing is that the ability to get along with vastly different personalities is a critical skill to finesse departmental politics. If I'm leading a committee made up of my peers, I need to be aware of who gets along and who doesn't. Even things like who has dated and then broken up or who is currently stressed out over his or her dissertation and is about to burst are important to be aware of. Part of respecting my peers, in my context as an administrator, is getting to know them personally. I need to know who will be furious over the new textbook we've selected, who will take on extra committee work without complaint, and who is sure to arrive at a meeting on the wrong date and time if I don't send out three reminders.

PAUL: Dan is just wrong on this one! Well, that is a bit of hyperbole, but don't let departmental politics dull your sense of the academic world. Much of academics is about positioning yourself and your opinions. Sometimes you have to take a stand, especially with your peers; however, there are ways to go about it. For example, I know that I can come across as very self-confident when I want to discuss something (some would call it brash and arrogant). I don't really care if people think less of me for my confidence. I come from a family and region of the country where people state what they want and what they believe. I refuse to indulge people who lack the security to express their ideals and try to suppress mine. However, that doesn't mean I advocate treating their opinions with disdain or allowing personal attacks to surface.

Our department has a vibrant electronic Listserv for graduate students, and I was an active member for a number of years. Though I may have alienated some, most knew I was opinionated but also knew that my strong beliefs did not lead to personal differences. I often disagreed with some of my best friends on the list. I also never—and I repeat never—made any statements that I thought disparaged my department or faculty. I would jokingly make fun of other graduate students, and I would question their beliefs and support my own. In short, I would take political risks with other graduate students, but not with faculty. Part of the reason I got into this field was to argue and debate important issues. I love it and won't walk away from a good intellectual fight. With peers, you can cut your teeth on how to fight/debate fairly.

Of course, you can also take stands with professors in classrooms, but that's a different political arena. Allow yourself to take stands, but consider the consequences. Also know that as a grad student you are not a peer of faculty members. In an ideal world, we would all be peers working toward the same wonderful goals. In the real world, you need to prove your worth. Of course, I'm not telling you to play the sycophant (that will impress no one), but, as Dan mentioned, knowledge of the realistic political atmosphere is important. Some professors may treat you as a peer, but others will see you only as a student and preserve a strict teacher-student relationship. Learn to recognize the difference.

DAN: I think one of the reasons I'm more reluctant to question the beliefs of other graduate students has to do with my role as an administrator. In some respects I'm a peer to my fellow graduate students, but there are also times when I have to play the administrative roles of a mentor or an authority figure. First-year writing teachers come to me for advice and guidance in their classes, and sometimes I have to talk to them about their policies or about problems that they're having as teachers. Because of this, I often find myself holding back when there's a political or religious debate on the Listserv, even if it's a friendly debate. Of course, I'm also a humble and friendly midwesterner from Cleveland, while Paul is a loudmouthed, arrogant New Yorker!

PAUL: Dan's humility and insecurity aside, be careful about how you release any pent-up opinions you hold back because of departmental politics. For example, it seems prudent not to infuse your classroom with political rhetoric as a release from restrictions with peers. Poor teachers use their classrooms as forums for presenting, for example, Republican or Democratic ideas. It reminds me of TAs who teach first-year writing classes like literature classes because they really want to teach literature. Find out the departmental goals for the classes you teach and follow them. Don't turn the classroom into a place where students must learn about your pet projects and opinions. Listservs and parties are good places for politically biased talk, but you should be more evenhanded in the classroom. I think of the classroom as a place to offer options rather than a forum for imposing specific ideas. Don't let personal beliefs counter departmental needs in the classroom. Or, at the very least, realize that extolling the virtues of the Green Party in a writing class can be a politically poor move. Since I'm quite opinionated, and because I remain evenhanded on many issues in the classroom, I often find myself in search of an arena in which to unload my "real" beliefs without any censor. Graduate students searching for that venue just need to be careful.

Respecting and Failing to Respect Professors

DAN: I'm not someone who likes pecking orders. I have my students call me Dan, and if they ever refer to me as Dr. Melzer, I pretend to gag. My favorite professors are usually the ones who ask their students to refer to them by their first name. For example, when I first met one of the editors of this book, I called her Dr. Bishop. She smiled and told me to call her Wendy from now on. On the other hand, a few months ago I was talking to the Director of Graduate Studies about my coursework, and as I was leaving I said, "Good-bye, David" instead of referring to him as Dr. Johnson. I'd always called him Dr. Johnson, and this was just a slip, but he arched his eyebrow and I could tell I had made him uncomfortable. Dr. Johnson is also one of my favorite professors, but he prefers to maintain a little more distance than Wendy. These name games may seem like a small thing, but they point to something larger, and that is the need to be aware of the personality of each faculty member when you interact with them both socially and "politically." Some faculty will join you for a drink and talk about their families; other faculty are so focused on their research agendas that they see you as yet another distraction. Some faculty respond best to flattery; other faculty will not tolerate a phony. This is not to suggest you treat your graduate career like Machiavelli, jockeying for favor "by any means necessary." After all, ideally faculty are mentors, and the quality of your thinking counts for more than the quality of your schmoozing. But you do need to approach each interaction you have with a faculty member on an individual basis. As long as you start with respect as a baseline, you'll be fine.

PAUL: I agree with Dr. Melzer on this one. I knew a graduate student who had a legitimate grievance with a faculty member over a teaching assignment. The situation was not handled to his satisfaction, and the student brought the problem to others in the department. He went over the original faculty member's head. Did he have a right to do so? Yes. Was it smart politically? Absolutely not. Department administrators have more to worry about than the teaching assignment of a graduate student. The event made a faculty member look poorly in front of other faculty, and it wasted the time of others. It would have been best to simply let the situation go without making a major fuss. To make matters worse, this student was in the last year of guaranteed funding; not surprisingly, he was told that he might not have funding for the next year. Am I saying that he was denied funding because of this one incident? No. However, many students obtain funding, without any problems, years after the guarantee is over. Part of their ability to do so stems from political moves. They don't anger faculty or present themselves as troublesome over relatively minor issues. Faculty members often can find positions for politically savvy graduate students. Your job is to impress faculty during your time as a graduate student. You have to make professors want to work with you. You have to give them a reason to want to help you when you need funding or require extra assistance. Foolish political moves usually don't impress anyone.

Respecting and Failing to Respect Administrative Assistants

PAUL: So much of politics in the graduate arena comes down to intelligence and basic interpersonal skills. So would you like to know an effective way of testing your people skills? Think about how you treat the staff in your department. Do you look at them as your servants? Do you see yourself as smarter and more important than they? If so, you probably have a lot to learn about departmental politics and dealing with people. And let's not forget, departmental staff have power over you in ways you couldn't imagine. Most important, they deserve your respect as people. Our department has wonderful staff members. They are an important part of our department, and departmental politics includes everyone.

DAN: Sometimes when I'm in the copy room, I overhear the administrative assistants talking in the English Department office next door. I often hear them talking about lack of respect from graduate students. I've heard a hundred of these stories from the administrative assistants: graduate students becoming furious because the administrative assistant was on a lunch break when they needed her; graduate students blaming an administrative assistant for a rule or requirement he had nothing to do with; graduate students asking administrative assistants to bend rules or change deadlines and then getting upset when they won't. Sometimes graduate students respect faculty but fail to give the same kind of respect to administrative assistants. Administrative assistants are your colleagues, just like faculty. And like faculty, they can make your life easy if you treat them with respect, or miserable if you don't.

A Few Final Thoughts

We hope that our advice will prepare you for both the positive and the negative aspects of departmental politics, and help you better finesse politics as you advance in your academic career. But we also hope that you do more than just accept departmental politics as they are and simply try to work them to your advantage. We also hope you will try to help change the political climate of your department, whether it's something as small as serving on a committee or as large as treating everyone—and every field of study—with respect.

14

Staying in Town: Life after the Program

LAURA NEWTON

During my first semester as a PhD student in creative writing at a large state university, a young, ambitious colleague said to me, "We all want to know why you are here."

"To get a degree and to write," I answered.

"Yes," he pressed, "but didn't you leave a job that paid pretty well to do this?"

I've since discovered that he's not the only one bewildered by the idea that someone would do all this work without plans to seek a tenure-track job.

Many students enter graduate school with their adult lives already well established. Often these students have been in the work world as professionals in other fields. They may have families, children in school, and spouses with jobs and ties to the community, and they may own their own homes.

Many of these students intend to follow the traditional career path and will enter the job market looking for tenure-track jobs at colleges and universities. However, some of them plan to stay in the town where they get their degree and view the PhD as an end in itself. Sometimes graduate students fall in love with someone or with the city where they attend school and are so deeply connected to the place by the time they finish the degree that they decide they don't want to move.

I've lived in this town for twenty-six years. Twenty-two years ago, I earned my master's degree at the same university where I am now a PhD candidate. I had intended to earn a doctorate immediately after finishing the master's degree in 1981, but I dropped out of the PhD program after one semester. My reasons for dropping out were many. As I was starting the PhD program, I was also getting a divorce. My husband and I had agreed on joint custody of our children, so we needed to live in the same town. I already had a BA and an MA, and he had not yet graduated from college. At that point, going on with a PhD seemed foolish when, as the more financially responsible parent, I needed immediately to provide a home, health insurance, food, and clothes for two kids. At the same time, after three years as a graduate student, the academic life had begun to seem less

151

appealing than it had originally. The female faculty members in the department were struggling to be taken seriously, fighting for tenure and for recognition of the importance of family. (In this regard, the university hasn't changed as much as I hoped. Between 1998 and 2001, three female professors in the English department were denied promotion and tenure.) In addition, I could see that the university operated as a parallel universe to the rest of the community. The rich, exciting world outside seemed not to exist to many who spend their entire lives in one university department.

I love this beautiful, southern town full of live oaks, camellias, and azaleas, very near the Gulf of Mexico, and the same university that seemed so insular to me then provides a wealth of cultural opportunities from dance to theater to a very cool circus. There is also a politically progressive, alternative community that provides great music, a food co-op, alternative schools, and several intentional communities, one of which is my home. This is also the state capital.

And so I stayed. Then, eighteen years later, my very political job with a state department of education, a job I loved, began to lose its charm, largely because the agency had taken a hard turn to the right. My children were on their own. I was happily remarried to someone who was glad to see me take a teaching assistantship and begin work on the PhD I'd put aside so many years before.

I could have continued to work part-time in my position with the state. The director of my program was eager to keep me, but the Department of Education wouldn't have paid my tuition unless the degree was in educational leadership, something I didn't want to pursue. By the time I factored in the tuition, the clothes to keep working in my suit job, the changing political climate, and the transition time between work and school, it made more sense to work at the university as a teaching assistant and to take the pay cut. I decided to put both feet in the university life again, at the age of forty-eight, to surround myself with other writers, and to put myself in a situation where people expected to me to write poetry, not as an avocation, but as a vocation. I've never regretted the decision.

There is a pretty clear assumption in Research I universities that if you're getting a PhD you plan to look for a tenure-track teaching job, which means moving to where the job is. In the current climate, when the academy is becoming more corporate, the push for students to be job-focused is even stronger than ever before. Yet, like me, many graduate students don't want to make that move, or they make the move and regret it. Still others discover over the course of their graduate program that they don't like to teach or don't like some other aspect of the academic life.

Because I wanted to know how other students who stay in town reconcile the time and expense they've spent on an advanced degree if they choose not to enter the traditional academic job market, I have interviewed several English Department graduates who have found jobs in the town where they earned their degrees. I wanted to know how such students find jobs or establish careers that are satisfying without leaving town. Are there other measures of the value of an advanced degree? If so, what are they?

The graduates I interviewed are Michael and Mary Jane (who are married to each other,) Faith, Karen, Cadence, and Dean. Mary Jane and Michael now have non-tenure-track faculty positions at the university where they got their degrees. Cadence is also employed full-time by the university in a professional position

providing technical support and training in distance learning to faculty. Their stories defy the conventional wisdom that you can't get hired at the university where
you get your degree. Karen and Dean are working as editors. Faith is a public information specialist writing an oral history of the Apalachicola River.

Michael, Mary Jane, Faith, and Karen all started graduate school with plans
to become teachers in a college or university setting. Michael, Mary Jane, and
Faith were hired for tenure-track positions at other colleges or universities and left
those jobs to return to the town where they had earned their degrees, the place they
had come to consider home. All three of them are relatively happy with the
decision even as they recognize that they have traded some benefits for others. Like
me, Dean and Cadence entered graduate school without plans to seek tenure-track
faculty positions. Both of them saw the PhD as a valuable end in itself.

All the people I interviewed now have professional positions, good salaries,
and benefits. The degree to which they are happy with their current work lives
varies, of course. Each of them expected and gained different things from the graduate school experience, and it is in the discussion of those expectations and how they
were or were not met that these interviews are most revealing and most useful.

Faith: Stories I Never Could Have Invented

I interviewed at a dozen colleges and universities and was offered a position as
assistant professor of creative writing at a college in a small, blue-collar,
Pennsylvania town with a coal mine rising right out of its center. The salary was
$30,500. The course load was four classes each semester. I gulped but reasoned that
it was a beginning position. We painted our house and put it on the market. My
scientist husband resigned his job at the national lab and we drove to Pennsylvania,
fifty percent poorer, to rent an apartment.

I cringed as we entered the garage-front town, grimy with coal dust. I began
to feel the impossibility of moving my husband out of his science community, my
high schooler and middle schooler from live oaks and Spanish moss to eight
months of winter. I obtained legal counsel and broke my contract.

Immediately, I began hunting for another job in Tallahassee. The Northwest
Florida Water Management District wanted a writer-editor to write an oral history
of the Apalachicola River and Bay. Within two weeks of breaking my previous contract, I was hired to conduct an enticing new project.

The last steamboat pilot, the last sharecropper, the first black mayor of
Apalachicola, and a Creek Indian chief have all entrusted stories to me that I never
could have invented. Some of them I recorded just before they died, adding special weight to their words. On the side, I have started a novel based on my research
with more emotional value than a transcribed oral history will permit.

I have pangs about giving up teaching too easily, but then I recall how jeal-
ous I was of my students' output while I did pedagogy. Two of my most admired
female professors with children were denied tenure for not producing enough new
material to equal a book in their first seven years of teaching. After two years in public
information, I'm earning the equivalent of a professor's salary, at a small college
and will produce a book within three years. I race home every day at four o'clock

to spend my free time with my husband and my children. When I look forward, I see myself rising in public information or opening cross-curriculum study in a university someday—recording oral histories, developing public service or environmental education, and writing.

Mary Jane: More to Life Than That

Michael and I got jobs at a university located in a midwestern beef slaughterhouse town that smelled like dog food. I understand it was the blood burning. The weather got to 50 degrees below some days in the winter. The department was in pretty unhappy shape, and I felt I was wasting my writing life and my family life in faculty meetings and on doing tenure-track committees and other duties to get the tenure status. So I quit and came back here with my family.

The adjustment was cruel and punishing at times. I did adjunct work, but I'd been a regular faculty member, so I hated the bad pay and the lack of benefits. Michael had been freelancing for a women-and-children's-shelter newsletter, and the director mentioned to him that his college, the College of Business at the university where we had gotten our degrees, was hiring writing teachers for the next year. He decided to do it. They were hiring three that year, then two the next. I thought I'd apply for the job myself if he did okay, and he did.

I interviewed and got the job. So I am still in academia, but sort of below the radar, where I like to be—non tenure-earning, no research required, no meetings required. I teach a business communication course to juniors and seniors with a wide variety of majors, everything from future accountants to future hospitality management folks.

Meanwhile, my first collection of short stories has been published, and I have toured. My students didn't know or much care about all that. Probably a good healthy dose of reality for me, frankly.

As a faculty member (I'm not tenure-earning, but I am promotion-earning), I get to teach in the overseas program, and my husband and I are now writing a textbook on intercultural business communication. I've finished a novel, which is circulating right now, and started a mystery novel. The writer in me never stopped working, though she wanted to retire several times during my first years at the College of Business. Now it's a manageable thing. I enjoy the teaching.

I miss the camaraderie that I had in an English department with folks who love books, writing, the literary life. But this is a rich place to live. There's always a good movie or play to see, or an interesting art exhibit, or an amazing longtime friend to have lunch or dinner with or afternoon coffee. My kids are in great schools, and we have a billion writers here now. I always can workshop my fiction with one group or another. I also work as a fiction editor for a literary magazine. I think this is the way to go, especially for a woman—getting higher degrees. They just seem to open up more avenues and opportunities for different kinds of work. The key is not thinking along a narrow pathway of "the tenure-track job in English." Not only are they going extinct anyway, but there's far more to life than that.

Michael: True Gritty Realism

I suppose I had big ambitions to be an integral part of creating a community of writers somewhere in the States as a faculty member of some creative writing program. After getting an understanding of the job market, I saw myself doing a 5/5 or 4/4 load at some community college somewhere. That wasn't my ideal, but that was my realistic view. True gritty realism.

Simply staying in town and being happy with it didn't happen until after I accepted the fact that teaching business communication would be an OK fate. I think it took me about three years (or maybe four) at the university business college to finally become okay with that. The dream of becoming a full-time creative writing teacher is very far in the back seat now. Getting over the need for having the ideal "tenure-track" job takes a while too, because that's what academia grinds/pounds into your head. In some ways, I think it's a lot better not to have to live with the tenure-track pressure/earning tenure issue hanging over your head. But it took a while to come to that realization.

The teaching has become satisfying. It was very difficult at first. The course and textbook seemed rather superficial and a bit uninteresting. I would have never imagined myself in a million years teaching for a college of business. Business was anathema while I was in grad school. But after teaching business communication for five or six years now, I've finally learned enough about the subject and business and the type of student at the College of Business to make the course interesting to me and my students (hopefully). I still imagine doing my ideal, teaching writing and literature, as being more satisfying. I do get to teach Article and Essay Workshop when I teach in the university's overseas program, so I'm lucky to still get a little taste of it every so often.

To me, the greatest part of that PhD experience was being part of the community of teachers, writers, readers, and critics, and having the WORD be the most important thing in everybody's mind. I'm probably a bit lucky. I'm not sure if the average PhD experience is as enjoyable and community-oriented as mine was. I think I valued the experience of the community much more than I saw the value of the PhD degree.

Karen: Struggling to Accept the Consequences

I began to realize that my personality was not as well suited for the profession as I had initially thought. I was too far into the program to quit. I really just hoped that I could find some niche that I would fit into. Much as I enjoy intellectual banter, I like some type of implementation or practical action as a result of all this thought and debate. I found myself leaving some graduate classes thinking, "So what?"

In contrast to my coursework, my teaching was very stimulating and meaningful. I was drawn to my topic (war literature) because it was grounded in history and culture as opposed to theory. I often lectured on history and psychology to establish a context for a work we were reading. I thought that if I could get a position as a professor, the teaching would be enough. I've been published, but life is short, and the type of work I would have to produce is really not very interesting to me anymore, so the requirement to publish is a major disadvantage of a professorship.

I already had doubts about my former career goals. I feel most at home in the South. I really like the beauty of this town, and because I worked for the state, I have friends here outside the university. I know myself enough to realize that I'm not going to be happy just anywhere and that place and community are very important in one's life. Also, as a single female I have to rely on a support network of friends, and I have such a network here.

Currently, I work as an editor for a government-funded education agency. The work is relatively stable, but I can't do this forever. I don't really like editing, and I would have to take about a $20,000 pay cut if I had to get a job as an editor somewhere else. I'll ride this job out as long as I can, and I hope something else, at least an idea for a fifth career, comes to me.

I have a great deal of regret and even anger at myself for making the decision to pursue the degree. I wish I had pursued a doctorate in public health or a law degree with an emphasis in public health. (My past work experience as a CPA and policy analyst is all in health care, and even my doctoral work in English dealt with trauma, psychological and physical, in the context of war.) However, at thirty-eight, with $15,000 worth of student loans to pay off, I don't have the money or the mental or physical energy to get another degree. I'm struggling to accept the consequences of the decision I made and to get past the regret and move on. Right now I have no idea where to go, careerwise, from here, and one of my regrets is that I will probably eventually have to move. I'm my only means of support, and I'll have to go wherever I can get employment in whatever field I can find it in.

Cadence: Doing Something That Contributes

When I started the PhD program, I had a one-year-old daughter, and sons four and eight. I had stayed home for a year from a lucrative consulting practice that required a lot of travel. When I discovered that I could be paid to teach and go to school, it seemed like a great job, a lot of time at home and intellectually enriching.

How academe defines success can be damaging when the opportunities to succeed in that defined way are severely limited. I just kept putting my energy into doing what I really loved doing. I fought hard against the despair that was all around me in my peers, and the disdain from faculty because I made no secret of the fact that I wanted a university job, and I wanted it here. I didn't have my mind set on a tenure-track job. I even made a little list of what I wanted in a job that I kept in my planner: flexible, pays well, allows for some teaching, in an environment where I am valued.

I applied for the summer enhancement workshop on using the electronic campus. This proved providential. Now I have a full-time job in instructional development. I work with faculty in improving their instruction, and get to teach a course as part of my job. Teaching a course helps me do my job even better, and I am valued, even by the English Department; they get those hard-to-cover classes covered for free, because my salary is paid for by Instructional Development. The flexibility isn't as great, but it is still there should I need time for my family, and the salary more than makes up for it.

My years of thinking about my teaching yielded this job, and it uses all those years of experience prior to returning to school (factors that were not valued in my years as a grad student or instructor): my MS in psychology, my years as a consultant, and my years as a training director. Since the office I work in now loves creative solutions, it is more satisfying to me than creative writing. It feels good doing something that contributes, working in a collegial atmosphere, paying my share of the bills, and still teaching. Learning from young adults and thinking about how I can increase their learning really "floats my boat" now, and all that can go into helping other faculty.

The time in the PhD program was great; I was at home and paid some while I was with my young kids. My only regret is that I took financial aid and now am paying those loans just as my oldest son is getting ready to incur his own. That was the worst planning decision I made. If I had stayed in my other profession I would be making more by now, but the degree wasn't the main goal: the process was and the time with my family. A lot of moms have interrupted careers, but they didn't come out the other end with a PhD and a university job.

Dean: Living Is Learning

I was thirty-seven and recently divorced when I started grad school. I chose this university because my ex-wife had brought my kids here, and I wanted both to be near them and to have the time and the environment to write. I still had no idea what I wanted to be when I grew up. I only wanted to write. Not to write for a living but just to be among writers and talk about writing and write. It wasn't until I got a teaching assistantship to pay for grad school that I realized I loved to teach.

Education was never about getting a job, but if one came along that I liked, that would be cool. What changed along the way was everything: I found that I loved everything about the classroom and the students and hated everything about academia outside of that: grading people and spending all my spare time doing just that. There are lots of days spent away from the classroom, that's true, but there never seems to be a single minute away from the work. No time to write and no time to live a life that might stimulate writing.

The job at the Department of Education came through friends, and it has worked out beautifully so far: I make twice the money I was making, drive five minutes one way to work, and have every moment I'm not in my office to spare: no homework. The work I have found has very satisfying parts to it: the people I work with are wonderful, and the people we are doing the work for need it.

Reconciling time seems crazy to me: my life is what it is, and everything I've done or will do contributes to my life. If I'm happy, that's all the reconciliation I need for everything that has happened in my life, so of course, it was all. The value of my degree is the people I've met and the things I've learned about myself and others from it. Living is learning, so if you get to spend some part of your life on a campus where learning is available all over the place, what a great life opportunity. All I ever really wanted to know was what it takes to be happy, and I've learned that that is a lifelong process. I'm still working on it.

Messages in a Bottle

Some of you may find that you don't want to pursue a job that requires you to move. Some of you may decide that a tenure-track job is not what you are most suited for, after all. My hope is that the personal stories of others who have faced these difficult career choices will serve as cautionary tales, as pep talks, as career counseling, but most of all as what they are: heartfelt and eloquent personal narratives, messages in a bottle from people who have gone across the graduate school sea before you.

15

Surviving Alienation: How Junior Faculty Reconnected with the Classroom and Why They Needed To

GAY LYNN CROSSLEY AND KIM HAIMES-KORN

Irony is best appreciated from a distance. Perhaps that is why some of us, while quite adept at discussing irony in literature, are slow to identify it in our own lives. When we set out to study the experiences of our graduate school colleagues once they gained full-time positions, after earning their doctorates, we intended to study the conflicts that they faced in their early years of post-graduate-program life. Our experiences as junior faculty members inspired this focus on conflict, since conflict, in some form or another, stands out in our memories as we've worked to create the professional lives we wanted.

Before we start sounding pessimistic or bitter, let us explain: While uncomfortable in the midst of it, we value how conflict, ultimately, can motivate renewal. Once on the other side, we find conflict brings us clarification or affirmation, spotlights the possibility in negotiation, and creates new allegiances. Even unresolved conflict has made us more aware of priorities and taken us to happier places, both literally (one of us did change jobs) and figuratively (both of us find ourselves living more fulfilling professional lives today than when we started).

So we studied conflict as planned, examining the experiences of faculty at seven institutions (two men and four women in positions ranging from full-time tenure-track composition specialists or generalists to temporary full-time instructor positions). We asked them to reflect on the often tacit expectations of entering faculty, to identify successes, surprises, and disappointments, and to share strategies they use to negotiate conflicts that they've experienced. Their responses landed us in territory both surprising and familiar.

Alienation is the strongest theme: geographical alienation; philosophical alienation; and the alienation resulting from disciplinary isolation (many of these teachers were the only "compositionist" at one time or another, whether they specialized in composition studies or not). We are familiar with alienation. It is why we anticipate annual conventions with such joy. It is what drives up our phone bills as we confide in and console one another. But each of these teachers also spoke of some change in his or her relationship with the writing classroom and with students. This change was (and is) perceived as a threat to their teaching lives. To varying degrees the respondents also spoke of the irony they found in the changes they experienced. Down the line, the very thing—the classroom—that had attracted these teachers to the profession was jeopardized in the first years of full-time employment. More than anything else, these teachers emphasized the alienation they felt from their classrooms. In fact, the other mentioned forms of alienation were often directly related to this alienation.

We immediately identified with what these respondents told us of their experiences, yet there was the element of surprise that comes any time we recognize irony in our own lives. Like these teachers, over the years, we had struggled to maintain an emphasis on teaching, to reimagine and renew our classrooms, to create productive relationships with students, and so on. We expected these struggles as any teacher should, but we didn't fully recognize how they were intensified and complicated by our transition from graduate student to professor. In retrospect, it all seems obvious, but we didn't *name* our own alienation from the classroom until we read the responses from these teachers. How this alienation was created and these teachers' responses to it is the focus for the remainder of our discussion.

Setting the Scene

Irony is born of context, so we'll begin by describing the institutional contexts—specifically, the expectations of the individuals operating within them. Predisposed as we are to recognize the significance of institutional context in an individual's professional experience, we had anticipated a need to structure our discussion around the kinds of institutions represented in respondents' first jobs. While institutional contexts do remain significant to understanding particular experiences, the theme of alienation transcends context.

This alienation is not mere coincidence in our minds. All the teachers we surveyed attended the same graduate program as we did. We had all taught in a first-year writing program that encouraged expressivist and process pedagogies. Equally significant, if not more so, is that we participated in a strong and supportive community of writing teachers. Whether chatting about classroom experiences and sharing assignments and activities in our offices or attending in-training workshops or a composition-studies reading group, we were immersed in conversations about the theory and practice of teaching writing. Finally, in large part because of the strength of this community, we experienced extraordinary autonomy in the classroom that inspired us to experiment in the classroom as well as to share and grow from those experiences. Much of the alienation discussed here seems a direct result of our sense of community and autonomy as graduate teaching assistants.

Even though all the teachers (whose names have been changed for this discussion) attended the same graduate program, we believe that our early experiences as full-time faculty members are not unique to us, or if they are, only in degree. Like the majority of doctorates who enter the job market, we began, and some of us currently teach, at midsize or small colleges and universities.

Four of the respondents began full-time employment at regional state universities (two in the West and two in the Southeast):

> While completing her dissertation, Annie was hired on a two-year contract as a Lecturer in Composition; however, as she points out, she was "generally considered an adjunct." In this position she was expected to teach "four classes per semester—all composition, though Intro to Lit was also available." Evaluation of her work was based solely on student evaluations. (She has since completed her degree and taken a job at a community college.)
>
> Daniel's first and current position is tenure track; in fact, he has already earned tenure and been promoted "without much difficulty." He is expected "to teach a variety of writing classes, including first-year, journalism, and business, technical, and creative. [He has] also taught sophomore literature survey, senior seminar, and a graduate writing class for master's in education students."
>
> Dana returned to her alma mater for her first tenure-track position (where she remains). While her situation is more complex than those of the other three respondents at regional state universities in that her current colleagues are her former professors, what is expected of her falls in line with what is expected of the other three: "I teach three or four classes a semester, direct the Writing Center, serve on two standing departmental committees, and serve on varied university committees, such as Annual Fund and Screening Committee for A&S Dean Search. I teach mostly writing classes, usually three or four different preps: Writing for Teachers, English 102 for honors students, the tutor-training class, and a perspectives class titled 'The Myth of Southern Womanhood.' I have taught graduate seminars twice, directed two theses in Rhet/Comp, and done a graduate directed study."
>
> Unique among our respondents in that she completed her master's and doctoral work in women's literature (with a minor in film studies), Adrienne was initially hired by a regional state university to teach two sections of composition and to assist the director of writing for twenty hours a week; in her own words, she was "jack of all trades, master of none, and/or chief cook and bottlewasher." After two years, Adrienne became the director of writing, during which time she focused her energies on reeducating herself "in what had become, by caveat, [her] new major field." In this position, Adrienne was responsible for training and supervising graduate teaching assistants as well as adjunct instructors. She resigned from this position after five years to move across the country with her husband.

The last two respondents began at small private institutions:

To be close to her parents, who were in declining health, Deidre accepted a position at a liberal arts college for which, she recalls, "I may have had a job description, but no one ever told me what it was, and I didn't ask. I taught nine courses, five in fall and four in spring. Of these, eight were in the first-year writing sequence; the ninth was a general creative writing course."

Isaac also began full-time employment at a liberal arts college as a division chair for developmental studies and English as a second language: "The position involved teaching four five-hour developmental studies classes on the quarter system (later five three-hour classes of the same on the semester system), supervising teachers within the programs contained in the division (e.g., math, reading, writing, and ESL), developing and evaluating the division's curriculum, and supervising the college's writing center."

At first glance, these job descriptions are strikingly dissimilar. Three of the respondents were primarily (or solely) composition instructors; one was in charge of developmental students and ESL programs. Two directed writing centers. Teaching responsibilities ranged from first-year writing to business and technical writing to creative writing to tutor-training classes to literature courses. One respondent became the director of writing at a state institution with an enrollment of twenty thousand students. However, these dissimilar job descriptions resulted in a common alienation that ultimately distanced each of these teachers from his or her classroom.

More Work Means Less Time for Students

I have some wonderful students . . ., and I wish I had more to give them. I'm tired.
—Deidre

According to Isaac, the first year at a full-time position is spent learning "how to juggle all the responsibilities we encounter in our jobs." Workload is usually the first reason we recognize for our changing relationship with the classroom. As the job descriptions show, these teachers juggled a great number of responsibilities. In addition to teaching twelve to fifteen hours of writing courses, some of these teachers are serving in administrative positions (developing curriculum, training and supervising teachers, etc.), on top of the usual department and college service expected of them. In our experience, on job searches and in our current positions, such job descriptions are the norm at regional state universities and small colleges. This reality quickly changes how (and how much) we are able to work with students. As Dana puts it, "I don't have as much time for students as I did as a graduate student. Now, it's up to students to seek me out for help rather than my requiring conferences for most papers."

Isaac also emphasizes how the time he spends with students and their writing was the first casualty:

My workload was easily the most challenging element to my teaching. Taking a job at a school where the standard teaching load was five classes a semester, sometimes with yet a sixth class as an expected serv-ice to the institution, meant that I had to step back from or modify some of the practices that I had been taught to idealize in graduate school. For example, whereas in graduate school I would write fairly in-depth responses to my students' drafts and final compositions, at my new institution I had to reduce the amount of commentary that I wrote on student work and in some cases had to abandon writing comments altogether on intermediate drafts, journals, and other pieces of writing. Other aspects of my teaching, such as student-teacher conferences and portfolio grading, were affected in much the same way.

Annie echoes his experience:

At [my first position] the biggest challenge was the increase in course load. Working with one hundred students in as many as three differ-ent courses forced me to find ways to reduce my workload. Often that meant giving less attention to individual students and cutting back on the amount of writing I required in those classes. I also found I spent less time responding to rough drafts of essays and rushed through grading just to get it done.

Consider us the backup singers, since we, too, have searched for ways not only to respond and conference less but also to justify (feel good about) devoting less time to writers in our classrooms. But it's hard to feel good for long when we take into account the students at our institutions. Isaac says it best: "It is no small irony that I had to make these compromises in response to my workload even though the students with whom I was working needed these elements even more than the students I taught in graduate school." Such is often the case for the major-ity of compositionists who find their first full-time jobs not at the far rarer major research institutions whose admissions policies recruit the "cream of the crop" but at the midsize to small college or university with a far greater proportion of first-time college students and nontraditional students. These students often exhibit weaker skills and stronger insecurities than the typical first-year student at PhD-granting universities. For many of us, these are just the kinds of students that contemporary composition pedagogies were intended to address.

The Lone Compositionist

The most fundamental cause of alienation grows from traditional definitions of English departments (whether independent or combined with other humanity disciplines) in which literature is emphasized, regardless of the number of first-year writing classes taught by most English faculty and/or to address the rec-ommendations of outside reviewers. In these departments, a compositionist is generally hired to remove some of the "burden" of first-year writing instruction from literature faculty. Rarely is more than one compositionist hired, creating a fun-damental alienation: "Worst of all, because I was the lone compositionist and there wasn't an English department, there was little support for my policies—and some of them ran counter to administration's wishes" (Deidre).

For example, two respondents have risked alienation by representing the concerns of adjuncts. As a temporary instructor, Annie brought adjunct issues (hiring, pay, and continued employment) to the attention of the department. Dana also "challenged the teaching load of full-time temporary instructors in a department meeting when [she] was still an untenured (but tenure-track) assistant professor." This moment stands out, since, she recalls, "one of my mentors opposed our taking a stand on the issue."

Daniel spends the most time articulating what seems a common experience:

[In my department of twenty tenure-track and twenty full-time non-tenure-track instructors] most faculty members here have a clearly defined role or area of specialty, in addition to teaching composition. As someone who was needed in several areas and who has the experience/education/interest to teach in those areas, I often feel . . . at odds with the department's need to fit everyone into a "niche." I suppose that some of this tension is historical in that the department follows a traditional literature-based model, with each faculty member representing a defined period or type of literature. Also, the upper-division writing courses are divided into distinct tracks with little crossover in terms of faculty interaction or teaching. As someone who practices and enjoys teaching creative/journalism/professional writing, I guess I don't fit the pattern. At times, I sense resentment and/or fear from other faculty about what I am up to in terms of encroaching on their "territory." Curiously, because of my ability to teach a number of kinds of upper-division writing courses, I teach far fewer sections of first-year composition than my literature colleagues.

Finally, Deidre reminds us that, as "lone compositionists," we may be the only teachers in our departments (and in our students' experiences) to require, for example, workshopping and conferencing. In these situations, little administrative support exists for teachers wanting to introduce these practices to students: "students wouldn't come to conferences. They simply saw it as not having class; they disrespected me, the pedagogy, etc., and without administrative support (no writing program, no other compositionists, not really an English department but just a humanities division), there was little I could do besides wave reduced grades over their heads" (Deidre).

The Return of Personal Lives

When many of us look back on our graduate careers, we can point to marriages beginning and ending, the birth of babies, life going on in one way or another; however, most of our energies were necessarily devoted to completing our degrees and obtaining jobs that would bring us above the poverty level, if only marginally. It is not surprising then that once we earn our degrees, much of our time immediately following graduate school is spent wrestling with a personal life long neglected. Only one respondent talked in these terms; however, her experience was shared by the authors of this essay and many others, as those conference reunions and lengthy phone conversations remind us. Therefore, the distraction our personal lives create those first few years seems well worth mentioning. As Deidre puts it,

> I was probably more interested in figuring out who I was than I was in teaching. I had taken the job I did because it was relatively near my parents' home, and spending time with them was more of a priority for me than thinking about my teaching, since my mother's health declined abruptly during the year I was there. During grad school I had divorced, and taking the job I did meant moving away from my ex-husband and both of my grown children. That was a big adjustment; leaving behind good friends was just as bad. Then soon after I moved, I fell for someone new.

Deidre also points out that one need not face such stressful situations as divorce, distance from children, or seriously ill parents to become distracted by personal life. The health and car maintenance we could not afford in graduate schools now become pressing needs, and simply adjusting to the culinary limitations of another region of the country eats up time and energy:

> All of this was confusing, and trying to figure it out occupied most of the free space in my brain (what was leftover after teaching nine classes that year). Then there was the new environment, the budget, the car needed a valve job, the college didn't have e-mail, I needed new glasses, there were no fresh bagels within a hundred miles so I couldn't figure out what to eat. Away from [my grad school home], I didn't know how to live.

The lesson here: Expect (we can't really plan for it) personal lives to demand center stage. Personal lives will always demand our attention in surprising ways, but we don't always have to feel blindsided, as some of us have. And time invested here has to come from someplace—usually the classroom.

Changing Student Perceptions and Student Populations

Respondents brought to our attention two ways that students themselves may alienate us from the classroom, or at least make us feel like aliens in our own classrooms. The first involves students' changed perceptions of us when we walk into the classroom as members of the full-time faculty. As one respondent put it, we are now, "The Professor." That comes as little surprise, on the one hand: it's what we've been working for all along. On the other hand, if we've grown comfortable with the relationships we cultivated with students as GTAs, the difference can take some getting used to:

> It was disconcerting and disturbing. They treated me differently, much more distantly. They were suddenly "afraid," as they would tell me, to come by my office to chat, to linger after class just to shoot the breeze,

and certainly they would not talk as much in class. I tried dressing "down" to make them more comfortable, but that got me in trouble with my colleagues. I tried finding new "fun" writing activities, but I found that [they took the emphasis off the *quality* of writing]. Finally, I simply accepted their distance and proceeded as I used to do, with a concern for their writing and thinking. (Adrienne)

The second way that students may contribute to alienation stems from changes in student populations. As we move to different parts of the country and to institutions that, more likely than not, bear little resemblance to our PhD-granting institutions, we intellectually recognize that these changes will probably be reflected in the student population. Seems simple enough, until we walk into the classroom and face students more conservative or more liberal than those we are accustomed to, with different understandings of power and their relationship to it, with different conventions. Whether resulting from regional differences, class differences, or the similarly complicated differences that arise when we simply move from college towns or universities in urban settings to rural colleges and universities, these changes take time to recognize, not to mention to understand.

While a couple of other respondents mentioned changing student population as one of the challenges they faced, one respondent in particular focused on the challenges she faced when learning a new population of students. According to her, " it took . . . most of one semester to understand that [the] students had very different attitudes, perceptions, and needs than the ones [she] was used to (and the ones [her] pedagogy still addressed)." Not only did these students exhibit weaker skills than she was used to, but also, and more disarmingly,

> [t]heir ideas about power and power relations in the classroom were also very different. In several classes I taught, students scorned the whole idea of student-centered classes or strategies designed to empower students: they knew they had no power, and they knew they never would. They perceived me as being powerless, as abandoning the power I possessed. This was not a good thing, since they couldn't understand why anyone would do that. In my experience, [my former] students were comfortable with assuming power and authority in the classroom. The last thing I expected in my new job was for students to say, 'Yeah, right!'

To complicate matters further, at Deidre's college, "failing a student . . . was almost impossible." Consequently, "students took it for granted that they could receive the grade they wanted most of the time. So in a strange way they felt absolutely powerless but at the same time more powerful than their teachers."

The Pressure to Fit In

Just when we think we've earned the right to call the shots, experience our autonomy, be the teachers we were meant to be, we meet our new colleagues and learn the tenure and promotion guidelines. The pressure to fit in was the most mentioned reason that respondents gave for feeling (at least briefly) disconnected from their classrooms, and posed the greatest challenge, not only for those hired as the only composition specialist, but also for any teacher expected to teach first-year writing courses and whose training as a GTA emphasized contemporary composition pedagogies. For those of us who experienced autonomy as graduate teaching assistants, it can be disheartening (okay, downright discouraging) to

1. Join a department that has instituted a standard syllabus (and textbooks and assignments) for first-year writing courses.

   At my first job, we had common textbooks for first-year writing because the bookstore thought it would be too expensive to send back so many different books; in addition, we had a common syllabus because we had government funding that required certain language in the syllabi. There was some individual choice allowed, but not much. (Deidre)

2. Join a department as "the lone compositionist" who is trained to recognize the need for that department to rethink its theory and practice of teaching writing, only to learn that the department is not interested in doing so.

   Although I was hired because of my varied teaching experience and ability to work in several genres as a writer and teacher, I sensed the department—which seems to think of itself as a literature department—really did not want to hear much from me in terms of helping to focus the writing program or reform current classroom practices. (Daniel)

   When I started at [my first job] I jumped in with the assumption that because I was hired I was welcome and needed. I faced some resistance because really all they wanted was someone to teach comp and that's about it. (Annie)

3. Join a department faculty who does not share (or out and out rejects) the theories and practices we take into the classroom but who will evaluate our work as teachers.

   I was scrutinized and criticized fairly intensely and worried for several years that I would not receive tenure if a class plan did not go well or if the dean remembered the way the department chair wrote about my grading policies in his annual letter of evaluation. (These were not idle worries, by the way: they were backed up by the Promotion and Tenure Committee.) I hated being scolded like a backward child. (Deidre)

   [G]iven that I now had to "earn" tenure not only by being an effective teacher and scholar but also by "fitting in" to the department, I felt the need to be somewhat cautious in what I did in the classroom.

I discovered that methods and practices routine in the writing program where I learned to teach—use of expressive writing, extensive drafting, peer responding, reflecting on the writing process—were not in use or even not valued at my new job. I was aware that as part of the extensive job review process—pre-tenure, tenure, promotion—I would have to submit syllabi, assignments, and graded essays for inspection by a committee that I would not be allowed to interact with face-to-face and whose members more than likely would have a much more narrow and traditional view of composition instruction. (Daniel)

Such experiences typically lead to safer, duller teaching lives. Daniel found himself "becoming a bit more wary and less likely to be innovative. I did stick to the basics of what I knew to be good teaching, but I quelled my urge to reform and inform the others about the approaches to writing that I valued." Similarly, as Deidre became more sensitive to "institutional mandates," she felt her joy in teaching "vanish."

As graduate teaching assistants, we may have been supervised, even evaluated, but it's likely the case that we would have had to commit a crime (and we are not speaking in hyperbole here) before we would jeopardize our jobs. That's the upside of being cheap labor. The whole game changes when we assume full-time positions and face the pressure to fit in. It is natural, in the first years of professional life, to overemphasize the expectations toward tenure and promotion. During the process we feel uncertain and vulnerable. Although this vulnerability may never entirely disappear, the process does give us a light at the end of the tunnel that offers refreshing possibilities for a return to richer teaching lives:

Now that I have recently earned tenure and promotion, I am feeling a sense of liberation — almost like a teenager who has just gotten a driver's license and stays out late just for the hell out it! So I am trying some new things, and not worrying quite as much what the others in the department or university may think. My two goals this semester are that my writing students and I do some work that we can call our own and that we have fun doing so. (Daniel)

Overcoming Alienation

Well, all the normal advice applies: find out as much as you can about the department, the institution, and the community; attend meetings; chat with colleagues for various perspectives;ask for sample syllabi of the courses you'll be teaching; and so on.

—Annie

Fortunately, over time, these teachers have found ways to reconnect with the classroom, and that's how we want to end our discussion—with the common-sense, insightful, ordinary, and inspired efforts of these teachers. Their advice challenges, reminds, and always encourages. We offer it as a survival manual for teachers who love teaching and wouldn't have it any other way.

Learn Your Priorities

Dana puts it best: "Figure out what in your pedagogy is essential and hold on to that. But also figure out what isn't that helpful, and be willing to negotiate on those parts." Ditto.

"What Are You Prepared to Do?"

That is the question Sean Connery's character asks Kevin Costner's character in *The Untouchables* as they prepare to go after Al Capone. It works when committing to a teaching life, as well, since, for some of us, creating the teaching life we want requires us to make unconventional career decisions. The model for teachers in higher education is to start out at a small place, if one has to, and publish in order to earn a position at a larger (more prestigious) school. Lateral moves are at times necessary, but pose great risks. "Downward" moves are understood as failure, little else. This model does not account for those teachers who choose the "downward" move as a way of transforming their professional lives into more valuable, satisfying lives. For Annie, the "downward" move was the best way to protect her life as a teacher:

> I think the best change I have made to improve and protect my teaching life was moving from the university setting to the community college environment. Teaching really is valued more here than at [my first job], and I think the students here expect more from me as a teacher in some ways. . . . While it was suggested I review the course plans of other teachers prior to my first quarter here, I am free (in fact encouraged) to develop my own courses, select texts, and so on. In an evaluation session with my dean today, she strongly encouraged me to find ways (next year) of sharing my content knowledge of composition with other faculty members, and working with the developmental education program to improve the prerequisite courses students take before the composition courses that are required for the associate's degree. . . . Ultimately I think if the institutions we work for do not support teaching, it's very difficult to develop strategies to maintain a focus on students and our classroom work.

Similarly, after two years at a major state institution, one of us set out to find a job at a small liberal arts college, and has never looked back.

Learn to Say No

Graduate school fueled our interests and developed our expertise not only in our areas of specialization but also in matters concerning teaching ranging from professional development to curricular development to assessment. Consequently, as we work to achieve respect for our discipline and expertise, we are also often exploited for it. As Isaac points out,

> It helps to learn the word "no" because without it you'll be asked to and will take on more and more work until you burn out. It helps to realize that many administrators believe we work only twenty hours a week and therefore one should not be disappointed when the sixty-hour workweeks aren't recognized by the school.

Step Out of the Fray

The pressure of our workloads and student loads can fragment our lives. It is easy to feel overwhelmed and exhausted, and important to understand our own sense of balance and time. For some, like Deidre, achieving that balance is as simple as adjusting to the pace of our institutions:

> I teach at night . . . the place I teach now is morning-centered, so there's much less administrative interest in the night classes. And the students are more likely to be mature, thoughtful, and involved with the work. How they remain cheerfully interested in a writing class after a full day at work and two Snickers I do not know, but many of them do.

Reimagine the Classroom

We all need to find that balance between the comfortable predictability that comes with teaching classes again and again and the need to keep our classes dynamic and ever changing. Like our respondents, we have developed new classes and approaches and have often refocused through fostering strong student relationships. We have found that often our renewed interests in the classroom lead us toward rich, productive research directions that also satisfy institutional expectations. Committed teachers, like Deidre, can find ways to reinvent their teaching and the way they see their classrooms. She explored the possibilities of a new technology as a way of gaining a different perspective on her teaching life.

> I teach on line. I am no longer a doubter when it comes to on-line instruction: it's allowed me to create a whole new teaching persona; take a different perspective for reflection, questions, and research; and collaborate with students in designing and evaluating new teaching strategies. The on-line teaching environment is very structured in many ways, and it certainly isn't as open as being a TA was. But at the same time, the on-line classroom constitutes a very different kind of space to explore, occupy, and compose; doing so challenges and excites me.

Create a Community

Community answers not only our need to belong in the midst of negotiating the politics of our institutions but also a desire for intellectual growth through examining classroom experiences with other teachers. Coming out of our graduate programs, we are used to the kinds of relationships in which we which we could freely share ideas and get counsel from those who have been through similar experiences. Many times, when we move to our professional environments, we neglect this need. Deidre remembers the importance of her graduate school community and is inspired by those memories to "foster collegiality":

> One of the most wonderful, freeing, empowering things about being a TA was the teaching community; I felt like part of a big, active brain, and also supported, encouraged, and questioned in a positive, helpful way. It was all learning-centered. So here I try to work within the writing program and with the adjuncts, of whom we have dozens. I don't feel different from them; many are my age, wonderful writers, and great teachers. We work in a hierarchical and deeply divided department, which tends to bury the excellent teaching community here. I want to counter that. Foregrounding collegiality is a selfish move for me as a teacher; it will also, I hope, make things better for others.

The community you want may not be present in your first year, but these teachers have found ways to create them, as we summarize in the following:

> *Talk to people.* Talk about books you have read, your kids, and your weekend plans. The most unlikely person can become a vital part of your teaching and learning community.
> *Cross disciplinary boundaries.* It is not only our area of study that creates common bonds. We can never know when the math or science or architecture teacher shares similar concerns about students and innovative teaching. Connections between/among disciplines are thought provoking and intellectually stimulating. Sometimes we have more in common than we realize.
> *Create opportunities to talk about teaching and exchange ideas.* This can be in the form of in-service workshops for others or through the informal teacher talk that might happen when you share an article with a colleague or discuss student papers in the department workroom.

In short, take the initiative to identify and seek out the other people who value teaching and students as much as you do—they are out there, as Isaac reminds us:

> [i]t isn't hard to find the dedicated faculty members at a new school. You already know them. They're the ones who have students hanging around their offices, who are in early and leave late, who are doing obscure departmental duties for little recognition, who take the time to show you around or ask you how your classes are going and really listen when you tell them. Seek those people out. Ask their advice. Talk about your concerns with them and what you're unsure about. Listen to the stories they tell and the history they reveal to you. And if by chance you find yourself at a place where these people don't exist or

where they are so few that they are like isolated islands, dust off that vita and move on or resign yourself to finding joy in places outside work.

I see . . . enthusiasm in many of my colleagues at my current post, people who are in some cases in their third or fourth decade of teaching. That's heartening and tells me that the initial interests that drew me to teaching in the first place, while naive and untested at the time, are really the foundation of my teaching and will carry me a long way. —Isaac

Ultimately, it is a matter of remembering that our most satisfying times in graduate school involved drawing together theory and practice and learning from our students and classroom stories. We have found, over and over again, that when the irony becomes less than amusing, when alienation colors our days, we turn to the part of our jobs that comes with the most rewards—teaching and student relationships. For our final words, we turn to Isaac who reminds us to draw from the rich, fulfilling potential of these moments:

I guess I have an overwhelming pessimism when it comes to institutional matters and an often romantic optimism in regard to my students. I've come to expect the worst from the bureaucracy that issues me a paycheck; that way I am never surprised except for the good. But with my students, it's another thing entirely. I have never had a semester or quarter in which I did not meet students who inspired my teaching and who made me want to do my best in the classroom. It is for these that I try to improve the quality of my teaching. It's been over a decade since I taught my first class, and I still feel a rush when I go into a new class for the first time and a thrill every time one of my students makes a breakthrough in her or his writing.

Teacher-Scholars

DANA C. ELDER

Those who can say their avocation is also their vocation have blessings to count. If the cost is too high, they'll say, then don't make the investment. However, as these forthright essays attest, the "cost" of being teacher-scholars continues well after the initial decision to join their ranks. As graduate teaching assistants and graduate students, we learn the ropes; yet, the ropes might be different in the actual rigging of today's professorships, and sea changes abound. They always have.

Now we have state-mandated and institutional assessment, for example, and accountability to many stakeholders. These are in addition to our traditional obligations to students, colleagues, disciplines, institutions, and regions. Fortunately, the lengthy novitiates of our profession prepare us for new challenges—even when these commutations are not specifically anticipated in our training. We know how to read, write, and think. These skills inform our lives and our teaching; they are what we do. The authors of these excellent essays show their skills in responding to the unexpected. To them I offer praise and a few cautionary remarks.

In Essay 12, Maggie misses few of the essentials in her survival-manual essay on graduate studies and teaching in our discipline. Her advice on time management is excellent. Her realistic observations about taking energy into the classroom, front loading, and staggering the paper load are accurate and perceptive. The admonition to keep students well informed is essential, to which I might add candor about course objectives and assessment criteria. We all need to make "sure to eat right and sleep enough," but this mandate remains a challenge for many. To Maggie's question "Why work harder to keep track of an irresponsible student than that student is working for you?" one could surely add, "Why spend more time responding to a student draft than the student spent writing it?"

My cautionary remark here involves "days off" and the privilege to "cancel classes." In many learning communities, these options are not condoned by local practice or state law. In many locales, assuming such authority could be a big mistake. Nonetheless, staying healthy and working smart are keenly presented in this essay.

To Dan and Paul, the authors of Essay 13, I offer praise for their acknowledgment of politics as a staple of all academic environments. Politics are always present, and ignoring or denying them can be an error. Nor are efforts to "break down divisions" among tracks "within the structure of the department" without peril, but this is important work. These men's call to respect staff, students, faculty, and others in our learning communities is exactly right, and Paul and Dan's willingness to choose when to bend and when to stand straight is wise. My only caution goes to Paul. Even when we "fight/debate fairly," there will be winners and losers. In politics, losers never forget, so fight selectively and rarely. Success in life depends on positive ongoing relatedness. Just a thought.

In Essay 14, Laura and her friends have earned unconditional accolades. Their wonderful sense of purpose and place incite envy. Their community values its members, learning for the sake of learning, surrounding themselves "with other writers," having "careers that are satisfying," and teaching because they love to teach. And they acknowledge that there are many ways to serve the greater good. That people can still see "the PhD [and learning] as a valuable end in itself" warms my mature bones, and the respect Laura shows for our colleagues who serve community colleges is more than earned. Good for you, Laura. Ditto her praise for those who share our formal training and serve in roles beyond the academic. To all, write on!

Gay Lynn, Kim, and their collaborators present in Essay 15 a candid and balanced perspective on situations junior faculty too often face. As the authors point out, this collection of scenarios constitues a cautionary tale rich in irony. Alienation, nonsupportive work environments, and second-class citizenship (a dream deferred?) are widespread. Many faculty suffer overloaded teaching schedules and nonteaching tasks that limit their time with students. The thought of being "the lone compositionist" on a campus or the "lone" anything is especially frightening. And we do need to call foul on the exploitation of any educators while recognizing the dangers of so doing. Is it unusual for teacher-scholars to find themselves "wrestling with a personal life long neglected" (and neglected still)? I think not. So this essay's stories and advisory conclusions deserve the full attention of those seeking for the first time, or still, a community of learners that offers both a job and a life. Do they exist? Yes, and they are legion. Many colleges and universities enjoy "enlightened" programs, departments, and divisions. More and more academic leadership roles are admirably filled by compositionists and those who appreciate them. Will the many challenges of academic life abate? No, but we are moving in the right direction.

Are our work and lives as literate adults meaningful and rewarding? Absolutely. Are they easy? Absolutely not. Do we love the work of teaching and writing and speaking (often, I confess, at length) and thinking, and do we serve a greater good? You bet! The contributors, editors, and publishers of this book make their voices heard and have their hearts in the right place; undeniably, they are teacher-scholars, within, without, and beside the academy.

Tips from a Traveling Composition Instructor

KATHLEEN ASHMAN

I figure I got a head start on this traveling lifestyle, since my dad was an insurance salesman and every three years he got a promotion. A promotion for Dad meant a change of scenery for me—usually somewhere in the Midwest—always a new school. Adapting to a new environment, new friends, and new school policies became an art form for me. Moving from Loves Park Elementary School in Illinois suburbia to 66th Street Elementary School, an inner-city school in Milwaukee, Wisconsin, opened my eyes to people who went to art museums, played in professional marching bands, ate kielbasa, and danced the polka. Yes, different locales, even in the same "heart of America," offered up quite a smorgasbord of culture. Each of the four new schools, in as many states, housed different course requirements, different extracurricular activities, and, of course, different fashions and friends, providing plenty of opportunities to embrace new cultures. The skills I took away from my twelve years of public education on the road proved worthwhile, because they helped me to adapt to life as a traveling composition instructor.

With a master's degree in hand, I began my teaching odyssey: full-time and part-time, in private and in public, two- and four-year colleges. I did pick up quite a few tips along the way—some of them are echoed in the many voices in this section.

Echoing Voices

Both Dan and Paul in Essay 13 discuss the need to "know" the departmental politics—to lie low, ears to the ground—before a grad student chooses a major professor and a doctorate committee, or joins departmental committees. Once the grad student jumps into the ring, how much "extra work" she or he takes on

175

should be a consideration. The same caution should be used by the part-time instructor or the new professor in the department. As Isaac points out in Essay 15,

> It helps to learn the word "no" because without it you'll be asked to and will take on more and more work until you burn out. It helps to realize that many administrators believe we work only twenty hours a week and therefore one should not be disappointed when the sixty-hour workweeks aren't recognized by the school.

From my own experience as a part-time "migrant instructor," I have often found myself saying yes to any and all people and projects. I remember well the many portfolio workshops I conducted, courses I constructed, and classes I taught for absent instructors—only to find that the department, thrilled to allow me to work twenty more hours a week, had no intention of paying me. I knew that it was free for the short term but presumed that in the long haul—when a full-time position did open up—I might seriously be considered. I wasn't.

Why should they pay me to do the work I already did for free? So, I guess the Chinese cookie fortune here is to *know your worth and expect to be paid for your expertise*—a hard lesson to learn. But after twenty years, I think I got it.

More Echoes, Different Voices

Coming back for a PhD after two decades of teaching at the postsecondary level, I felt that I was the luckiest person alive. I could be a student again, and most of the classes I took were in my field of composition and rhetoric. Discussing pedagogical theories with others as enthusiastic as myself was, as Michael says in Essay 14, "the greatest part of that PhD experience." I garnered a great deal from classroom readings and peer discussions, but the greatest epiphany—as I reflect back on it now—happened outside the classroom.

Rick Straub's Rhetoric of Fiction course required a lengthy paper which outlined and discussed rhetorical use of language in a novel of our choice. Straub wanted us to peer-respond to working drafts. Terra, a fellow TA in the composition and rhetoric program, was in my small group. While reading Terra's draft in what she would call "Terra speak," I realized that indeed this was a rough draft—very closely akin to what some might call a brainstorm. Her words charted thoughts that were loosely associated, that folded back on themselves, and that opened up to new ideas. The draft was not coherently structured. Indeed, it was a discovery draft: every third or fourth sentence opened up new ideas, jumped to new territory. After reading the draft carefully, I just stared at it for a while. I began to see patterns of thought emerging—sort of like one of those Magic Eye pictures from the mid-1990s—you stare at it for a while and finally you see the image. Terra, discovering ideas as she wrote, left an indelible trail of thought patterns for me to follow.

I learned something very valuable from that colleague. Even though I had witnessed the discovery of ideas in my own writing, I hadn't seen patterns emerge in those discoveries until Terra's brainstorm draft. The singular discovery moved me into a new realm—multiple discoveries could create visual avenues of critical thought. Since then, I have been fascinated with what I have come to call "aha" moments in writing—whether these moments reflect the writer's forgotten memories pulled up during a brainstorm, the juxtaposition of seemingly unrelated ideas that provide insight on a topic, or flights of ideas circling unknown destinations. Close reading of the last might reveal patterns—much like the ones I saw in Terra's draft. Both colleagues and students continue to supply me with "aha" moments in writing. These moments have rendered the classes I teach as much of a learning situation as the classes I've taken.

Indeed, as Dean in Essay 14 states, "Living is learning, so if you get to spend some part of your life on a campus where learning is available all over the place, what a great life opportunity!" Traveling to and working in so many different educational institutions sort of speeds up the whole learning process. Much like the lightning rod attracts the powerful bolt, experiencing different institutions, departments, cultures, and peers condenses knowledge and speeds up its delivery. There is little time to acclimate to the surroundings; total immersion—sink or swim—becomes the sole strategy for survival, especially for new teachers. Maggie Gerrity in Essay 12 talks about this "cultural immersion" she found herself in when she came to teach and take classes at a university. She compares it to the flying monkeys in *The Wizard of Oz*.

> Students want feedback to their drafts. Teachers want thesis essays, annotated bibliographies, and revisions to critical essays. Sometimes friends actually want me to leave my apartment to go somewhere other than campus.

Whether it's flailing about in deep water, gasping for air with legs kicking, or dodging hundreds of sinister black flying monkeys, the effect is the same: Learn to adapt to the "culture," to life's situations to work within them; learn to swim—even dog-paddling is better than drowning. Even gauging how and when to avoid the monkeys' attacks is better than cowering in a corner. While submerged in these circumstances, it is indeed difficult to see their worth. The "aha" moments come afterward, in the brainstorming and writing about, as well as in the close reading of, such events: in the reflections or, perhaps more important, in the shared stories of others who have immersed themselves in the varied "cultures of academia."

In Essay 14, Dean finishes his "living is learning" quote with this statement: "All I ever really wanted to know was what it takes to be happy. . . . I'm still working on it." Echoing Dean, I'm still working on it too, and sharing the lore of my experiences and listening to others' stories is part of life's learning process for me.

All Dressed Up and Nowhere to Go

GREG BEAUMONT

Each of the essays in Part III is a true story; your task is to sift your own kernel of truth from the life experiences of those who have "made" it to a terminal degree and are generously sharing their knowledge, all of it hard-earned. To be sure, much of the advice given and many of the experiences rendered do not or will not apply to you. But if you think that you will dodge all the issues presented among these essays, read them again in a year, and then again in two years, and . . . you get the picture. As an academic administrator at the school where I got my PhD, I see my own experience mirrored closely in a couple of the essays. Beyond that, however, all four essays offer continuing truths that most of those I know and respect in academe practice in order to survive, and have fun doing so. Don't be intimidated by the thought of adding teaching to the already mammoth task of earning an advanced degree. Most of all, though, as you already have read in the essays and will hear again and again, do not forget that your own education, your own degree, is paramount.

The topic in "Finding the Twenty-fifth Hour" is time management. From my perspective after six years in administration, along with usually teaching one course per semester, the topic is still time management. Maggie Gerrity suggests many time-saving strategies and tips that should get you thinking immediately of what you can do to make your life more efficient. This is doubly true if you are new both to graduate school *and* to teaching. Some of what Ms. Gerrity offers may seem obvious or only marginally incremental in benefit, but you must realize that you are hunting precious minutes that add up over the course of a semester whose deadlines arrive as quickly as they do inexorably. More to the point, however, is that this essay should prompt you to examine critically your own style of teaching and learning with an eye toward efficiency and compromise. Yes, you *will* often need to compromise many aspects of your personal and professional life, but please remember that the operative verb here is "compromise," not "sacrifice."

The temptation for all of us who love teaching is to strive to be the perfect teacher while putting everything else on hold. Academic employers often look at the transcripts of potential candidates, and a graduate record littered with "I" grades implicitly suggests that time management has been a problem. You don't want to defend your transcript; you want it to be as unassailable as possible. Remember, the person who hires you has probably taught while in graduate school—he or she knows what it takes.

In "The Art of Academic Diplomacy: How to Finesse Departmental Politics as a Grad Student" by Dan Melzer and Paul Reifenheiser, you may feel bewildered by the evident importance of politics, or perhaps even fear of the political arena into which you may be thrust as a neophyte. Relax and remember that you have a lot of peers; in a large institution there is safety in numbers, while in a smaller college you may have the benefit of closer mentoring. However, no matter the size of the institution, politics are a very real part of survival in academe. The important lesson in the essay is that you probably will be in a political environment that is not only survivable but also manageable and integral to the training of junior faculty members. In addition, both writers make it obvious that if you approach politics with good humor, you will enjoy the ride much more; this is as true in the subunits of an English department as it is in the university as a whole.

Dan Melzer makes a particularly good point about serving on departmental committees; obviously, one learns much about a department's inner workings when serving on these committees. However, don't ignore the fact that there are also numerous opportunities to serve on college or university committees. Just because a committee doesn't directly relate to your department does not mean that there is little to learn from the experience. Indeed, if your career progresses to any reasonable level of faculty status, you will be serving on outside committees. Let your major professor know of your interests; ask him or her if there are any standing committees that include graduate students. Talk with the director of graduate studies about search committees, university welfare committees, academic policy task forces, and so forth. In particular, as you read the last two essays, you will realize that there is a good chance that you may end up working in academe in a satisfying, though not traditional tenure-track, position.

I can relate particularly well to Laura Newton's dilemma in "Staying in Town: Life after the Program." As I was approaching the end of my program, my wife's career as a public high school teacher of English was approaching its zenith; she had tenure, was department chair (and was likely to remain so until she retired), and had just a little over ten years left until possible retirement. By mutual agreement, it was not unthinkable that we would pull up stakes and start over someplace else, but our first choice was to remain as close as possible to the town and the institution where we had earned our degrees. As the essay demonstrates, it is entirely possible to remain in the same town to which you have perhaps become attached during your tenure as a grad student.

One important point that the essay does not dodge is that if you stay in town you will be something other than a tenure-track faculty member at your doctorate granting institution. The "rule" against your, or anyone else's, being hired into a tenure-track position at your doctorate granting institution is, for all practical purposes, inviolable. Those who truly want permanent full-time employment in the town where they earn their doctorates actively explore the job market outside tenure-track academe. As you have read, this doesn't necessarily mean that you can't go to work for your own institution; it just means that you won't be an assistant professor in the English Department. However, the essay also contains excellent examples of those who leave town initially, almost always for perceived greener pastures, only to return in several months or a couple of years. In my own situation, I never left town but was able to transition immediately from school to employment just about a year before I was due to finish my dissertation, which, in the actual event, took two years to finish. This last point is important because if you gain employment before you finish writing, plan on that writing taking twice as long as you tell your prospective employer it will take to finish. If your prospective employer is savvy, he or she is already making this delay to degree adjustment mentally. However, don't pass jobs up just because you haven't finished your doctorate. If you have advanced to the writing stage, most employers in a university town will work with you, especially during those anxious days that surround submission and defense. After all, it is in any employer's best interest to have well-educated employees.

In "Surviving Alienation: How Junior Faculty Reconnected with the Classroom and Why They Needed To" by Gay Lynn Crossley and Kim Haimes-Korn, we are reminded that we teach because it is at the bottom of who we are. It has been said countless times, but if you don't feel a "calling" to teach, you probably should not. It can be officially thankless, will have mediocre pay and benefits at best, and can be absolutely overwhelming in what it demands. Take heart, for if you have the calling, the sheer joy of teaching, of reaching and helping people to know more about themselves and their universe, is endlessly rewarding. However, the other side of this truth is that not all who teach necessarily feel called to it. Such may be your own experience. I have known many TAs who absolutely hated to teach and did it just to get the fee waiver and some financial assistance. (Indeed, it is obvious to me as an administrator at a large university that there are some teachers who would be better off in another line of work.) While the important point of the essay is that connectivity with the classroom and peer teachers is what inspires the dedicated teacher, implicit in all this is that you love to teach, that teaching is a part of your very essence.

As I said in the opening, the essays in this section may seem remote right now; give them the opportunity to come closer as you grow as a teacher and a student. I hope that you take advantage of the experiences generously shared by those who may be sadder but wiser, happier but wiser, or, most often, somewhere in between.

RESPONSE

Stepping into the Minefield: Employment in and beyond the Classroom

RESA CRANE BIZZARO

A few years ago, I saw a poster that expressed some basic wisdom from Robert Fulghum's *All the Things I Really Needed to Know I Learned in Kindergarten*. The poster was a list of seemingly simple statements, including "Share Everything," "Play Fair," "Don't Hit People," and "Be Aware of Wonder." Much of that wisdom is repeated in essays included in Part III: Beyond the Classroom, although it emerges in slightly different language. In addition, I can see from these essays how much all teachers of writing over the past two hundred or more years have in common.

While all the essays here remind us of Fulghum's directive to "live a balanced life," Maggie Gerrity offers some specific advice for how to achieve that balance. Her time-saving tips have allowed her a "personal twenty-fifth hour" in a world where tasks can be overwhelming. Her strategies may prove invaluable to people entering the profession, whether they are graduate students, instructors, or assistant professors. And this advice transcends disciplines; teaching writing is not the only profession in which students and faculty feel overwhelmed by their responsibilities. Some of Gerrity's best advice is directed toward managing the workload of teaching, including staggering due dates for assignments and organizing work so that teachers can be more flexible at the most stressful point in the semester: the end. Gerrity recommends establishing an eight-to-five routine every day because this kind of schedule allows teachers to maintain social lives alongside their professional ones.

Dan Melzer and Paul Reifenheiser offer important advice about the politics of academia. Their insights might be added to those of Fulghum's book, and these observations are equally applicable to graduate students and faculty members. Melzer and Reifenheiser note the difficulty of staying out of political situations.

Students should take time to learn the culture of their departments; this knowledge allows them to avoid the "land mines" of academia. The authors' best observations include paying attention to relationships, respecting your peers, *never* disparaging others, treating everyone well, and considering individuals and their situations individually. The examples provided elaborate upon situations that most of us have encountered in some fashion as part of our experience in graduate school. These lessons are important across all disciplines and—in fact—in all aspects of the working world. While the primary focus in this book is on English departments in postsecondary education, I find that Melzer and Reifenheiser's advice applies equally well to employees in most every field of work.

The authors also encourage graduate students to become involved in departmental activities—not simply to use such experiences as lines on their vita but also to provide useful exposure to the "workings" of academic departments. While professional experience may be the primary goal, the added opportunity may exist to participate in developing courses, choosing textbooks, and modifying policies—all of which allow graduate students to participate in permanent change within the institution. These opportunities also teach professional diplomacy, what Fulghum calls "play[ing] fair."

Laura Newton discusses nonacademic employment opportunities for students. As we all witness the shrinking employment options at universities, we must be broad-minded enough to encourage graduate students to enter other professions, which may be equally satisfying and financially rewarding. Newton offers several examples of people who work in situations which provide alternatives to traditional, tenure-track positions. While these types of jobs pose their own challenges, they may be rewarding in their own right.

Gay Lynn Crossley and Kim Haimes-Korn's essay reminds me of the age-old conflict between composition and literature. For over a century composition has been thought to have little or no subject matter. This perception of composition as subjectless developed into a marginalization of composition teachers. Over the past two centuries, many compositionists have internalized a sense of inadequacy, which contributed to their feelings of alienation from their colleagues, students, and profession. Crossley and Haimes-Korn emphasize how many who enter the field of composition continue to feel these emotions. For some academics, these feelings of isolation are so extreme that they leave the profession. Others manage to create communities of support networks, learn to say no to unreasonable demands, and avoid becoming embroiled in conflicts that are not their own (that is, to choose battles wisely). These skills are all *absolutely necessary* in every profession, and—in particular—in academia.

Finally, I see commonalities among all the essays—ones that might appear on Fulghum's poster. Their wisdom includes maintaining a sense of humor and humanity; being honest with yourself and students; loving your work; working hard *and* playing hard; and sharing everything—the bad and the good—with the community you've built around you. All the authors note that graduate students should seek to understand, as fully as possible, the demands that will be placed upon them when they graduate, particularly if they enter the academic world of work. These are lessons from which everyone can benefit.

Some people may think it is discouraging to realize that these essays could have been written twenty, forty, or even a hundred years ago. Rather than suggesting that the academic institution should change, I believe that individuals in the institution must change. These are ongoing *human* issues that have been well documented over time; accepting responsibility for changing these problems can set us on the path to resolving them. Only our efforts to eliminate the human problems will allow the institution to progress. The authors here have identified several problems and potential solutions; it's up to us now to attempt to implement them.

Work Cited

Fulghum, Robert. *All I Needed to Know I Learned in Kindergarten: Uncommon Thoughts on Common Things*. New York: Villard, 1988.

RESPONSE

On Advice beyond "Being Smart and Working Hard"

DOUGLAS HESSE

As if their new careers needed any more complexity, graduate students and fledgling teachers should appreciate how the essays in this section sketch professional challenges that may be surprising: the interactions between studies and teaching, between professors and graduate students, between careers that the academy would have us make and the ones we make ourselves, between professorial life as we dream it and life as it is. At least, the issues surprised me early in my career, and even twenty years later, they still have some force. I first read these essays at the same time I was reading Richard Preston's *The Demon in the Freezer*, a frightening book about engineering smallpox strains resistant to vaccinations. While I'm pessimistic that any amount of foreknowledge can inoculate graduate students against certain lessons learnable only through experience, the wisdom in these four pieces can mitigate a too-harsh onset.

Maggie Gerrity's suggestions for managing time strike me as absolutely sensible—which is different from saying that they are easily doable, at least in my own experience. You would think that having taught for twenty years would by now have certified me as a time-management genius, but just yesterday, a Sunday, I spent nine hours responding to lengthy papers for a graduate seminar, papers I couldn't in good conscience keep yet another day. The good news is that I'm better at this now than when I began teaching. The bad news is that an active career teaching writing means that the number of opportunities that pull for your time and attention only increase. And, of course, this is partly good news, too. It's hard to stagnate in a job when so much is going on.

The most important piece of general advice that Gerrity provides new teachers is to "treat graduate school as a full-time job." Especially for graduate assistants straight from undergraduate degrees, this requires a tough change in perspective, although I'll say that even folks coming from the world of full-time work can be seduced by the apparent freedoms of graduate school. Gerrity recommends keeping a set routine. Routines work for some people and don't for others, but you should at least keep in mind that the graduate student/teaching assistant combination is a fifty- to sixty-hour-per-week job. Routine or not, reflect at least weekly on how efficiently you're accomplishing your work. When teaching and scholarship become so overwhelming that you don't have time for relationships or relaxation, take this as a warning sign. Recognize that you need to set parameters. Gerrity offers plenty of reasonable strategies for doing so.

At the heart of Dan Melzer and Paul Reifenheiser's essay on departmental politics is the hybrid status of graduate students, especially if they're teaching. Because you're teaching, you're a colleague, yes, but however egalitarian we'd like to imagine academic departments, you're not an equal. Many factors contribute to this inequity—some good, some bad—but the most important is that you're renting intellectual space for a fixed term in a department where faculty consider themselves property owners.

Melzer and Reifenheiser unveil troubling secrets of departmental life, including the most troubling one: professors don't necessarily all get along with one another, and this may have consequences for their graduate students. Certainly when it comes time to set up exam or dissertation committees, it makes sense to foresee possible conflicts. Yet the good news, at least in my experience, is that faculty generally put aside differences when it comes to working with graduate students in such situations, just as a troubled marriage may hang together for the sake of the children. Faculty save most of their differences (and these can range from petty to justifiably profound) for situations where it most matters: hiring, tenure and promotion, merit evaluations, and the curriculum.

The blunt—almost shameful—problem, then, is how to act around professors. Be the best scholar you can. Come to class prepared, write well, attend lectures and readings, and so on. Whether it should or not, your seriousness as a student shapes almost every response you'll receive. Professors like to work with students they believe can work independently, students who will finish and leave to get good jobs. Most of us work very diligently with students who show these efforts. We do somewhat less so with the merely convivial, eager-to-please student who seems to spend more time schmoozing than reading and writing—including on the department Listserv, which is not very often a friend. Finally, you need to take your cue from faculty themselves. As Melzer and Reifenheiser point out, professors can vary a good deal on intimacy issues; you need to follow their lead, with one caveat: the relationship must be a professional one. You (and they) need to find drinking buddies and sex partners elsewhere, which is not to say don't forsake all social occasions, even ones that happen in bars, but rather to say that crossing certain lines can easily create all sorts of problems for you.

As for departmental service, be judicious. I've seen too many graduate students spread themselves thin joining committees and ad hoc efforts, racking up lots of experience at the possible expense of their teaching and scholarship. You ought to do some, but a little bit of service work goes a long way on the job market. This is even true of important positions, such as that of program assistant for freshman composition. Remember that you are traveling through the department, not homesteading it, and while you want to leave it a better place and leave your-self a better person, your goal is to leave.

Or maybe not. At least, that's the import of Laura Newton's clutch of tales from those who chose not to move into tenure-track markets away from people and places they love. Lots of conference coffee chatter over the years convinces me that this kind of decision is more common—or more visible—than it was years ago, when graduates took a tenure-line job no matter where. Probably this is a sign of our profession's better health, a realization that life is not the job, however much the field presses that expectation. I agree with Candace's observation that "how academe defines success can be damaging." Surely the only honorable outcome of a terminal degree cannot be tenure.

And yet part of me whispers "caution." Newton observes that all the tellers "have professional positions, good salaries, and benefits." But there is the troubling voice of Karen, struggling with regret at lost opportunities, with shame and anger, and PhD programs everywhere have people like Karen, whom I respect and about whom I worry.

With the exception of programs in professional writing (technical or cre-ative), doctoral programs prepare people for careers as university professors. If you end, by accident or design, outside this trajectory, just recognize that you have to be your own agent in a discourse not set up to help you, just as medical school is not set up to find professional situations for people who decide not to practice med-icine. The only wisdom I can offer is that you have to be intentional about your decisions—to stay in school, to leave, to apply far and wide, to stay near home, to rut yourself in the tenure track, to strike a wholly different path. Newton has col-lected stories from people who have made good decisions, and I take consolation in them. But there is Karen.

Still, alienation doesn't plague only those who abjure tenured life, as Gay Lynn Crossley and Kim Haimes-Korn eloquently illustrate. When I landed my first tenure-line job, I thought life was set. While pretty realistic about tenure and pro-motion, I did imagine professorial life as relatively easier than graduate-student life. I'm here to tell you that it isn't, notwithstanding the undeniable advantages of some certainty, some status, a real income. A teaching career has more demanding facets than most people imagine, the complex of teaching, research, and service inter-acting epoxylike to fill more space and time than any of them alone. Like Crossley and Haimes-Korn's six colleagues, I felt the pull away from students and, even, away from some writing projects that most attracted me.

One compensation for all these complexities is a network of professional colleagues who become friends, who invite you to read engaging work about pro-fessional life and to contribute such work yourself, as in these essays. That's no small solace.

RESPONSE TO THE COLLECTION AS A WHOLE

Realistic Idealism

IRWIN WEISER

I've chosen to title this response "Realistic Idealism" because I think the fifteen essays that make up this collection offer a wonderful blend of thoughtful, critical reflections on becoming a teacher-scholar and pursuing a PhD while maintaining a tempered idealism about the work of teacher-scholars that is so vital to anyone's success in academia. We must be realistic about the social, economic, political, and personal aspects of graduate school, postsecondary teaching, the academic job market, but we must also hold on to those ideals that have led us to choose to spend our careers teaching and learning and reading and writing.

As I read these essays and the responses to them, I found myself thinking about them in four ways, each reflective of a particular aspect of my own career. I read and thought about them as a former TA, finding my own way into the classroom and profession; as a person who has continued to think of myself first as a teacher; as a mentor of new teachers of writing; and as a writing-program administrator (WPA). What follows are reflections from each of those four perspectives.

Finding My Way into Teaching

In the first week of the second semester of the 1972–73 academic year, a faculty member stopped me in the hall to tell me there was an opening for a teaching assistant and asked if I was interested. I'd begun my MA program without support from the university, mostly, I think, because I was so naïve about how graduate school worked that I didn't realize I should apply for an assistantship. So I jumped at the opportunity to get into the classroom, to get a fee waiver, and to earn some money.

"Sure! When do I start?"

"In about an hour. I'll take you to the class and introduce you."

There are two good things I can say about that situation. First, I didn't have time to be anxious about meeting my first class. Second, I don't think I did any harm to the students I taught that semester (and I hope that's held true over the past thirty years). The course I taught was a combined literature/composition class, with a faculty member lecturing and TAs leading discussion sections, assigning writing, and reading and evaluating that writing. The TAs and the faculty member met before each paper assignment and discussed what we thought we'd assign and what we expected from students, but basically we were on our own.

For the following year, I was assigned to teach my own section of composition. At that time, few universities provided new teaching assistants with the "boot camp" experience that the authors of this collection describe. In my program, we learned by lore and by talking with more experienced TAs. There was a director of composition, but (perhaps because I was more or less thrust into a teaching assistantship in the middle of a year) I didn't really know what my relationship with him was or when I was supposed to consult with him. Instead, I talked to people who'd been savvy enough to apply for assistantships when they applied to graduate school, and borrowed syllabi and got ideas for textbooks. In August, I began teaching my first class, and I did exactly what Fadi Al-Issa describes doing in Essay 4: I got to the room early, and I sat at a "student" desk and watched and listened and chatted as students came in. Then I got up and introduced myself and told them I was their teacher and passed out the syllabus and off we went.

I wonder how many new teachers do this. I wonder if we understand why we do it. Al-Issa writes that this was his way to overcome nervousness, to make himself and his students feel more at ease, and to break down "that hierarchy of teacher-student." I think that's right—but I don't think it's the whole story. For Al-Issa and for other international teaching assistants, that feeling at ease and helping students feel at ease is particularly critical, but for all new teachers, particularly for new TAs who are not much older than their students, there's a desire to relate to our students as peers, not as authorities. In fact, as many of the authors explain—and describe so effectively—becoming a teacher means developing both a teaching philosophy and a teaching identity, what Kate Brown calls "a constant series of adjustments." Our teaching identities, as we learn from Brown and from all the other authors in this collection, are reflections both of how we choose to represent ourselves and of how our students see us. Sometimes, we have choices—to be out or closeted, Rita Mae Reese and Brandy Wilson and Jay Szczepanski remind us, is an issue that GLBT teachers address. Our politics, too, can be either out or closeted—how directly do we want our classes to be sites of political and ideological discussions? How much about our own views do we want to make clear to our students? There are some features of identity that teachers can't help but reveal: their race, gender, nationality, ethnicity, size, approximate age, pregnancy are visible aspects of their identities that affect how students see them from the very first minute they walk into a classroom—the "Oh! No" syndrome that Pavel Zemliansky and Hsi-Ling Huang write about. (And of course, there's the less obvious "Oh! Yes" response, which is sometimes an unstated response to the familiar or, as Kristi Marie Steinmetz's student Jeremy more blatantly asserts, "I never thought a college English teacher could be so hot.") And what teachers do, particularly when the response is not to the familiar, is decide how to address those aspects of their identity and of their personality that affect their interactions with students.

Still Teaching, Still Learning

It's been a very long time since those first classes I taught as a teaching assistant, but I know that I'm still experiencing the "constant series of adjustments" Kate Brown writes about. So as a teacher, I found myself learning from the authors as they described their decisions about what to teach and how to teach it and how to interact with students. I'm reminded, in particular, that as a teacher—particularly, perhaps as a white male with children as old as many of the graduate students I teach and mentor and whose dissertations I direct—I'm an authority. Yes, I have an informal manner; yes, I'm comfortable with graduate students calling me by the nickname I've gone by since I was an infant; yes, we joke and banter. But as Carlyn Maddox, Jay Szczepanski, and Edward Tarkington explain, there's always the line between the personal and the professional, and it's a line we need to be mindful of for a variety of reasons. Ultimately, we evaluate students, and we can't let our personal feelings for them—whether we like them or not, whether they're fun and smart and interesting or whether they're annoying or boring or pests—affect how we work with them as students, how we counsel and advise them and teach them.

Other essays in this collection challenge me to think about my own professional values. I've been a faculty member at a Research I University for over twenty years and inevitably have developed a set of values and prejudices about the profession and about what people with PhD's should aspire to. Kenya Thompkins's and Laura Newton's essays remind me, as do the annual experiences of graduate students at Purdue on the job market, and as should my reflections on my own professional life, not only that each of us needs to recognize our interests and goals, but also that as their teachers, we need to value the choices students make as well as be sensitive to what Michael, in Laura Newton's essay, "Staying in Town," calls the "true gritty realism" of the job market. I began my career as an adjunct, then accepted a non-tenure-track assistant professorship, then a tenure-track position at a place that I should have recognized as a bad fit (my reluctance to throw away the packing boxes should have been a clue), and then moved to Purdue. My family and I moved four times in six years. The people who stayed in town—or left and came back—made decisions that were different from mine. So do the graduate students I work with who know that they want to be at small college or at a comprehensive university where their primary responsibility will be to teach. As a faculty member and advisor, my responsibility is to support students in these decisions, to avoid implying that everyone's goal should be to teach in a PhD-granting university, and to remember always that not only is this not everyone's goal, it's also not a possible goal for everyone who wants it.

Newton's essay, as well as the other essays in Part III, reminds me that graduate students' lives are complex; their reasons for being in school are varied; their goals differ not only from one another's but also from ours. These authors remind us, their teachers, that we have to honor their decisions to change their minds, to leave the program, to seek other goals. The lesson holds true for new teachers as well: the students in our classes, especially in our required first-year composition classes, are in school for reasons that are often very different from ours, and we will struggle—and sometimes fail—to reach all of them. Carlyn Maddox finds a way to inspire her Marching Chiefs trumpeter, but we're not always going to be so successful. We can, however, learn from our failures, even the difficult conflicts such as dishonest students that Amy Hodges writes about.

Reading and Learning as a Mentor

Almost every year since I've been at Purdue, I've been a mentor for new teaching assistants. It's an enormously rewarding kind of teaching, because it allows me to support people who are learning to teach, to indirectly support the students they are teaching, and to learn from the talented and creative and smart teaching assistants who bring their own ideas and experiences to teaching. Reading the essays in this collection has been an extension of that learning, offering me new insights and new ideas about how to support and teach and advise new teachers of writing.

For example, in "When You Look and Sound 'Un-American': Advice for Foreign-Born Teachers of Writing," Zemliansky, Al-Issa, Huang, and Raja offer advice for mentors (and WPAs) that is increasingly important as the number of international students coming to study as both graduate students and undergraduates increases. We need to be attuned to the special challenges foreign-born teachers face when they're asked to teach writing to native speakers of English, and we need to be prepared to suggest the strategies that these authors offer us: to be prepared to talk with students about their previous studies of English and how those studies have provided them with a kind of detailed understanding of the language that native speakers take for granted; to be prepared for students who nevertheless mistrust them; to recognize that their foreignness and lack of experience in the US educational system may be taken by students as an opportunity to get away with things they might not try with an American teacher; and so on. As Hsi-Ling Huang and Juli Hong both point out, being foreign, being a woman, being young, being small each can be a disadvantage for a teacher, and being all or several of these is particularly difficult. Many international teaching assistants come from cultures where a teacher's authority is taken for granted, so the readiness of American students to challenge them or resist them can be quite a shock. And cultural differences that are not indications of disrespect can be interpreted as such: wearing caps in class, speaking without being called on, joking with the teacher or calling her by her first name. As mentors, we need to be ready to talk with international teaching assistants about these issues, and with all new teachers about the more broadly applicable issues of authority that age, gender, race, or nationality can bring about.

As mentors (and WPAs) we should also realize that experienced teachers, whether they are experienced in the United States or in other countries, have much to offer us and the other teaching assistants in our programs. I found it interesting to learn that some experienced teachers are excused from "boot camp" as an acknowledgment of their previous experience, since at Purdue, every new teaching assistant, regardless of her or his prior teaching experience, participates in the same orientation and mentoring program during their first year as a TA. Our intention, though I'm sure to some experienced TAs it appears that we're interested in indoctrinating them in "our way" of doing things or devaluing their experience, is to help create a teaching community, one in which experienced and new teachers learn from one another. The authors of all of the first four essays of this collection talk about this kind of learning, and what I think is important for those of us who mentor or direct writing programs to keep in mind is that we can do a lot to create an environment that takes advantage of what people bring with them to our programs.

Mentors (and WPAs) also need to be aware that our experiences, as teachers and as observers of teaching and learning, have shaped our reactions to a variety of teaching situations and thus the way we would respond to them, but that our responses and the advice we might give new teachers may not work for them. A number of the essays in this collection serve as examples. As a mentor and WPA, I have advised teaching assistants to recognize that they are not counselors or therapists and that they need to be cautious in advising students about personal matters. I, and other mentors in our program, generally give teaching assistants advice about how to direct students to the appropriate campus resources—the counseling center at psychological services, the adaptive learning program, the office of the dean of students, and so on. But Jay Szczepanski tells us that not only is he comfortable counseling gay students, he in fact feels obligated to do so. What Jay reminds us, quite explicitly, is that teachers need to know their own comfort zone, where to draw the line between the personal and the professional, when and how much to listen to and to offer advice about.

Rita Mae Reese and Brandy Wilson, Kristi Marie Steinmetz, Amy Hodges, and Edward Tarkington also offer these reminders. For Reese and Wilson, as for Szczepanski, the comfort zone concerns their own sexual identity. For Tarkington, it's how to address the "frankness regarding their private lives—especially related to sex and sexuality" in students' writing and conversation and behavior, and how to address the very real fact that students and teachers can be attracted to one another. For Steinmetz and Hodges, the comfort zone has to do with how to work with difficult students. Steinmetz, for example, makes decisions about how much time and space she'll give difficult students to come around, and from my perspective, following the advice of her program director, she gives Jeremy more latitude than he deserves. But things work out.

I'd probably have reacted differently than Steinmetz's program director, probably would have called the Dean of Students, probably would have been concerned about Jeremy's inappropriate behavior and the safety of the instructor, and would have erred on the side of caution. Jeremy, it seems clear to me, is harassing his teacher. She doesn't have to put up with harassment. But Steinmetz, guided by good advice from her supervisor, is able to recognize her own comfort zone and is able to deal with Jeremy and to learn from that experience and apply that learning when she finds Dennis in her next class. Why was Steinmetz able to handle these students? She suggests that it helped to be from New Jersey and to have two brothers—she knew how to be tough and to deal with difficult people.

She knew what kind of behavior she was comfortable with. But not every person has the same comfort zone, and not every Jeremy turns out to be harmless. TAs, mentors, WPAs—we all need to be aware that every situation can be responded to in a number of ways, and that the right response for one person is not the right response for everyone. The essays in Part II have all helped me, as a mentor and WPA, recognize the importance of tempering counsel with an acknowledgment of helping new teachers find their comfort zones. I'll be reminding myself to ask the question "How would you like to address this?"

The WPA Perspective

As the number of times the acronym WPA appeared in the previous section suggests, I often can't separate my mentoring and my administrative experiences. Being a mentor has made me a better administrator; being an administrator has made me a better mentor. Both have benefited from my own classroom experiences and have shaped them as well. So I'll acknowledge the leakiness of these categories and offer some reflections that I think are more or less administrative. The authors of the preceding fifteen essays have provided readers with rich and varied insights and perspectives on what it means to become a writing teacher at the postsecondary level, to join an academic culture that can best be understood as made up of a variety of subcultures and contexts and individuals. Writing-program administrators, like other university administrators, sometimes take these subcultures and contexts for granted. We forget that we've had to learn them and that the learning curve can be steep. Several of the essays in this collection address these issues directly; all of them address them in one way or another.

Kenya Thompkins, Edward Tarkington, Maggie Gerrity, Dan Melzer and Paul Reifenheiser, and Gay Lynn Crossley and Kim Haimes-Korn place the institution at the center of their essays. Thompkins emphasizes the importance of learning about and adjusting to a new institutional culture and its assumptions and reminds readers that institutions are highly political. All of us—TA, staff member, tenured faculty member, or administrator—shape and are shaped by the institution and are players with more or less power in its politics. This is an important lesson for new graduate students and TAs, who may think they've come to graduate school to learn to be better scholars, writers, or teachers and will soon realize that they are also players in the institution in a way that's different from what they experienced as undergraduate students. They are, as Melzer and Reifenheiser point out, always in the position of negotiating their multiple roles of teacher/student/employee, sometimes able to contribute to major change, and sometimes affected, often in significant ways, by changes they have no control over. And these multiple roles, as Maggie Gerrity suggests, demand that TAs/graduate students become effective time managers. That means not just finding the twenty-fifth hour or putting oneself on an 8:00–5:00 schedule but also recognizing that one's time is not always one's own (something Doug Hesse emphasizes in his response to the essays in Part III) and can't always be managed.

Tarkington, as I mentioned earlier, addresses in a sensitive and sensible essay, issues of responsibility and professional behavior, particularly as it involves the complex matters of sexual attraction and romance between instructors and students and the hazards that the closeness of teaching, especially teaching writing, presents. His essay elaborates on the advice most WPAs provide: "When in doubt, don't." When we say that, we mean all the things Tarkington addresses: Be mindful that it's flattering to have students like you, find you attractive, flirt with you. Be mindful that you may be attracted to students as well. But be mindful that as a teacher you have a particular responsibility because you have both influence and power over students. When you have the authority to evaluate a student, you can't have an appropriate romantic or sexual relationship with her or him because the differences in power render the relationship inappropriate. As Tarkington points out, such relationships do take place; we all know of them. Some work. Some don't. But life is long and semesters are short, and relationships need to wait.

Crossley and Haimes-Korn and the faculty members whose experiences they include in their essay provide one more important lesson about institutional life: the lessons one learns in graduate school don't always prepare one for what comes next. In many ways, Parts I and III of this collection, and Thompkins's first essay and Crossley and Haimes-Korn's final one, are mirrors. They remind new teachers, experienced teachers, mentors, and administrators of the importance of understanding and adjusting to new cultures, whether those be cultures of graduate school or faculty positions or administrative jobs. The adjustments can be—will be—challenging, but they can be—and will often be—rewarding.

And Finally

In some ways, even a fairly informal response to the essays of this collection seems unnecessary. Each essay invites readers to reflect, to question, to take issue, to learn, to make decisions about how to become a teacher, how to respond to the complexities of being a TA, how to develop one's own professional identity. While the essays speak most directly to relatively new teachers of writing, this experienced teacher/mentor/WPA has learned from each. The collective wisdom of these essays urges us all to think about who we are when we enter the classroom, what responsibilities we have to our profession, to our students, and to ourselves. The authors tell it as they've experienced it, and the experience isn't always pretty. In fact, each author has given us insights into the challenges he or she has faced in becoming a teacher—challenges of authority, of failure, of disappointment, of frustration—and in doing so each author has helped us understand that the rewards of teaching come hard. But they come. And that's why each semester we go back into the classroom with renewed enthusiasm and joy.

RESPONSE TO THE COLLECTION AS A WHOLE

The Character of a Teacher

ROXANNE MOUNTFORD

> *The dumb demon is not merely our fear of the audience—the teacher, the class, the congregation, the faculty meeting; it is our deep and accurate knowledge that to speak is to commit, to assert, to assume the outrageous authority of a self, to announce to the world, "I am here."*
> —Gail B. Griffin, *Calling: Essays on Teaching in the Mother Tongue*

Who should I be in the classroom? How should I act? The reflections by beginning and experienced teachers that appear here remind us that, fundamentally, teaching is a material act of bodies acting with other bodies in space. And these spaces are written over with a history that accompanies each gesture the teacher makes. As a rhetorician, I've thought about these two questions in a different location with another set of "newcomers": churches in which a woman is the first of her gender to stand before a congregation and lead. The disadvantages of age, height, ethnicity, race, sexual orientation, and gender cited by the authors in this volume are problems also faced by ministers. The struggle over how to be in order to respond to an audience's deeply socialized reactions to visual cues (like bearing Asian features and being under five feet tall) are struggles shared by all speakers who must also lead.

The traditional caretakers of teachers of writing, scholars in rhetoric and composition are accustomed to separating their twin fields. But because teaching is fundamentally an act of oral and visual performance, it seems appropriate to bring rhetoric into this discussion as a way to expose the nature of the questions being asked and answered in the volume. What I argue is that new teachers are fundamentally interested in the question of character, which must always be *performed* in order to be earned. For an audience of students or congregants, it is not enough to be a good person; to be thought of as a good person by the audience, one must *appear* to be good. Such questions of performance have always been addressed by the rhetorical canon of delivery, which has largely been abandoned by our field.

As a 22-year-old woman newly graduated from a small college, I faced my first semester of teaching English 110 at Ohio State University with some of the same angst that is articulated so well in these essays. I anticipated that I would be younger than a number of my students (and I was), and I feared that they would learn all too quickly that I knew little about the teaching of writing. I was fortunate to be admitted to a university with an outstanding TA training program. But while the program helped me understand what to do, it did not answer the questions, who should I be? and how should I act? (I was so young that my colleague and friend Patricia Sullivan later remarked that I appeared to be about twelve years old.)

Youth has been a problem for orators for thousands of years. George Campbell and other rhetoricians encouraged young men never to apologize for their youth, for they only lost credibility in the eyes of their audience. Wise advice, perhaps, for young men whose social status as white men of the middle or upper classes, educated at universities, was mostly secure. But suppose you have other liabilities, such as gender, or ethnicity, or a strong accent? What then? And suppose you have several in combination, as some of the writers in this volume do? The audience is thinking about what sort of character you are, and as we see in Part II, the expectations aren't always flattering.

I wanted to snuggle up to the patches-on-the-sleeve, serious, kindly white male professor image, because at base it signified a character type with the confidence I lacked. So on Day One I put on a blue blazer, gray corduroy skirt (below the knee), and blue pumps. In one hand I carried a hard-sided briefcase my parents gave me as a graduation gift, and in the other hand I carried a diet Coke (the only prop in my performance that I actually needed). I dropped the props on the table and then turned to write my name on the board, speaking in as deep a voice as I could without sounding ridiculous. No need for the bra with molded cups— my body was as hidden as possible under layers of suit. But when I found I could speak without trembling and teach without falling down, I loosened up. I tossed in a self-deprecating joke. Students laughed. I talked to the back row. They responded. Though I had arrived at graduate school without a clear sense of what I wanted to do, within the first term I taught, I fell in love with the performance of teaching. It took a few terms, but eventually I perfected my character: young woman, confident, optimistic, tough, funny, and a motivator.

To teach, one must find one's character, and to find one's character is ultimately about delivery and rhetorical performance. Since ancient times, speakers have worked carefully on their appearance, their gestures, and their mannerisms, and fretted over those features they could not control. In preaching manuals (often still focused primarily on men), one finds occasional references to seminarians' anxieties over having feminine features, such as a higher-pitched voice. In fields that presume that familiar, deep-voiced, tall, kindly male speaker (like preaching), speakers without these features worry that their audience will infer that they lack the appropriate skills and necessary character to perform their task. After all, audiences rely strongly on character types (e.g., older, tweedy male for college teacher).

But the good news is that rhetoricians since Aristotle have considered the performance of character (understood as *ethos*) to be a skill that one performs and that has much more to do with excellent delivery than with innate physical traits. One rhetorician who wrote about delivery in the nineteenth century argued that, in fact, a speech could not be separated from its performance: the delivery of the speech is the speech act itself. So while having patches on one's sleeves, white hair, and masculine bearing may be helpful for convincing a class that one is in control and intellectually competent (that one is, in fact, "a professor"), what is more important is to perform "control" and "intellectual competence" through one's teaching. Aristotle argued that speakers must seem to embody the attitude they hoped to engender in the audience. A speaker who hoped to move a crowd to action against a perceived wrong would need to seem angry about it himself. Because orators must embody a range of emotions to win over their audiences, rhetoricians have long recognized that acting and speaking are, perhaps, the same skill in different guises. Teaching is theater, production, performance—and it is an art that can be learned.

Actors always draw on perceived cultural stereotypes of certain kinds of people: how they act, what they look like, how they sound, what they wear. Likewise, when in the course of a speech an orator stops to quote someone, often she will "mimic" that person's gestures, facial expressions, and voice. Called *ethopoiia* by ancient rhetoricians, this method draws on the same skills that actors use to momentarily "embody" a character. But as some rhetoricians have argued, *ethopoiia* is in miniature what delivery is on the whole: that is, a presentation of the self in appropriate character. No matter how marked an orator's *particular* body is by physical features inconsistent with the role she is supposed to be playing, she still has options open to her. The body in motion creates new realities. Orators can use eye contact to establish their connection with individuals in the audience. They can step down from the podium and walk up the aisle to establish intimacy. They imitate a favorite gesture or manner of speaking of an orator they admire. Most important, they can project confidence they do not feel through a strong voice, a smile, and smooth, deliberate movements.[1]

In a culture that prizes "finding oneself," with self-help books designed for this purpose taking up huge sections of every bookstore, the idea of "acting out" or "performing" good character takes on the pejorative sense of, well, so much "rhetoric." Indeed, many of us were told to "just be yourself" when up in front of our new class of students. Behind this invocation is the romantic notion of the "true" self, which has been thoroughly critiqued in literary and rhetorical theory. If it were possible to rely on the idea of "just being yourself" in order to be a successful teacher, surely this book would be unnecessary.

---

[1] For further information about delivery, I recommend Reynolds's *Rhetorical Memory and Delivery: Classical Concepts for Contemporary Composition and Communication*; Crowley and Hawhee's *Ancient Rhetorics for Contemporary Students*; and Mountford's *The Gendered Pulpit: Preaching in American Protestant Spaces*.

The question, who should I be in the classroom? suggests that being a good teacher is all about creating a character in whom one's students have confidence. It is not a question of identity. In the end it is a question of where to stand, how to move without falling down, and how to look students in the eye, as well as how to present the writing task to inexperienced writers, how to honor students for their efforts, and how to set boundaries so that learning can prosper without distraction. I think of Carlyn C. Maddox's story of Mr. B, a teacher whose "excitement [for writing] was [so] contagious," that "it hasn't left [her] yet." I think of Juli Hong's wise undergraduate sister who advised, "'[D]on't think about students liking you, but about the teaching.'"

In the latter part of graduate school, I served in the Center for Teaching Excellence as a universitywide consultant for faculty and TAs. Among several other jobs I performed, one was to observe the classes of faculty (particularly assistant professors) who were receiving negative student evaluations for their teaching and to help them find ways to improve. One particular day, I found myself in the back of a class of fifty students, listening to a scientist give a lecture. This thirty-something professor sat on a tall stool reading from notes resting on a lectern. Behind him was the outline of his notes, meticulously chalked onto six blackboards, obviously written there before class, which he repeated in his lecture. Professor X said three times in his fifty-minute lecture that he was a graduate of Harvard. He held his chin high in the air when speaking, rarely appeared to look his students in the eye, and never moved from his stool—for fifty minutes. If one were to play the role of the arrogant professor, out of touch with students, one could not have given a better performance. In their evaluations, his students wrote, "Professor X does not respect his students," and "Professor X thinks the only good ideas come from Harvard." Professor X was baffled. My advice? Give a better performance: get off the stool and move, make eye contact, and drop the Harvard pretense. I didn't say, "Respect your students more." He insisted that he *did* respect his students. Instead I said, "*Act* like you do."

At the end of my first term of teaching, my students and I were working on persuasive writing. I was teaching them about various appeals they could employ to win over an audience, so I asked them to act out scenarios in which they put these appeals into practice. Two of my younger male students paired up for the exercise. One strode in through the classroom door wearing a blue blazer and gray corduroy pants and carrying two props: a brown hard-sided briefcase and a can of diet Coke. He sat down at my desk and proceeded to set a tough tone with the hapless student who attempted to persuade him to change the grade on his paper. We all had a good laugh. I had abandoned that buttoned-up character of a teacher after the first day, and my students trusted me enough to give me a good ribbing about it.

The essays in this collection remind us all that students are a flexible audience, who face us at the beginning of each semester hoping to learn something (even if not as much as we would hope). Even the young men at the back of the classroom with their ball caps turned backward and arms folded defiantly hope in some way that they will learn something from us. They dare us to teach them. They are in character, too. And what we perform for them and for the eager students looking brightly at us from the front row is the character of a teacher, embodied and material, even if at some level we are just feeling our way and finding our way.

Works Cited

Crowley, Sharon, and Debra Hawhee. *Ancient Rhetorics for Contemporary Students.* 2nd ed. Boston: Allyn & Bacon, 1999.

Mountford, Roxanne. *The Gendered Pulpit: Preaching in American Protestant Spaces.* Studies in Rhetorics and Feminisms. Carbondale: Southern Illinois UP, 2003.

Reynolds, John Frederick, ed. *Rhetorical Memory and Delivery: Classical Concepts for Contemporary Composition and Communication.* Hillsdale, NJ: Erlbaum, 1993.

Appendix

Possibilities for Your Teaching Bookshelf

Conditions, institutions, students, teachers: they vary. Only you, then, can amass your own best resources for enlarging your teaching. Some books you'll be assigned; others you'll look to for quick advice and then for deeper consideration.

Begin, perhaps, by acquainting yourself with the on-line Bedford bibliography prepared by Patricia Bizzell and Bruce Herzberg. Many of the regularly reprinted essays found in the anthologies listed in this bibliography are annotated at this site: http://www.bedfordstmartins.com/bb/.

Also, consult http://www.ncte.org, the Web site of the National Council of Teachers of English, particularly the Conference on College Composition and Communication. You can find out about membership and publications, including relevant teaching journals: *College English, College Composition and Communication,* and *Teaching in the Two-Year College,* and several others. Other journals to consider include *Composition Studies, Computers and Composition, Dialogue, Fourth Genre, Journal of Advanced Composition, Pedagogy, Reader, Research in the Teaching of English, Rhetoric Review.* Many of these have Web sites.

Classroom Lives

Introductions

Anson, Chris, Joan Graham, and David Jolliffe, eds. *Scenarios for Teaching Writing: Contexts for Discussion and Reflective Practice.* Urbana: NCTE, 1993.

Elbow, Peter. *Writing Without Teachers.* New York: Oxford UP, 1973.

Lindemann, Erika. *A Rhetoric for Writing Teachers.* 4th ed. New York: Oxford UP, 2001.

Rose, Mike. *Lives on the Boundaries.* New York: Free P, 1989.

Anthologies

Corbett, Edward P. J., Nancy Myers, and Gary Tate, eds. *The Writing Teacher's Sourcebook.* 4th ed. New York: Oxford UP, 2000.

Hawisher, Gail E., and Cynthia L. Selfe, eds. *Passions, Pedagogies, and 21st Century Technologies.* Logan: Utah State UP, 1999.

McDonald, Christina Russell, and Robert L. McDonald. *Teaching Writing: Landmarks and Horizons.* Carbondale: Southern Illinois UP, 2002.

Reynolds, Mark, ed. *Two-Year College English: Essays for a New Century.* Urbana: NCTE, 1994.

Spurlin, William, ed. *Lesbian and Gay Studies and the Teaching of English: Positions, Pedagogies, and Personal Politics.* Urbana: NCTE, 2000.

Tate, Gary, Amy Rupiper, and Kurt Schick. *A Guide to Composition Pedagogies.* New York: Oxford UP, 2001.

Villanueva, Victor, Jr., ed. *Cross-Talk in Comp Theory: A Reader.* 2nd ed. Urbana: NCTE, 2003.

Classroom Practice

Bishop, Wendy, ed. *The Subject Is Writing.* 3rd ed. Portsmouth, NH: Boynton, 2003.

Brooke, Robert, Ruth Mirtz, and Rick Evans. *Small Groups in Writing Workshops: Invitations to a Writer's Life.* Urbana: NCTE, 1994.

Moore, Cindy, and Peggy O'Neill. *Practice in Context: Situating the Work of Writing Teachers.* Urbana: NCTE, 2003.

Newkirk, Thomas. *The Performance of Self in Student Writing.* Portsmouth, NH: Boynton, 1997.

Newkirk, Thomas, Elizabeth Chiseri-Strater, and Patricia Sullivan, eds. *Nuts and Bolts: A Practical Guide to Teaching College Composition.* Portsmouth, NH: Boynton, 1993.

Rafoth, Ben, ed. *A Tutor's Guide: Helping Writers One to One.* Portsmouth, NH: Boynton, 2000.

Roen, Duan, ed. *Strategies for Teaching First-Year Composition.* Urbana: NCTE, 2002.

Smith, Frank. *Understanding Reading: A Psycholinguistic Analysis of Reading and Learning to Read.* 5th ed. Hillsdale, NJ: Erlbaum, 1994.

Tobin, Lad. *Writing Relationships: What Really Happens in the Composition Class.* Portsmouth, NH: Boynton, 1993.

Tucker, Amy. *Decoding ESL : International Students in the American College Classroom.* Portsmouth, NH: Boynton, 1995.

Young, Art, and Toby Fulwiler, eds. *When Writing Teachers Teach Literature.* Portsmouth, NH: Boynton, 1995.

Response, Evaluation, and Assessment

Straub, Richard. *A Sourcebook for Responding to Student Writing*. Cresskill, NJ: Hampton P, 1999.

White, Edward M. *Teaching and Assessing Writing*. 2nd ed. San Francisco and London: Jossey-Bass, 1994.

Yancey, Kathleen Blake, and Irwin Weiser, eds. *Situating Portfolios: Four Perspectives*. Logan: Utah State UP, 1997.

Exploring, Revising, and Refining Drafts

Bishop, Wendy, ed. *Elements of Alternate Style*. Portsmouth, NH: Boynton, 1997.

Heilker, Paul. *The Essay: Theory and Pedagogy for an Active Form*. Urbana: NCTE, 1996.

Laib, Nevin K. *Rhetoric & Style: Strategies for Advanced Writers*. Englewood Cliffs, NJ: Prentice, 1993.

Murray, Donald M. *The Craft of Revision*. 4th ed. Boston: Heinle, 2000.

Quinn, Arthur. *Figures of Speech: Sixty Ways to Turn a Phrase*. Davis, CA: Hermagagoras P, 1982.

Starkey, David, ed. *Genre by Example: Writing What We Teach*. Portsmouth, NH: Boynton, 2001.

——. *Teaching Writing Creatively*. Portsmouth, NH: Boynton, 1998.

Grammar and the Teaching of Writing

Hunter, Susan, and Ray Wallace, eds. *The Place of Grammar in Writing Instruction: Past, Present, Future*. Portsmouth, NH: Boynton, 1995.

Kolln, Martha. *Rhetorical Grammar: Grammatical Choices, Rhetorical Effects*. 4th ed. New York: Longman, 2002.

Noguchi, Rei R. *Grammar and the Teaching of Writing: Limits and Possibilities*. Urbana: NCTE, 1991.

Weaver, Constance. *Teaching Grammar in Context*. Portsmouth, NH: Boynton, 1996.

Composition and Rhetoric

Connors, Robert J. *Composition-Rhetoric: Backgrounds, Theory, and Pedagogy*. Pittsburgh: U of Pittsburgh P, 1997.

Corbett, Edward P. J., and Robert J. Connors. *Classical Rhetoric for the Modern Student*. 1965. 4th ed. New York: Oxford UP, 1999.

Crowley, Sharon. *Ancient Rhetorics for Contemporary Students*. New York: Macmillan, 1994.

Enos, Theresa, and Keith Miller, eds. *Beyond Post Process and Postmodernism: Essays on the Spaciousness of Rhetoric*. Mahwah, NJ: Erlbaum, 2002.

Theories and/of Composition

Anson, Chris, and Christine Farris, eds. *Under Construction: Working at the Intersections of Composition Theory, Research, and Practice*. Logan: Utah State UP, 1998.

Clifford, John, and John Schilb, eds. *Writing Theory and Critical Theory*. New York: MLA, 1994.

Heilker, Paul, and Peter Vandenberg. *Keywords in Composition Studies*. Portsmouth, NH: Boynton, 1996.

Kennedy, Mary Lynch, ed. *Theorizing Composition: A Critical Sourcebook of Theory and Scholarship in Contemporary Composition Studies*. Westport, CT: Greenwood, 1998.

Kent, Thomas, ed. *Post-Process Theory: Beyond the Writing Process Paradigm*. Carbondale: Southern Illinois UP, 1999.

Kirsch, Gesa, Faye Spencer Maor, Lance Massey, Lee Nickoson-Massey, and Mary P. Sheridan-Rabideau, eds. *Feminism and Composition: A Critical Sourcebook*. Urbana: NCTE and Bedford, 2003.

Rose, Shirley K., and Irwin Weiser. *The Writing Program Administrator as Theorist*. Portsmouth, NH: Boynton, 2002.

Schilb, John. *Between the Lines: Relating Composition Theory and Literary Theory*. Portsmouth, NH: Boynton, 1996.

Teaching Lives

Bishop, Wendy. *Teaching Lives: Essays and Stories*. Logan: Utah State UP, 1997.

Bishop, Wendy, and David Starkey, eds. *In Praise of Pedagogy: Poetry, Flash Fiction and Essays on Composing*. Portsmouth, ME: Calendar Islands P, 2000 (now distributed by Boynton).

Bloom, Lynn. *Composition Studies as a Creative Art: Teaching, Writing, Scholarship, Administration*. Logan: Utah State UP, 1998.

Elbow, Peter. *Embracing Contraries: Explorations in Learning and Teaching*. New York: Oxford UP, 1986.

Haswell, Richard H., and Min-Zhan Lu, eds. *Comp Tales*. New York: Longman, 2000.

Roen, Duane, Stuart Brown, and Theresa Enos, eds. *Living Rhetoric and Composition: Stories of the Discipline*. Mahwah, NJ: Erlbaum, 1998.

Trimmer, Joe, ed. *Narration as Knowledge*. Portsmouth, NH: Boynton, 1997.

Villanueva, Victor. *Bootstraps: From an American Academic of Color*. Urbana: NCTE, 1993.

Yancey, Kathleen Blake. *Reflection in the Writing Classroom*. Logan: Utah State UP, 1998.

Institutional Life and the Conditions of Instruction

Dethier, Brock. *The Composition Instructor's Survival Guide*. Portsmouth, NH: Boynton, 1999.

Harris, Joseph. *A Teaching Subject: Composition Since 1966*. Upper Saddle River, NJ: Prentice, 1997.

O'Neill, Peggy, Angela Crow, and Larry Burton, eds. *Field of Dreams: Independent Writing Programs and the Future of Composition Studies*. Logan: Utah State UP, 2002.

Schell, Eileen E. *Gypsy Academics and Mother-Teachers: Gender, Contingent Labor, and Writing Instruction*. Portsmouth, NH: Boynton, 1998.

Schell, Eileen E., and Patricia Lambert Stock. *Moving a Mountain: Transforming the Role of Contingent Faculty in Composition Studies and Higher Education*. Urbana: NCTE, 2001.

Research and Writing Classrooms

Bishop, Wendy. *Ethnographic Writing Research—Writing It Down, Writing It Up, and Reading It*. Portsmouth, NH: Boynton, 1999.

Hayes, John R., et al. *Reading Empirical Research Studies: The Rhetoric of Research*. Hillsdale, NJ: Erlbaum, 1992.

Johanek, Cindy. *Composing Research: A Contextual Paradigm for Rhetoric and Composition*. Logan: Utah State UP, 2000.

Macnealy, Mary Sue. *Empirical Research in Writing*. Needham Heights, MA: Allyn, 1999.

North, Stephen. *The Making of Knowledge in Composition: Portrait of an Emerging Field*. Portsmouth, NH: Boynton/Cook, 1987.

Ray, Ruth E. *The Practice of Theory: Teacher Research in Composition*. Urbana: NCTE, 1993.

Rose, Shirley K., and Irwin Weiser, eds. *The Writing Program Administrator as Researcher: Inquiry in Action and Reflection*. Portsmouth, NH: Boynton, 1999.

Contributors